Love You Mom

GUIDED THROUGH GRIEF
FROM THE AFTERLIFE

Charmaine & Carter Roud

 FriesenPress

Suite 300 - 990 Fort St
Victoria, BC, V8V 3K2
Canada

www.friesenpress.com

ISBN
978-1-5255-5213-7 (Hardcover)
978-1-5255-5214-4 (Paperback)
978-1-5255-5215-1 (eBook)

1. SELF-HELP, DEATH, GRIEF, BEREAVEMENT

Distributed to the trade by The Ingram Book Company

This book is worth its weight in gold. It's my hope the content will be a gift of comfort and peace.

Patricia Brezden,
Grief Counsellor

Charmaine's the genuine article. After I lost my son Ryan, there was not a day that I wasn't ready to pack it in. All that changed when Charmaine allowed me to connect with Ryan once again. As a devout Christian, I find it hard to make sense of Charmaine's ability. But I'm a Christian because I have known for certain God's touch in my life – similarly, I'm now certain that we're able to know the presence of our loved ones who have died.

Rob Martyn,
Bereaved Parent

As bereaved mothers, we were navigating a life that was new to us. We forged ahead not knowing how we'd carry an unbearable burden, hold our marriage together, and mother our remaining children. Carter always had a joke to share and a loving embrace for his mother, and he remains so. He is a teacher, as is Charmaine. Our children help show other bereaved parents the way to re-establish our most cherished relationships but in a new way for our new lives.

Heather Scavetta
School of Miracles

DEDICATED WITH MY ETERNAL LOVE

TO MY CHILDREN CARTER, VICTORIA, AND OLIVIA

Table of Contents

Introduction

My life as a stay-at-home wife and mother, happily raising three wonderful children, was shattered when our son was killed. I wasn't sure what I believed in up untill then; I grew up without any strong beliefs in terms of religion or spirituality. However, shortly after our son's death, a series of strange events began to occur, and I felt compelled to try to find some answers if I could.

I couldn't understand then how or why these things were happening, but with every new odd occurrence, I grew more hopeful my son was trying to let us know he was still with us. I have never been much of a reader, and I was never interested in philosophy or spirituality before this time. I wouldn't consider myself a writer, and yet here I am, driven by all that I have learned. This is the story of my search beyond our "seen" world. As my journey unfolded, I experienced many surprising events that helped me find a path through my grief.

I am not trying to convince or change anyone's beliefs; we all have to come to our own understanding. I do hope that after reading about my experiences and following my thoughts, you will be more aware and open-minded to allow yourself to find a truth that you can believe in. My lack of beliefs and my desperation to find my son compelled me to question even what I believed to be true. Ultimately, my life has been enriched beyond measure. I hope I can help ease others' journey through grief by sharing my story. You may come away from my story feeling content and more at ease, you may feel more confused about life and death, or you may just find this an interesting read. Use this information however it serves you best.

Our son Carter was a fun-loving boy who lived his life with enthusiasm and joy. He loved people and lived life to the fullest. He never took a philosophy class or wrote with any great skill, in fact, his sentences ran on and on with little punctuation, something which I find very funny because he still does this. Yet he often speaks now with enlightened wisdom and understanding he did not have when he lived among us. How interesting I find this to be.

"No man is an island," and truly to take that thought further an island does not stand alone. It is surrounded by water, (the love, support, and energy of unseen existence fully supporting it always). It is held and supported by the earth itself, rooting it solidly on its strength. Upon this island are plants, trees, insects, animals—it is abundant with life, definitely not an "island." Even a totally barren island void of all "life" and composed of only sand or rock, this island is not isolated for there are billions of grains of sand required to make it. We are all but grains of sand in the real scheme of existence, it is not the grain of sand that holds importance; it would be lost in obscurity if it was alone. It is when all the sand works and stays in unity you see the true beauty. A single grain cannot compare in beauty no matter how lovely it is to the wonder of the desert. The goal in life is people uniting together for each other, we need the wisdom to try to see, understand and work toward this reality. People are wise in many ways, but the human mind, in its unique vision of importance, stops the truly important from being seen. The mind will busy the body and slow the strength of spirit. Spirit taking the lead and reigning in the mind, will allow a greater wisdom to come forward. (Carter, writing received May 22, 2012.)

All truths are easy to understand once they are discovered;
the point is to discover them.

Galileo

Shattered Lives

My life was shattered when our nineteen-year-old son Carter was killed in a car accident, and I began to face an unbearable future that couldn't be changed.

I sat frozen inside an ambulance, engulfed in a pain that was incomprehensible, as I saw my son looking as if he were just sleeping while lying on a stretcher. As tears streamed down my face I began screaming at the two attendants who were in the ambulance with me. "Why are you just standing there? Look at him! He's fine! DO SOMETHING DON'T JUST STAND THERE, HELP HIM PLEASE!" They looked at me helplessly, but said nothing. I held Carter tight and told him I loved him. Oh God, please don't let this be happening! Outside, beyond the open doors of the ambulance, the world had looked black, punctuated only by the flashing lights of the emergency vehicles.

Only yesterday I had enjoyed an idyllic day at the lake with my husband John and our three children. My youngest child Olivia had decided that was the morning for her to learn to water ski. I went into Carter's bedroom and rubbed his head gently.

"Morning buddy, time to get up, Olivia would really like to learn to water ski this morning."

He raised himself up on his elbows and rubbed his right eye. "Okay Mom, I'm up." I thought he'd fall back to sleep, but to my surprise, he didn't. He wasn't scheduled to work until noon, and since it's easier to learn to water ski in the morning when the lake is calm, this worked well.

By nine o'clock we were all on the lake. Carter went wakeboarding first with all of us watching him from the boat as Victoria, our middle child, had also woken up and joined us. I was sublimely happy in the complete perfection of the morning with all of us together. After the wakeboard run, John brought the boat back to our dock. Carter and Olivia got off the boat while the rest of us stayed aboard. Carter helped Olivia put on her water skis, and supported her as she sat on the edge of the dock. He then jumped into the water and she slipped in beside him. While treading water, he handed her the ski rope, then he held her in a starting position. John drove the boat forward, the rope straightened then tightened, and when they were ready Carter shouted, "OKAY, GO!" Carter, still treading water, held and guided Olivia up as the rope began to lift her out of the water. Olivia was startled; she wasn't expecting to actually get up on the skis, and she fell.

Attempt two was the same routine, Olivia rose partly up out of the water—nope. She didn't find her balance and fell. On the third attempt, Carter arranged her skis with the tips up out of the water then held her in position with his hands on her waist as he treaded water to keep them both afloat. "OKAY!" he shouted. John quickly drove the boat forward to get tension on the rope. Once again Carter continued to hold Olivia as she rose out of the water, and when he let her go she stayed balanced and was skiing. Victoria, John, and I were all excitedly shouting at Olivia from the boat as Carter watched her happily from the water. Olivia stayed up on her skis as the boat circled around, and as we approached the dock she let go of the rope and sank gracefully down into the water. She had done it! We were all so happy for her, and at that moment I was aware of how special this experience was with all of us sharing it together. Also, it had meant a lot to Olivia that her brother and sister both happily got up early to share this with her. As teenagers, they enjoyed sleeping in during summer holidays when they could.

After lots of excitement from all of us, Carter decided he would go for a slalom ski, so the girls hopped into the boat for a ride. As the rope tightened and began to pull Carter out of the water, it snapped and he sank below the surface of the water.

"That's okay," Carter said. He said would go get something to eat before he had to go to work. After a few moments, I followed him into the cottage and gave him a really big hug to thank him for getting up and doing that for his sister.

"Nobody else in the family could have done that. You're the only one strong enough to raise her while treading water; that was fantastic." We chatted about it, and then I hugged him again and said, "I'm so proud of you and I love you so much," before I went back outside to rejoin the others. We were all relaxing on the dock as I watched Carter come down the spiral stairs and walk across the grass to ask which car he could take to work. Then off he went as we stayed in the sun, happy and content with our wonderful morning.

At nine o'clock that evening, the phone rang, John answered it.

"Hey Carter, what's up?" happy to hear his voice. Carter said he was going to his friend Kevin's cottage, and he would see us tomorrow after work.

The next day was another lovely warm summer day. While John and I enjoyed watching the girls and their friends swim and kayak on the lake, he suggested we could surprise Carter at the restaurant he was working at that summer and have supper there. What a good idea, as we hadn't been there yet.

We all arrived, unbeknownst to Carter, and ordered items he often cooked. We planned to ask him later what he was cooking that evening. We were all surprised when our server asked Olivia if she was Carter's sister. Olivia smiled and said yes.

"You look so much like Carter," the server added. We were amazed because no one working that evening knew who we were, yet she could see the resemblance to Carter. What a nice moment. It was around eight when we finished dinner, and wondered if we should wait for Carter since he would be finished at nine. No, we decided we'd meet him at home. On our way out, we asked the server if we could say hi to him. She opened the kitchen door and shouted teasingly, "Carter, your family is here to see you!" He was wearing a white T-shirt and was cooking on one of the griddles on the line. He looked up and gave a great big silly grin that he often did with his mouth wide open. He didn't say anything, he just had this huge smile as he worked, but he saw us all.

We arrived home and contently settled into the evening. Carter would be home soon. I was in the laundry room folding his laundry when the phone rang; I walked into the living room just as Olivia picked it up then passed it to me saying it was a server from the restaurant. A bit puzzled, I took the phone. I have no real memory of her words; I just know she said something about Carter having been in an accident and a truck. John was standing beside me, and I thrust the phone toward him. I couldn't bear to hear this. John spoke to her and quickly said were on our way. All of us were stunned as we told the girls Carter had been in an accident and we had to go. John and I knew without speaking that the girls shouldn't come with us. We gave them both a big hug and walked out to the car. I had no idea what was going through their minds as they waited for our return; thank goodness they had each other. It was not yet 9:30; we had left the restaurant just over an hour ago.

I tried not to let my mind race uncontrolled into terrifying thoughts because I had no idea what was happening. Only minutes into our drive, I did something that was very odd for me; I began to concentrate on sending my thoughts to Carter in the hope that he would somehow be able to receive them. I had never believed in anything like this, yet as we drove to the accident scene I felt the need to try to reach him. Carter had never liked being confined, even as a baby, and I was worried that if he was trapped in the car he might be panicking. I thought it might help if he could hear me, so I closed my eyes and put every ounce of effort into sending a clear thought to him that we were coming.

I guess John saw me sitting with my eyes closed and, trying to help, said, "if you want to do something, maybe you could call the police and see if they can give you any information." I was annoyed by his statement. I thought *they aren't going to tell me anything, how could they? Knowing won't change anything anyway, and I'm trying to do something here*, not that there was any way John could have known this.

Abruptly, I said to him, "I'm trying to concentrate and send my thoughts to Carter." As I said these words, I heard how strange they sounded. Could this be done? And if I could send my thoughts, would he be able to hear them? As my mind began spinning out of control with these questions, I also began to send thoughts to my father, who had died three years before. *Dad, I don't even know if you're there, but if you are and you can hear me, can you go stay with Carter so he's not alone and let him know if you can we're coming?* I didn't know if I even believed any of this was possible, but at that moment I hoped it was. Looking back, I see now in that one awful moment not only had our lives been forever changed, but that my mind was already reaching toward a world that I wasn't convinced existed.

Our car approached flashing lights where a police officer was blocking the road going north. John pulled up and said, "It's our son who's been in the accident." The police officer radioed ahead and said the parents of the victim were coming through. "The victim," chills went through my body and our fears grew as we drove through total darkness along the empty road. Would we never get there? I remember feeling sick as we approached the scene and saw the mass of flashing lights from the many rescue vehicles. We got out of our car and stared at the nightmare before us. The firefighters were still trying to get Carter out of the car. I ran toward the car to tell Carter we were there, but a firefighter blocked my rush forward, asking me not to go to the vehicle, and to let them do what they needed to do to help him. I stopped and stared at him as he spoke, unable for a moment to comprehend what he was saying. I struggled to understand his words as my only focus was getting to my son who was only a few feet away. I certainly didn't want to slow them down, so I said something like, "Whatever's best for him, but please tell him his mom and dad are here." He promised he would tell him, then walked me back towards our car where John was standing, frozen, staring at the wreckage his son was in. Workers from the restaurant came and talked to us, but I don't know what was said. Finally, we saw them lift Carter out and place him on a stretcher. I thought, *good he's out,* with a huge exhale, but only seconds later John said, "Oh God, they're working on his heart." We couldn't see Carter as they had screened the stretcher, but we could see them performing CPR as they walked alongside the stretcher toward the ambulance. No, not his heart! My mind hadn't and wouldn't allow me to think of that possibility. Within moments, a firefighter came over and told us they were bringing him to the hospital, and for us to meet them there. We went immediately to the car and waited for the ambulance to go ahead of us so we wouldn't slow them down.

As we were enduring the worst moments of our lives, John and I tried to keep functioning. We discussed whether we should get the girls or go right to the hospital. We had also decided to call our friend Shari, a nurse at the hospital. We would ask her to please do whatever she could in the hope she could get the best help possible in place for Carter when he arrived. As we were quickly trying to put some thoughts in motion, I suddenly had this terrible realization; it had been several minutes, and that ambulance hadn't moved.

Horrified I asked, "John why haven't they left yet?" Stunned by the thought, he left the car to find out. I waited, so frozen by fear I that couldn't phone Shari. I wasn't even able to breathe. What was going on? My eyes locked on the car's side mirror, searching for John's return. I saw nothing for several minutes, and then finally out of the blackness I saw John and a rescue worker walk into view. They were walking, side by side, slowly, with their heads down. I gasped—oh my God, what's happening? Panicking, I bolted out of the car and ran toward them. I don't know who spoke or what was said to me I just know I began running to that ambulance and climbed in.

I screamed and cried as I saw Carter, "They're wrong they must be wrong! He's perfect, he doesn't even look bruised. Why won't somebody help him?"

I guess someone eventually got me out of the ambulance and away from Carter, though I have no memory of it. John and I, both broken and crying, now needed to face our daughters. I don't remember the drive back to our cottage, except for us asking each other how are we going to live without him, and how can we possibly tell his sisters. I vividly remember getting out of the car and seeing my legs walk the path to our cottage, then looking up through the glass in the front door to see Victoria and Olivia holding tight to each other. Opening the cottage door, we hugged and cried before words were even spoken. We sat them down with us on the couch and told them that Carter didn't survive the crash. They screamed and cried, and we just tried to hold them, crying with them, knowing there was nothing we could do to make any of this better for anyone.

We all went to the hospital together. The nurses were very helpful and kind, some of them were crying with us. I touched Carter's hand; it was already starting to get cold, and I thought, *oh my God, that's not right, that can't be*. I lifted his shirt and touched his stomach. It was soft and warm as it should be. I leaned down and kissed his stomach; I still can feel exactly what his skin felt like. At some point we needed to leave for the girls' sake, but how could we leave him there all alone? My son, whose presence lit up a room, now lay lifeless as we left him and walked out into the blackness.

The next morning arrived, we rose to face a world completely different than it was one day ago. Our lives were shattered; what do we do now? We told two of our dearest neighbours the horror of last night. They wanted to help, but how could anybody help us? As we were walking back to our cottage, Shari arrived with her husband and came running toward us in tears and hugged me.

"How did you know?" I asked, confused. Shari said she didn't know for sure, but she'd heard on the TV that a nineteen-year-old boy from Ancaster had been killed and right away she felt that she had to come over. She said that her husband and mother had tried to persuade her not to. They said it might not be Carter, but she said that she wouldn't be swayed, she had to come. We said we had to go home to tell my mother, who lived in a long-term care home. Shari immediately phoned the residence, telling them there's been a crisis. She said the family was on their way to her and to put a media ban on for my mother so she wouldn't hear it on the TV or radio.

John and I both drove cars home somehow since we had no idea when or if we would ever come back. The girls sat in silence in the car. John called several friends and relatives, so when we arrived home they were there to help us. The four of us all went to tell Mom. What an awful ordeal to live through at age eighty nine; we thought she might not survive hearing this. The nurses didn't know what had happened, but as we approached Mom's room, they were standing outside her door, prepared to help her with oxygen and medication if necessary. She had such a close and loving bond with her grandchildren and Carter would visit her almost daily. It was impossible to say this to her, crushing for her to hear, and impossible for our girls to witness her despair, though they wanted to be there for her.

Over the next week we focused on arranging a funeral to honour Carter's life. Friends and family were kind and helpful, but we were numb, walking vacantly through time. The outpouring of love for Carter helped us move forward, it helped knowing he brought joy to others and enriched many lives within his much-too-short life. After his funeral, the days seemed pointless and tortuously long. The girls wanted to go back to our cottage as soon as possible. They said we are always at the cottage in the summer and the only reason we're not there is because of what has happened, which made it worse to be at home. I also wanted to go, as every time I went out I always met someone, and even though they were supportive and kind, I would end up debilitated once again. I needed to get out of town. John felt the exact opposite; he didn't know if he could ever go to the cottage again. This was a major issue, as I couldn't go north and leave him alone. There was no way any of us should be alone right now.

Even if I hadn't wanted to go to the cottage, the girls were adamant that they did, and I felt we had to go for them. This discussion went back and forth for several days.

Finally, I said to John, "If you can't go that's fine, but the girls need to leave, and you shouldn't be alone."

He did find the strength to come, and as he and I sat in the cottage and watched the boats go by filled with young guy's wakeboarding and having fun, we both knew that should be Carter. I saw the lake and felt all the joy Carter had felt there. John saw it the same way, as the place that Carter loved, but he couldn't feel Carter's joy. He couldn't take anything but pain from it. We both saw the very same thing, through the same thought, but came to different states of mind. After several days, John said he had to go home. I felt awful for him being alone, but the girls and I couldn't go back. A few days later he returned to the cottage, but there was really no place that could ease any of our pain.

I was suffocating, imprisoned within a fortress of grief as I struggled to bear the unbearable, but I knew I must find a way to survive this for my family. My doctor said he could prescribe medication to help me, but I didn't want to do that. I knew I'd have to cope without the pills eventually, and nothing was going to change. I would still face the same awful reality; I might as well continue falling apart then. I felt I needed to do this for my children. I hoped to show them that the unyielding love I had for them could give me the strength to endure this grief and learn to cope, and I hoped I could somehow summon the strength to actually do this. I began to think that perhaps yoga and massage therapy might help, but it is only with the wisdom of hindsight that I can see their purpose for me.

Several weeks later someone from the local toy store called, saying the hutch and cow we ordered were in. Olivia collected small toy animals and as a gift, a rabbit hutch had been ordered for her, but nothing else. We assumed they made a mistake and asked the clerk to recheck the order. She did, and confirmed the cow was also under Olivia's name, which was very puzzling to us. We were startled when Olivia said it was from Carter, as she remembered telling Carter specifically that she didn't want a cow when he had mentioned it. She said it had to be from Carter and she was confident that she knew exactly how her conversation with him would have gone when he gave her this cow.

C: I got you the cow you wanted, Liv.

O: Carter, I told you I don't want the cow.

C: Yes, you do.

O: No, I don't.

C: Well, you like cows, don't you?

O: No, not really.

C: You like milk, don't you?

O: Yes.

C: Then you like cows, so I got you the cow.

We all had to agree that it sounded just like what Carter would say, and we could see him really enjoying this conversation. Olivia was adamant that it had to have been ordered by Carter, though we were certain that he hadn't, none of us had. We couldn't understand how this cow could be on the order. All four of us went to the store to pick them up, and once again I questioned the clerk if she was sure the cow was for Olivia. She picked up the piece of paper and showed us the request with my daughter's name along with the hutch and cow. Unfortunately, it didn't say who had placed the order. This cow was a very special gift to Olivia from her brother. The true value of love within this gift was completely unknown to us at this time, but it brought a smile to her face and that helped us through our tears a bit that day.

Olivia had been so excited the morning she successfully water skied, but after the accident, she hadn't wanted to try to water ski again. As the days went by, we continued to hope that she would be able to try again, but she was unyielding. She wanted Carter to help her, and she wouldn't do it without him. Our hearts were breaking; we absolutely understood but were completely lost for what to say to her. Our neighbours hired a ski instructor to come to their cottage in the hope she would join them, but she couldn't. Then one day John was reading the text messages on Carter's phone. He read me one out loud that Carter sent to his friend Cayley right after he helped Olivia water ski.

I gasped, "read that to me again." I couldn't believe what I heard. "Let me see the phone." The text read: "Ha-ha, its pretty good. Just taught Olivia to water ski and of course the weather is finally nice and I have a 9 hour shift."

"Taught, the word he used was 'taught!' Look, he said he taught her not he's teaching her." For the first time since his death, I actually felt excited. After a heart-wrenching discussion between us on whether this could help Olivia or be more hurtful for her to hear, we decided to show the message to Olivia, hoping it might help. With difficulty, we explained and tried to prepare her before reading his message. Though tearful, she smiled. We said that in Carter's mind he didn't need to help her again, he felt she could do it now because he didn't say he was teaching her, he said he had TAUGHT her, so his job was done. This message that he sent Cayley was a gift; Olivia now had his thoughts on that day. The very next day she said she wanted to try to ski—fantastic! I asked if she wanted me to be in the water with her and try to help.

"No, I'm doing this for Carter. He said he taught me and I'm doing it by myself for him!"

With tears in my eyes as I write this now, I can still find no way to express the relief, pride, and gratitude I felt at that moment.

As summer ended, I felt we had been trapped in this hell forever, but it had only been four weeks. Our family of five began the summer with joy and now only four of us returned home, destroyed. Our family would never be whole again and nothing would ever be right, but the girls had to return to school and we had to somehow help them continue their lives

My Journey Begins

Carter and his friends had stayed up all night, waiting for the sunrise.

Carter thought it was amazing and then captured the moment in a photo.

Early in the fall, I was shaken by a telephone call from the mother of Carter's friend Cam. She began by telling me that something had happened, something Carter's friends hadn't told me because they didn't want to upset me.

"But if I was you, I'd want to know," she added.

"Oh, okay, tell me then," I answered, having no idea what she'd say. She proceeded to tell me that only three weeks after Carter's death, on August 21, a group of his friends went to a baseball game in Toronto to celebrate the nineteenth birthday of their friend Sean. They went into a bar so he could have his first legal drink, and just as the bartender was passing the beer to Sean, Sean's cell phone rang. He picked up his phone; on the screen it said duplicate message, then the last message Carter had ever sent him appeared on the screen.

I was speechless and had no idea how to respond. Finally, to say something, I asked, "what did the boys think?" She said they were shocked, but felt Carter was letting them know he was with them. What I found most startling was not only that it happened but that it happened at that precise moment. The incident at the toy store confused me but didn't weigh on my mind as this did, and I began to wonder with the slightest hope—could it have been from Carter?

Over and over as I told this story to my friends, I struggled with what I thought were bizarre thoughts—maybe Carter did send this text message. Patiently they helped me explore my thoughts. Their questions always challenged my ideas and made me reach deeper to find a comprehensible thought. I could voice to them what I was afraid to say to others. I knew that I sounded crazy, but they were never judgmental and supported me in my grief.

Carter's high school football team dedicated the 2008 season to him. Carter had worn the jersey with his lucky number six on it, so that season every member of the team had a small six on their helmets and no player wore the six football jersey. No one would replace Carter on the field. The coach came to the house to give Victoria the number six jersey, and he told us that the team began the season with a service with thoughts and prayers for Carter. I wanted to honour their tribute to Carter, so in October I went to watch a home game. I was happy to see Carter's friend Ben helping coach the team. When I told him I'd brought my camera to take a picture of the six on the helmets, without hesitation he went over to the team and returned with a helmet. Repeatedly as I tried to take a picture the camera wouldn't focus, though every time I aimed the camera away from the helmet it focused. I was getting frustrated; I wanted this picture!

Finally, not really meaning it, but kidding to lighten the sadness we were both feeling, I jokingly said to Ben, "its Carter. He's goofing around." I looked up and said, "come on Carter, stop fooling around." Then I tried again, and this time the camera focused and took the picture. Hmm, that's strange.

Later that month, my friend Janice asked me to join her at yoga. It was suppertime and I was still in my pajamas, enduring another endless day. Repeatedly, I said I didn't want to go, but she insisted, and I'm thankful she did. The teacher began class by bringing our focus to our breath and ended with a short meditation to clear our minds. This was impossible for me, as thoughts of Carter flooded in and I started crying, but for those few moments when I focused on my breath at the start of class, I felt some ease. After class, I thought if meditation could clear my mind even for just a moment's break from the never-ending pain, it would be a worthwhile goal to work toward. So for ten months I persevered to learn, even though I had very little success. Day after day I'd get up from an attempt to meditate, frustrated or in tears, but I always tried again the next day. I never gave up because I had no idea what else to do.

For months, even the simplest tasks were impossible for me to do. I couldn't even clear the kitchen table of all the gifts of kindness friends continued to bring us in the form of food, necessities, etc. I'd begin, but couldn't decide where to put anything and then in complete frustration and overwhelmed, I ended up in bed, upset at my indecisiveness. *Why can't I do this?* Determined to succeed, I'd climb back out of bed and try again, but it was always an insurmountable task. I looked at the clutter on the table, and it could take me days to clear it. When I tried to make my bed, I would often give up and lie down on the jumble of blankets, not seeing any point in any of this. Even the mundane task of going to the grocery store was tortuous, as every decision was based on Carter's death. Before, when there was a sale I would buy multiples of everything, and it would all disappear in a few days because Carter was eating constantly, as teenage boys do. But now, I'd pick something up and think, *I can't buy this, Carter was the only one who liked it,* or, *we all like this, but I better only buy one.* Every choice was affected by the loss of Carter. Every item chosen caused me such pain, yet I had to do this because we needed to eat, I was barely functioning under the crushing grief.

I was also constantly bringing Olivia to the arena where all three children had spent so much time. I often walked in to face boys playing hockey, and all I could see was Carter. Although these were happy memories, it was also painful. Every place I went reminded me of the times that we had shared together. Yet I also knew that if I was to live somewhere where there were no memories with Carter, or where people didn't know him, that would be worse, because it would be like he had never lived.

One day at the cottage, I was overwrought with emotions and oblivious to appearances as I walked down the road with my friend in the pouring rain, wearing my pajamas and a full-length bathrobe. *What does any of this matter?* I thought. I couldn't think about anything but the death of my child.

I felt as if I was slowly dissolving away. I needed to find new ways of thinking that would help me cope better. My last conversation with Carter helped me through some very rough times. I had told him that I loved him and was proud of him. What else needs to be said? I am forever thankful I said those words. When my father was dying at ninety-three years old, he was being very positive and said, "I'm not afraid to die, but I don't think I should just roll over and die, either. I need to make an effort." I didn't have a final talk with Dad even though I knew he was dying, yet I had one with Carter, not knowing he was going to die. It was also a great help to me that we all went to see him at the restaurant that evening, and in his final moments, he knew we were think-ing of him. But now I questioned why we chose to go that night for the first time and why I had said those perfect last words in what turned out to be my final conversation with him? Although both brought me some sense of peace, I began to question why they happened.

Kevin told me that while he and Carter were having lunch that last day, they both said they had the best lives in the whole world. They said other people might have as good a life as they did, but nobody could have a better life because they were having the best life possible. Wow, what an amazing way to be thinking on the last day of your life! I can also relive how Carter spent his last day, and what a gift it is for me to know he enjoyed every precious moment.

Each day without Carter, I was aware could also be my last. This may sound overly dramatic, but I was just facing my new reality. Carter was here one moment and gone the next, and that overshadowed all my days. I also struggled knowing he was alone to face what—if anything—happened next, but I diverted my mind from these frighten-ing thoughts to tell myself he'd already done it, so I can too when my time comes. I was haunted by these thoughts, but I couldn't find a way past them. This added to my torment, as I was aware with each day, I was wasting what might be my final day.

Finally, I came to a pivotal decision. Carter loved life, and yes his life was too short, but he really enjoyed his time and lived his life well. I've had more days since he left but to what value? I decided I would try to live as he did, and to do this I attempted to find happy moments again. Some days were so hard for me to endure, and to add to my pain I realized at the end of the day that I hadn't enjoyed a single minute. As my emotions started to spin out of control, I thought if I didn't have another day on this earth then I've wasted my last day, and Carter certainly didn't waste his last day. If this is my last day, and we continue past this physical life, I want to look back on my final hours and be happy how they were spent and know that I touched others' lives in a positive way. And if this life doesn't continue, at least the people I was with will know we enjoyed our time together and will have no regrets. That's when I began to make myself think back over the day until I could remember one nice moment, there must be one! This seemed to help me, so at the end of each day I began to make myself think of three things that I had enjoyed that day. In the beginning, I struggled to think of any so I grabbed hold of moments. They might have been as simple as sitting outside and feeling the breeze on my cheek, or seeing my daughters smile at me, or hearing a bird sing. By searching backward to find these moments, I started to become aware of them as they happened and I no longer needed to think about it at days' end. When I saw a bunny, hugged a friend, or watched the raindrops fall, not only was I aware of the pleasure I felt but gradually they brought moments of ease within my day. This, however, was hard work and took a lot of time, patience and was an ongoing effort.

One day, Carter's friend Cam told me that he believed Carter had visited him in a dream. As he described his dream, I was amazed by how vivid it still was to him, but I was also hurt. If Carter can come into Cam's dream, why wasn't he coming to me? I'm his mother and I needed him. I pleaded for him to give me a sign if he was there.

By late November, the depth of my pain was unfathomable and getting worse. We had faced and endured Thanksgiving and my birthday without Carter, and now Christmas was staring me down. Could we ever enjoy anything ever again?

Then late in November, I finally had my own special dream. I was in bed, lying on my stomach and wide awake when I felt the mattress move slightly. I thought it was Olivia, so I started turning over while I said out loud, "get into bed Olivia," but I stopped halfway through because I saw there was nobody there. Right away I said, "Carter," and started to cry. "Are you here, Carter?" I tried to talk to him, but what do I say? I had a million things I wanted to say to him, yet nothing at that moment seemed to have any importance except saying I love you. So, over and over again I said I love you and I miss you, we all miss you so much, if I could just hold you one more time. Eventually, I fell back to sleep and had a dream that is still as vivid to me now as it was on that day.

First Dream Visit

In my dream, we were walking on a sidewalk with grass on both sides and trees to the left. Carter was on the sidewalk in front of me, with John and the girls walking on the grass to his right and a group of Carter's friends were also talking and laughing along with us. I could hear Carter's deep laugh, and I went up behind him and gave him a great big hug as I would often do at home. "I love you, Carter" I said. As I was hugging him, John and I looked toward each other with sadness, for even in my dream we knew he wasn't staying. Then John went back to laughing with Carter and the group. We all continued walking. Suddenly Carter vanished, and I woke up. I could still feel the pressure of his body in my arms from holding him, and I started crying because I realized that he had been right there with us; I had him and now I'd lost him again. For weeks after the dream my grief worsened. I was hurtled back to that sense of loss I had felt immediately after the accident.

Was it real, or was it just a dream? I could think of little else. I kept going over the first part, when I was wide awake and as I was turning over I was talking out loud to Olivia, so I was certain that I had actually felt the mattress move. Also, that wasn't a normal dream; I could physically feel Carter even after the dream ended. I began to allow myself to hope maybe it was Carter, and if it was, I began to picture him and realize how awful it must be for him to see us suffering for him. He would be upset, thinking, *Mom, I'm here. I'm trying so hard to help you.* It was at that moment of realization that I knew with absolute certainty I needed to determine whether these things were from Carter or not, because now I was not doing this just for myself, but hopefully for Carter also, and if he was trying to help me then I must find a way to let him help. I didn't want to cause him any more pain or upset than he'd already had to endure watching us grieve for him.

My desire to discover if he was there became an ever-increasing force within me as I opened my heart and mind to what I hoped might be. Before the dream I had asked, "if I could hold you one more time," then I held him in my dream, still physically feeling him when I woke. Going forward, I would need to critically examine things and not be closed-minded, but be open to considering thoughts that were inconceivable to me. I could never have imagined how unbelievable and far-ranging these events would become.

A Long Dark Winter

As Christmas approached we were all in a downward spiral, and I spent increasingly more time in bed. Victoria and John were concerned for me, so, trying to help they said we don't need to do anything for Christmas, but I felt Olivia was only eleven, she had lost her brother and she couldn't lose Christmas too. I was determined to do this for all of us so; I'd get up each morning planning to decorate, but end up in bed, waiting for time to pass. I finally managed to put up some Christmas decorations, but I couldn't bring myself to buy the tree. Each Christmas I had always bought the children an ornament that signified something special in their life that year, the girls called it a tree of memories. Every year we would chop the tree together then everyone would put on their ornaments.

In August shortly after Carter's death, Olivia asked who was going to put up Carter's ornaments. She was already thinking about it. The girls couldn't put up their ornaments without Carter doing his, and none of us could have even tried to put his up, so the tree was going to look very different that year. Two days before Christmas, after I dragged myself out of bed in the middle of the day, I grabbed a tree from the two ice-covered ones left at the store without even looking at it. I couldn't look; this took all my strength. John and I put the tree up, but our pain upon seeing it was indescribable and we both walked away. I went to bed, but forced myself up and said to the family that I would decorate the tree and call them when it is done. Our tree had never been done so quickly. I threw up lights, ribbons, and bows then called them. With total love and support for me, they said "it's beautiful Mom," and hugged me. I could see their hearts breaking, but to not have a Christmas tree would have also been heartbreaking. Carter wasn't here and everything was heartbreaking, but joined by my mom on Christmas Day, we all made it through the day because of an outpouring of love and an incredible effort for each other.

In February 2009, John woke up upset, saying he'd had a dream about Carter that felt real. I got very excited and I began to question him. He described it vividly and said that he was so happy to be with him until Carter said he had to go. John had said, "Don't go, Carter, I miss you so much." Carter said, "I have to go, Dad. I have to go see Olivia." John's dream was upsetting just as mine had been, but I was past the initial shock of mine and would have liked all the details of his, but understandably John needed time to deal with it, and I stopped pushing for information.

One or two days later, Olivia was very upset when I woke her. She said she didn't want to go to school. I thought something must be bothering her about school, but she wouldn't say what had upset her. After a lot of questions, she finally told me that she'd just had a dream about Carter.

"You dream of Carter all the time," I said.

Olivia responded, "Yes, but this one was different. It wasn't a normal dream. It felt real."

My heart started racing as Olivia told me about her dream. She and Carter were at the cottage having fun in the lake when Carter put his hands on her shoulders and tried to push her underwater like he sometimes did. At that moment she woke up, but she could still feel the pressure of his hands on her shoulders. This is why she was so upset, not only was the dream vivid, but she could still feel him when she woke up. That's exactly what I had experienced!

All three of our dreams were so real they brought us to tears, and I fumbled for words. I didn't tell Olivia about the dreams John and I had had. I desperately wanted to say, *Carter came to you too*, but I didn't want to tell her anything if my thinking was wrong. I may have crazy thoughts, but I had to stay responsible to help my children so I said nothing to her of my thoughts.

I was very excited though, as I could see only two possibilities. Olivia, John, and I were each visited by Carter in dreams, or in my grief I was going crazy. The thought that I might be going crazy came into my mind a lot throughout my search for Carter, and I was ready to accept the very real possibility that grief was causing me to lose my mind. I knew I needed to get advice from somebody before I spoke to Olivia about her dream, but who? A doctor would question my thinking and might worry about my mental health, and I didn't want that. I needed to talk to someone with a spiritual background, so I called the minister who officiated at Carter's funeral and had been so kind to us.

His eyes glistened as I told him about the dreams, then nervously I asked if he thought there was any possibility that these dreams could be from Carter. He said yes, he didn't think it happened often, but he absolutely believed it could be Carter especially after hearing so much about him as a person. I went home and felt comfortable as I spoke to Olivia about our dreams and my thoughts that it might actually be from Carter, adding that my ideas may or may not be true.

My meeting with the minister definitely energized me; perhaps crazy wasn't the most possible option for me after all. If he had said, "I think you need to work on your grief in a different way," I might have stopped trying to figure it out or at least been held back a bit, but what he said propelled me with greater determination to figure this out! I told myself that if I could know for sure Carter was alright I'd be able to learn to cope with his death and go on with my life. I had no idea how I was going to try to search for the answer to this, but I felt that I'd never give up trying, and my days became overshadowed by my need to know if these signs were from Carter.

As winter dragged on, John and I felt the family needed to get away. It was painful to make plans without our son, but we decided a cruise held no memories for us and once again our daughters propelled us to do more than just exist. If it wasn't for them I don't know how we would have gotten through this time, and we are forever grateful for them and all the love and support they gave us.

The cruise was a mix of emotions knowing Carter would have loved it as he tended to do with everything. One day for lunch we had a lovely corner table with a view out to sea. John asked, "What table is this? If we take this ship again we'll ask for it as our dinner table", which was table 127 on this cruise I lifted the table card and saw "six," and we all just stared at each other.

Elated, I said, "Carter's showing us that he's here with us." I know some of these things must be coincidences, but when you watch the timing and how meaningful they are to us, are they coincidences?

When we arrived back in Fort Lauderdale, Olivia asked if we could watch the ship dock. As we were watching, she said, "Look at the post we're tying up to, its number six." I thought, *if you're sending these signs, thank you, Carter.*

Carter was always my first and last thought every day. For years after his death, as soon as I opened my eyes in the morning I thought of him and silently said, "morning Carter." That awful reality bore down on me before I even took a breath, and the day would only get worse after that. He was my last thought of the day, too. "Goodnight Carter, I love you so much. Can you hear me? Please let me know if you are there." I begged from the deepest core of my existence.

Several months after his accident, I no longer allowed myself to think of the crash or the final images he saw; I simply couldn't cope with it. The sight of a transport truck approaching me as I was stopped to make a turn would bring me to tears and immobilized me in my car as I knew this was his last terrifying sight. The flashing lights or sirens of emergency vehicles would send me into a tailspin as I thought of all the hell that might be heading towards others' lives just as they did to ours. I would try to stop myself as my mind would begin to go out of control—this is only going to make these moments more tortuous for you to get through, so don't go there. Think of his happy moments; see happy times, his smile, his laugh. I can't change what had happened to him, remember our time together and how happy Carter was.

A war was raging within me between my mind that seemed fatally wounded and inner strength that was guiding and willing me to fight on. All of these thoughts were true, but I knew that focusing on our happy times made me remember how blessed I was. Memories that I could hold onto and know that he had a great life and we enjoyed the time we had together. I made myself focus on the quality of his life, and not the sadness of his death. Never did I allow myself to think what if ... hindsight is always perfect. Blaming myself or, even worse, others for choices that we make endlessly only caused more hurt. All decisions, even small ones, can change every outcome. I shouldn't torture myself by thinking *if only* ... if only we had waited for his shift to end, if only he had taken the other car ... none of this could change anything now. There was a part of me fighting to survive. My mind clung to the pain and horror, but there was an inner wisdom and compassion serving me that I had never been aware of before.

On April 3, 2009, I spent a wonderful day with my friend Nancy at a yoga conference. It took us a while to find a parking space. Nancy said we had better write down the section number so we don't forget where we parked. I looked, and couldn't believe what I was seeing: we were in green section six, Carter's favourite colour and number.

"I'll remember," I said, and as we walked between columns of green sixes into the building I began to cry, "it's like he's here, leading us in." I held onto Nancy for support. Afterward, we went to my cottage and I told her about the experiences I was having, and said I didn't know what to think. She gave me the book, *My Gift of Light,* hoping it might help me. Nancy wasn't certain if she should give it to me, but after we talked she felt confident that she should. I couldn't put it down. It was as if I was reading about my life, and it was reassuring that the author had also experienced and struggled with some of the same things I was. I was still trying to learn to meditate to calm my mind, and in the book, the author said that meditation led her to an awareness of spirit. Forget calming, I'd found an even greater reason to learn to meditate!

The Struggles and Blessings of Spring

From this point forward I will often begin with a date followed by a description of some of the selected events from my journals. I hope this allows your thinking to progress along with me and you become part of my journey.

April 8, 2009:

This was Carter's first birthday since his passing. I had wanted to ask his friends to be with us but hadn't because many were at university writing exams. Then on April 7th, his friend Curtis called to say that Carter's friends who weren't writing exams tomorrow would like to visit. How wonderful! I said we'd love to see them. My struggle over his birthday had been deepened by not being able to give Carter a gift, but this gave me a new idea. I could give each of them a gift from Carter on his birthday. Victoria made CDs with Carter's favourite songs from summer 2008, and I chose a photo of him holding a butterfly as the CD cover. This was a good distraction, as it kept us happily busy.

I had only expected a few friends, but when I opened the door, I was thrilled to see so many of them standing there. We talked happily about their lives and Carter. I kept waiting to hear Carter's voice amongst theirs, as it all seemed so normal to hear them talking and laughing in our home. They were exactly what we needed, it was our gift to get us through the day, and I hope we helped them too.

May 8, 2009:

Carter's football coach had a baby boy and named him Carter. We didn't know about this at the time, but a week later he came to our house and asked if he could bring in a surprise for us. I said of course, then watched as he brought two of his children and his wife holding a newborn baby. John, Victoria, Olivia, and I were honoured and completely speechless. I asked him what was it that he saw in Carter that made him choose to name his son after him, as this was an incredible tribute. He said that Carter was the most encouraging person he had ever met in his entire life, to both his teammates on the football field and in any situation where he would see him at school with his friends or with people Carter didn't even know. Whenever people were upset, Carter would stay with them until he cheered them up, either by being silly or just talking to them until he could see them feeling better. He said he'd never seen anyone do for people what Carter would do and he felt it was even more amazing for him to do this at such a young age. He also said at the daily football practices Carter was always happy, didn't complain, and did as he was asked.

Later that month at Victoria's water polo game, her coach (who had also coached Carter) and I were discussing what the football coach had said. He agreed completely, "I don't think Carter ever realized how much he did for other people. He was just being Carter."

I trudged through days that never seemed to end only to have to endure sleepless nights. When I did manage to sleep, woven into the storyline of my dreams was the understanding that Carter couldn't be in the dream because he had died; there was no escape from the grief. I not only couldn't sleep—I didn't really want to sleep. That longed-for sleep that I had waited for all day was no better than being awake.

May 10, 2009:

It was the day before Mother's Day. It would be my first without Carter, and I was dreading it. I had struggled to prepare to face Carter's birthday for months before it happened and I had barely recovered from that, and now Mother's Day was upon me. I knew the girls would try more than ever to make Mother's Day special for me and I needed to pull myself together. I wanted to try to find some enjoyment in the day and treasure all their memories.

To make things worse, it was a very difficult weekend for me at the cottage. John had decided it would be kind to launch the boat for our neighbours, who had bought it from us. We hadn't brought the car with the boat trailer hitch, so we called our friend

Roy to help and after he and John launched the boat, Roy headed back to our cottage with the boat trailer. Meanwhile, out on the lake, the boat had started making loud crackling sounds and smoke began pouring out of the engine. John phoned me in a panic saying he thought the boat might explode or sink and asked if I could find Roy and send him back. As I rushed outside I saw Roy driving down the road, and told him what was happening. Then I ran back into the cottage to tell Olivia that I was going to see if I could help and I raced back and got into Roy's truck. He had already phoned a friend with a barge to help get to the boat. We had no idea if the boat would be sunk or if John might have had to jump off into the freezing water. The men left immediately and I waited on shore; luckily they found John still onboard and towed the boat back to shore. In the past, we would have been able to handle a crisis like this quite easily, but now life's usual challenges became unbelievably stressful.

Mother's Day

May 11, 2009:

Neither of us could sleep that night, so at 2 a.m. Mother's Day morning John decided to drive home and switch cars for the one with the trailer hitch. He then returned to the cottage by 7 a.m. None of this was helping me; in fact, I was feeling more fragile by the moment. John had a nap since he had been up all night and we were going to tow the boat home later.

Unable to control my emotions any longer with all the chaos of the weekend on top of it being Mother's Day, I began falling apart. Shaking and crying, I went into Carter's room and sat on his bed. I missed him so much. Even this gesture of kindness for our friends had caused me such stress and panic; I felt everything in life seemed so painful right now. I opened Carter's drawers and took out his necklace of wooden beads and put them around my neck, then gently rubbed them with my hands as I tried to calm down. I hoped by having his beads around me it would be like him giving me a hug, and I *really* needed a hug from him right now. I began to feel a wonderful tingling sensation around my head and shoulders and I questioned whether I was doing anything to cause this. I checked my breathing—it was normal, my heart was not racing so I shouldn't be light-headed. There seemed to be no reason for me to feel this way. Then I smiled as I wondered, *Carter, is that you that I'm feeling?* The sensation around me felt wonderful and comforting, and the more I realized how good it felt the more I hoped it was Carter giving me a hug. I sat perfectly still for several minutes, my hand resting on the beads of his necklace as I allowed myself to enjoy the feeling. Thankfully, I felt a bit better. Had I been given the hug I so desperately needed?

May 23, 2009:

We were having a party for my mother's ninetieth birthday. Two years prior, we had held a big family party for her eighty-eighth birthday at our home. John had said, "Don't wait for her ninetieth. Have it now when we know she can enjoy it, you don't know what will happen in the next two years." As her ninetieth approached, the last party was all that I could think of. How could it possibly be that it's Carter who's not with us? He can't be the one who's dead.

We all wanted to celebrate Mom's special birthday, but it was going to be difficult for us. After what I had experienced on Mother's Day, I decided I might ask Carter to help us. I began by asking if that was him helping me on Mother's Day could he please give us a sign that he was with us at Mom's birthday also, to help us through the day. Victoria, Olivia, and I gave Mom her gifts before the party and one of them was a new frame for Carter's and Victoria's high school graduation photos. When Victoria took Carter's picture out of the old frame she turned it over and we saw for the first time that Carter had signed it – to Grandma Love Carter. Victoria looked up at me, smiled and said, "Mom I think you've got your sign." This was the only graduation picture that Carter had signed. Why did I feel such an urgency to reframe it that day? Mom had wanted it done for six months and I had never done it. I know this isn't a very convincing sign, but as the year progressed I would see that on special days when I was struggling and didn't know how I'd get through, that day something would happen to help me like it did here and on Mother's Day.

Two weeks after Mom's birthday, Carter's friend Richard and Victoria presented the first Carter Roud Team Player Award at his high school as we and Kevin and Sean tearfully watched. Next was Olivia's grade six graduation, followed the very next day by Victoria's high school graduation. Our girls smiled and looked lovely as they both received awards and we were so happy and proud of them, but every family celebration was incomplete without Carter and during all these important moments that mark life's passage we had to fight for happiness through our grief.

As spring progressed, anxiety, grief, and emptiness often overcame me. We had to face so many hurdles and I felt pushed to my limit, but somehow I found a way through each one. I knew the girls needed to have happy memories of their special days and I hoped we could all find a way to enjoy them. The waves hadn't drowned me yet, but I could feel a giant wave of grief and anxiety hitting me hard so I phoned Patricia, my grief counselor, saying I urgently needed to see her. She said she was sorry but she didn't have any openings for several weeks. An hour later she phoned to say she had a cancellation that afternoon. Coincidence or not, it was certainly what I needed.

The next day the whole family was visibly struggling with emotions, as we had all been weakened by the months of effort we had been enduring. That night Olivia slept in Carter's room as she often did. When I went into his room to check on her, I was instantly aware of a very strong and familiar smell.

Without thinking I immediately said, "Olivia, I can smell Carter." She looked up from her book, a bit dazed, as I said, "Can you smell him, Olivia? I really can." She said no, but she had a cold and couldn't really smell anything. I was shaken because this had never happened before, but I tried to compose myself and comfort her. "He could have been right beside you on his bed. Maybe he knows you're having a hard time and he's trying to help you."

Then Olivia said something startling. She said she had smelled Carter several times before.

"What? Why didn't you tell me when this happened?"

Olivia said, "I didn't know what to think. I thought it was kind of strange."

I asked, "Do you remember what you were doing? Or when this happened?" She said it was usually when she was really upset and she was either in her bed or Carter's. My mind instantly started searching back over the day. *Think Charmaine, think.* His window had been open and I had been in and out of his room throughout the day, yet this smell hadn't been there at any other time that day.

It took me a long time to fall asleep that night, as so many thoughts were racing through my mind. Why did I say he could have been there with her? Because I could still smell him, maybe that meant he was still there? Why didn't I think more clearly? Had we lost this chance to be with him when he was letting us know he was in the room? I promised myself that whether this was real or not, if it happened again I was going to sit down no matter what and spend that time with Carter. I woke up the next morning feeling both very excited at what had happened and very sad that I had missed a great opportunity.

Later in June during an appointment with Patricia, I became very emotional and upset so I changed the topic and said, "on a nicer note, I must tell you what happened."

She was sitting back, relaxed in her chair, and as soon as I told her that I had smelled Carter she sat bolt upright and said, "oh my gosh, yes!" I was startled at first, I then said that she didn't need to say another thing to me; her reaction was perfect for me. She didn't think I was imagining it. She said several other bereaved parents had told her the same thing. I went home feeling a little more positive about what I had been thinking. Could Carter be letting us know he was still with us? I spent a lot of time thinking as I continually re-lived these events, trying to figure out what was going on. I wished I'd asked Victoria if she could smell him as well since she was right beside his room. Patricia said don't doubt what you're experiencing if others don't have the same experience it could just be meant for you. Those words were helpful to me. I began to put together a possible explanation of that evening for myself. When I walked into the room, Carter wanted me to know that Olivia wasn't alone, that he was with her when she was upset. If this was true, then it would mean that he knows when she needed him, and if he could do it for her then he could do it for all of us.

My constant questioning tormented me. I needed to know beyond any doubt if Carter, and therefore all of us, were more than our physical bodies, if life was more than what we could see and if these odd but timely events were somehow from Carter. I yearned for peace of mind, but peace could only come by successfully finding Carter. I must be strong, courageous, and follow my heart even though I often felt that I was fighting a battle that couldn't be won.

The summer of 2009 was looming heavy in our hearts as it approached. We arrived at the cottage, knowing our summers would never have that unbridled joy again. Other years we couldn't get to the lake fast enough. This year we wanted to go, but how could we go without Carter? I don't know how to describe the feeling when we arrived—hollow, vacant, numb. We brought our things in from the car then we all scattered to different rooms, shattered yet again.

The Hummingbird

The weather that summer was terrible. Every day I opened my eyes, looking toward the lake and thinking it looked like I felt, horribly sad and lifeless. Gradually I realized that I was thankful for every grey day, knowing if I woke to see the lake shimmering under a bright blue sky I'd feel worse because Carter wasn't there to enjoy it with us. I felt that the lake was sad for its loss of Carter and was showing its respect for him. Though I knew this couldn't be true, it made me feel better to think it. Personally, I'd be happy if this weather continued all summer. As other people complained about the cold and rain, I thought to myself, *it's perfect*. As July wore on, the approaching anniversary of the accident was unbearable for us to cope with. I considered us going home to be with

Carter's friends since they had helped us on his birthday, but the girls definitely wanted to stay at the cottage. Their decision took the pressure off me to try to decide what was best, not that anything was.

July 29, 2009:

I couldn't sleep, so I got up very early, made coffee, and sat outside in the garden, trying to find some enjoyment in the flowers. I felt tortured, knowing this time last year Carter only had about fifteen hours left to live. I began to wonder, if we knew when we were going to die, how would we choose to live our last hours? I'm sure we'd try to surround ourselves with happiness and joy, which is just what Carter unknowingly did. I didn't know how I could survive this day, but it helped me knowing he had enjoyed every moment of those last precious hours.

As I sat counting down the minutes, a hummingbird flew into the garden and distracted me from my thoughts. How nice; I hadn't seen one yet this year. I was enjoying its beauty when suddenly the bird darted toward me. Then closer again, each time hovering for a few seconds before moving closer. When it darted closer for the third time, it was only inches from my face as it continued to fly back and forth with its eyes looking directly at me. I wanted to move away, knowing that if it came closer one more time it would hit me in the face, but I was frightened to move in case I startled it and it banged into me anyway. As our eyes continued to lock on each other, I realized this bird was behaving very strangely. Why was it right in front of me? Then an idea hit me like a bolt of lightning. *Could Carter have sent me this hummingbird?*

I asked him, "Carter, did you send me this hummingbird?" And as soon as I silently voiced this question, the hummingbird flew away. I continued to sit in the garden and wonder. It was inconceivable to me, but could it have been from Carter? As it flew in front of me, was Carter saying, "Mom, I'm right here with you," and why did it fly away as soon as I thought of this?

Each second of that day ticked by slowly, and every time I looked at the clock I knew what Carter had been doing at that time only one year ago, and how much time he had to live. These thoughts were eased a bit as the question of the hummingbird floated like a haze in my mind and seemed to ease grief's stranglehold on me ever so slightly.

As July 29 progressed, for one of the very first times this summer the sun shone, if only for a while, and even Olivia noticed and mentioned it to me later. Throughout the day, people phoned and left messages, but I couldn't talk to anyone. I had to try to be strong and somehow help my daughters. Cam was the only person I called back. He told me Carter's friends were all together and not doing very well, either. I told him I was glad they were together and I sent them our love. Would this day never end? The girls both had friends over and they were wonderful in helping them get through the day. I tried not to watch the clock, then finally thinking it must be well past the time of the accident, I looked at the clock. To my horror, it was 9:10—the time of the accident! There are simply no words to describe how that moment was for me as I stared at the clock, unable to move.

As the morning of July 30 began, for the first time that summer I opened my eyes to see a clear blue sky. I lay in bed thinking, *I don't know how we did it, but we've made it through that awful day and year and after a month of cloudy, cold and rainy days I must try to see the sun as a positive sign.* I felt thankful to our lake for giving me July exactly how I needed it to be and for the sun to shine as I woke on July 30. I told myself maybe now I could start to see the sun on the lake.

Throughout the summer I frequently went into Carter's room at the cottage, sat on his bed, and thought of him. I sometimes smelled his familiar smell, but it was never as strong and overpowering as it was in June with Olivia. I began going in and out of his room several times a day to see if I could smell him and to my great delight, every few days I did. Even though there was never anything different, his window and door were always open and the air was fresh, but his smell would come and go. I was growing more confident that when the smell was present, Carter was letting me know he was in the room with me, and I'd sit on his bed and send thoughts to him. Never again was I going to miss the chance to be with him like I felt I had back in June at home.

One day, feeling very sad, I went into Carter's room and even though I smelled him and felt he was there, it didn't help. I began to think about the last time I saw him in his bed the morning I asked him to teach Olivia to water ski. I missed him so much my heart was breaking. I lay down on his bed exactly as he had been that last morning. Consumed by grief, I gradually began to notice a sensation on my lower legs that slowly moved up my body that's hard to describe. It was a very delicate fluttering sensation like someone was moving their arms in circular patterns ever so softly along the back of my body up to my shoulders. I was amazed, what an incredible feeling and I let myself hope it was Carter. Later, I realized that for the first time I could both smell and feel him at the same time. I told myself once again to somehow find strength from this. If he was trying to help I must let him help me, but it still wasn't enough for me.

Meditation Opens a Door

In August during a massage, I mentioned to the massage therapist that I'd been trying to learn to meditate to help me relax. She said she had a friend, Sharon, who could teach me, then searched unsuccessfully for her business card. Coincidently, later that same day Sharon came into her office.

Sharon called me and asked, "Where are you trying to meditate?" When I said on my dock, she replied, "Perfect; I will come to you."

August 19, 2009:
Sharon arrived early in the morning. We sat on the dock with our feet in the water and she instructed me to rest my hands on my thighs with palms upright, then close my eyes and picture what she described as she guided me through a meditation. She began by describing a beam of light wrapping around me from head to toe first inside then out. Next, she described walking along a woodland path to a large rock, which I climbed onto. She said I could ask spirit to join me here and added that I might be able to feel something. Obviously, I asked Carter to join me and hold my hand. Almost instantly I felt a slight tingling in my left hand. When she ended the guided meditation, I took a deep breath, opened my eyes, and exhaled. WOW, so that's what a successful meditation feels like! That was incredible. After ten frustrating months, I had been totally immersed in what I was experiencing, and from that day forward I've had more success meditating. They aren't always with such clarity or without struggle, but once I began to visualize a journey and stopped trying to empty my mind I found a method that worked for me.

That same night, as Olivia and I lay on my bed, I began to feel a gentle vibration under my left side from my feet to my chest. I asked Olivia if she could feel anything since she was to my left.

"No; what?" she asked.

"That's okay; never mind." I didn't want to tell her if she couldn't feel anything. This must be my imagination, but as the vibration continued to get stronger I couldn't ignore it. Maybe Olivia was too far from me to feel anything because I certainly couldn't deny what I was feeling so I asked Olivia to come closer.

She moved toward me and after a few seconds said, "Oh!"

"What, can you feel it?" I asked, relieved that it was real.

She said, "The bed is shaking. No, it's kind of vibrating."

I was amazed but very glad that she felt it. The vibration lasted about ten minutes then gradually faded away. I didn't have any sense it was Carter, in fact, I felt that it wasn't Carter, but I have no idea what it was that we both felt.

After my success meditating I was committed to practicing each day. Reading the book *My Gift of Light* and my growing belief that Carter was trying to help me fueled my drive to keep searching for proof of his existence. Sharon said that she did Reiki, which I'd never heard of, but since I'd had such a wonderful experience with her I thought why not try it, so we scheduled an appointment.

I meditated before our meeting, hoping I might have a better experience. Sharon began by saying to relax and picture myself in a nice place as I lay down on the table. I didn't want to focus on Carter because I'd get upset, so I decided to picture myself with my parents and my dog at Queenston Heights Park where we often walked. Quickly, I began to see amazing colours that distracted me from continuing to visualize the walk. I was mesmerized by vibrant violet and neon green blobs moving in and out as if in a lava lamp. Next, violet circles appeared that were punctured in the middle by green that expanded until it filled the circle; one colour would fade, then reappear somewhere else. I knew Sharon was standing behind my head as I continued to enjoy watching the colours when suddenly a blinding white light cut through the colours in a brilliant narrow beam. I gasped as it startled me with its astonishing beauty and I began to cry. Sharon leaned over and asked if I was okay. I said yes, thinking, *don't distract me from this radiant beam of light,* which vanished when she moved her hands from above my head and she shifted to my side. I began to see soft pink and yellow colours that had no comparison to the vividness of what I first saw. She next worked over my heart center and I "saw" a beautiful blue sky with soft white clouds that appeared in my peripheral vision. They were forming simultaneously on each side and moving to the center to form a "smoke ring" that then rose up, fading until it disappeared. Over and over this happened as I watched, completely absorbed. After a while, I looked at Sharon with my eyes slightly open. I saw her as a black silhouette holding her hands over my chest. A beam of light shone down, touched her head then disappeared, reappearing on the other side of me beside my chest as if it was entering Sharon and exiting out of me.

When the session ended she asked, "Were you thinking about Carter when you were crying?" I shook my head no. I didn't really want to talk. I wanted time to absorb what I'd experienced. She said she stopped when she was working over my heart to see if I was okay because she couldn't hold her hands there. Each time she held them back above my chest she felt pressure forcing her hands up and away from me again and again.

I stared at her and then asked, "Can I tell you what I experienced?"

When I was seeing the smoke rings form, rise, and disappear, this was when her hands were being pushed away. She couldn't know this, but I could place what she said to what I had experienced. The beam of light was unbelievably beautiful, but it was only there when she was working over my head. When she moved away from my head the beam disappeared. She later spoke to her Reiki teacher and was told that the smoke rings were the emotional pain being released from my body. When she told me this several weeks later it made sense to me, I had been aware from that day on that I felt lighter, less burdened, and my days had more ease on an emotional level. What amazed me was that I knew nothing about Reiki; therefore what I experienced was not based on anything I had hoped for or ever known could be possible.

Sharon visited one month later to see how I was progressing. As we chatted, I began to feel a vibration underneath me, and though she was sitting beside me she felt nothing.

As I felt it get stronger she stopped talking, stared at me, then said, "It's you; your whole body is shaking, even your head and cheeks."

This unnerved me. "I really don't like this," I said.

She said, "Say that you don't like it and you want it to stop." Thinking that was ridiculous I said nothing, but she was persistent. "You need to say it."

I still felt the vibration, so I tried to overcome my embarrassment as I said out loud, "I want this to stop." Instantly I felt the vibration slide down and off my body. I looked at Sharon in complete disbelief.

She said, "I think in your desire to reach Carter you are opening up to this incredibly fast. Always remember you're in complete charge of your body. Never let anything happen that you don't want; you just tell it to stop."

I found this experience very unsettling, to say the least, yet it didn't slow me down as I pushed on in search of Carter.

Summer came to an end. We had all endured the first summer without Carter from beginning to end, including the anniversary of his death. We had endured an entire year of special days and moments without him, but to my amazement, I felt that I was actually making progress in my search for him, and this hope kept me moving forward.

September 3, 2009:

My last summer morning at the lake began in peaceful stillness with a meditation on the dock. I then woke Olivia and we enjoyed a cup of tea together as we dangled our feet in the water and watched the morning mist rise over the lake. Then with much reluctance we drove home, John and Victoria had gone home several days before so she could pack; the next day she was to begin university.

The roads home were empty. Olivia chose a CD of Carter's favourite songs to listen to, and as his music filled the car I was filled with sadness. *This is so unfair*, I thought, *it's your music, your favourite car. This should be you driving home to begin your second year of university!* As I began fighting back tears, I thought I felt Carter holding my free hand and as I drove along the empty road I wondered if he and I could drive together.

We have a great photo of Carter driving during his road trip to Florida with Sean in February 2008. I held that image in my mind as I repeated over and over; *this is your favourite car, your music, come on Carter, drive!* I hoped that I might feel his hands on mine against the steering wheel, but I was totally unprepared for what happened next. I felt so much pressure against my chest that I couldn't breathe, which caused me to lose focus and release the image of the photo from my mind. Immediately the pressure vanished. What just happened? Why couldn't I breathe? Was I holding my breath? I needed to try that again and make sure I was breathing normally. Again I held the image of him driving and said, *come on Carter, drive*. The pressure on my chest returned full force and stayed as long as I held that photo's image in my mind. I repeated this six or seven times exactly the same way so I could examine what I experienced, and each time I got the same results. The pressure always remained while I held the image of Carter driving in my mind and vanished when I released the image. Finally, I said silently *Carter, this has to stop. I don't know what I'm doing and I don't think you do, either.* Later at home, I wondered if he could have been "sitting" on me in the driver's seat and that was the pressure I felt against my chest. This was unbelievable, my mind raced with excitement; if this was Carter, had he ever ended summer with a big splash.

I had been apprehensive to leave the cottage. I felt it was instrumental in my learning to meditate and experiencing unique events that summer. I was worried that I'd lose all the momentum that I'd gained when I returned to the city, and that was nearly true. For days at home I tried to meditate with absolutely no success. This of course only made me more anxious and emotional, which didn't help. Meditation calmed me, and I felt the difference it made in my days. I knew I didn't want to lose it. After a week of frustration, I chose to try sitting outside to meditate. My mind easily drifted into silence, and I didn't even hear the lawnmower next door—success! That was followed by many more unsuccessful weeks as I tried to meditate in various rooms and locations, but there were always noises and interruptions. In frustration, one day I decided to try in Carter's room, no one else but me went in there very often during the day. To my relief, his room felt right, so though I continued to struggle, from then on I always meditated in Carter's room when I was home.

For Always

Einstein's theory of relativity (E=mc²)
At its most basic level, the equation says that energy and mass (matter) are interchange-
able; they are different forms of the same thing. Under the right conditions, energy can
become mass and vice versa.

For the first time since summer ended, we returned to the cottage in September to spend the weekend. I remained behind when the family left the cottage and waited for my friend Janice to arrive the next day for a visit. While I was alone, I found one of Carter's CDs on a shelf and placed it into the CD player and pushed play, but heard nothing. I wondered, maybe its blank (even though it was labeled) or damaged? I skipped to the next song just to be sure there was nothing on it, and a beautiful song began to play called, "For Always." I couldn't believe the words: "even though I am millions of stars away as long as I can reach out and touch you." Carter, this is exactly what you are doing, you reach out and touch my hand! When the song ended, I pushed stop and sat on the floor, all alone, crying. It was as if Carter was speaking to me through this song but that was crazy, wasn't it? I was stunned when I realized if there was music on the disc, why didn't the first song play? I turned the CD player on again and pushed play one more time, and this time the first song played. Was Carter orchestrating this? Was he using this to reach out to me? And if he was, how could he do this? The words in the second song spoke directly to me about what I had been experiencing, but when I listened to the first song it was meaningless to me. I was plagued by questions that couldn't be answered. Was my mind creating a story to answer my questions, or was there some truth to my thoughts? If the first song had played initially would I have been as focused on the words of the second song, or had he drawn my attention to the CD so I would be focused on the words he wanted me to hear? Also, why would Carter put this song on a CD? It seemed an unusual choice for a nineteen-year-old boy. Once again my head was spinning with inconceivable ideas as I struggled to make some sense of these odd occurrences.

When I returned home, I talked to Mom about these thoughts. I knew she wasn't comfortable with my exploration into the world of spirit, but right then I needed to be with my mother and talk to her. I was excited, and thinking positively about the song on the CD. I told her I had to find out if Carter was sending these signs to let us know he's with us. Mom was of course very worried about me. She was worried that I couldn't recover from this tragedy and worried that I was treading into dangerous areas. She counseled me not to go down this road.

"People get lost in that world trying to find answers. You have to have faith. I know Carter is safe and in a better place. He's fine, Charmaine. You just have to believe he is."

I gently wiped my tears away, upset that she wasn't excited with me, and tried not to overreact to her statement. I knew she was trying to help me, and I knew she truly believed what she was saying, but I didn't believe it.

This was my ongoing dilemma: I didn't believe! I tried to explain this to her. I wanted to believe it, of course I did. I wanted Carter to survive past this life, but there was no conviction in my heart to believe, only an aching desire for it to be true, and if I was just telling myself he's fine ultimately that wouldn't bring me peace of mind.

Though I was debilitated and confused as I tried to find my way through this increasing entanglement of ongoing thoughts, I couldn't let this search go. I had to know; there was no other way forward for me. I needed proof beyond any doubt, and it didn't matter to me what anybody else thought I was doing this for myself. *I have to find him if I can. I'll never give up searching and if he is doing all this to help us then I don't see why I can't prove that these signs are from him!* My unstoppable mission was to search for answers and find enough proof to know beyond any doubt in my mind that Carter was still in the now and not forever only in the past.

Thanksgiving 2009 was approaching, and Olivia wanted our traditional dinner. I struggled to find the strength as memories flooded into my mind of all the happy years with my parents and John's mom gathered for Sunday dinners and special occasions around the table. How could I do this now after the death of my father, John's mother, and, most painfully, Carter?

October 12, 2009:

I began Thanksgiving Day with a meditation in the hope that I could somehow find the strength deep within me to do this for all of us. I began my usual meditation of walking along a woodland path, creating a detailed vision of all that I saw, when a hummingbird appeared at the edge of the woods. Immediately I questioned how this bird appeared. I was creating what I saw, yet a hummingbird that I never thought of flew in; that shouldn't happen. The bird flew toward me and then hovered back and forth in front of my face, with almost identical behaviour to the one in the garden on July 29. I said hello to the bird while I simultaneously thought, *where did you come from?*

As I struggled for an answer I asked, "Carter have you sent me another humming-bird?" Once I formed this thought, the bird flew out of view. Inspired by the hope of Carter's participation in my meditation with the hummingbird I opened my eyes, smiled, and immediately went into the kitchen and started cooking Thanksgiving dinner. I felt I had much to be thankful for, and I was grateful that once again it seemed Carter had helped me face a very difficult day.

October 18, 2009:

We spent the next weekend at the cottage, and I was anxious to meditate on my dock again since I was still having little success at home. The day was cool but I wasn't going to let that stop me, so I wrapped a big blanket around myself, slid into a Muskoka chair, and slipped easily into meditation. I sensed a swirling motion around me that felt like I was sitting in a whirlwind. I was annoyed when I heard the neighbour's dog approach me and start barking. This was a distraction I didn't need as I was trying to figure out what it was that I felt around me. The dog became more agitated. Why is this silly dog barking? I opened my eyes and was stunned that I could actually see a swirling mass circling around me with bright lights that were changing colours within the movement. Beyond it, I saw the dog facing me, still barking. It became increasingly difficult for me to breathe as this swirling mass seemed to be drawing the air out of me, and I didn't have any idea what this was. It began out of nowhere and then disappeared, but while it was happening I experienced sensations through multiple senses and perhaps this was what the dog was barking at.

October 19, 2009:

The next day I was back home, sitting in Carter's room preparing to meditate when I felt pressure high on my chest similar to but not as strong as what I experienced on September 3 in the car. I was uncomfortable, so I tried a few times to pull myself forward and get out of the chair, yet something seemed to be holding me in place. I could feel something pushing against me, but there was nothing visible. I told myself this was quite the scene if someone should come into this room and see me struggling unsuccessfully to get out of this chair. They're going to either laugh or be really worried about my sanity as I continued to struggle against thin air to get up. Was Carter pushing against my chest or sitting on me? I didn't know what was happening, but I could definitely feel something unseen pushing me back in the chair, and this lasted for several minutes.

Finally, in frustration of not being able to get up, I said, "Okay Carter, get off of me." As soon as I said this the pressure vanished and I sat forward and got up. That was really weird. I had continued to feel the pressure until I acknowledged him by saying Carter get off me, then I guess he did. I left the room smiling as I imagined how much Carter must have enjoyed that, and I pictured him standing back from the chair with a great big grin when I finally thought of him.

In September I had brought the CD home from the cottage that had the song "For Always" on it, but I hadn't been able to listen to it again. Perhaps I didn't have the emotional strength, or maybe it was my lack of courage to hear the words of that song, to feel those raw emotions ripping me open and asking myself once again those unknowable questions about Carter. People who loved me were often genuinely concerned that my grief was pushing me to the boundaries of sanity, as was I, but I wouldn't be persuaded by anyone to stop. I was determined, and this fire that raged within me was being continually fueled by an ever-increasing awareness of odd but timely occurrences.

October 20, 2009:

While driving, I decided I was ready to hear the entire "For Always" CD for the first time. I listened to all the songs, which moved through a mix of both upbeat and inspirational songs. I started to cry as a song called "Remember Me" began, "as long as you remember me when I am gone I will always be with you, I will never leave you ..." My thoughts were streaming directly toward a vision of Carter I held in my heart.

"Carter, this song too speaks to me so clearly of your death and what I've been experiencing that I'm hoping is you." I couldn't understand why he would have recorded either of these songs. Was Carter using them as a way to speak to me because if he is, the songs are doing it perfectly?

December 23, 2009:

Carter's friends visited, and for the first time since the funeral, we saw Cayley. I had wanted to thank her ever since John found Carter's text message on his phone to her about teaching Olivia to water ski as that message was so helpful. Olivia and I took Cayley aside to thank her privately.

When I said I wanted to tell her about Carter's phone, her face went pale and she said, "Oh, the phone!"

My heart skipped a beat. "What do you mean, 'oh the phone'?"

She said, "Nothing; it's okay. Say what you were going to say." But my mind was racing ahead, wondering if she had also experienced something.

"Honestly Cayley, if something has happened I'd really like to know because a lot of weird stuff is going on and I'm trying to figure it out."

Then to my surprise, Olivia said, "There's a lot of things happening with Carter, a lot!" I told Cayley our water ski story, then asked her if she could please tell me what she had been about to say.

Hesitantly, she began telling us that after his death she got four text messages from Carter. They were all about one month apart, always near the date of Carter's death, the first coming toward the end of August and they continued for four months. She said the first text message she received after Carter's death was the last message he had sent to her. The timing of this first message is as startling as the timing of Sean's message, and to make it even more incredible, both of these messages were received in perfect timing on the same day! On Aug 21, 2008, Cayley was working at a summer camp, talking to a little boy named Carter. When she said his name she got upset, so she went behind a tree and tried to regain her composure. It was at that moment when her cell phone rang. She looked at the phone and saw "duplicate message," and then the last message she received from Carter appeared on the screen, and she began to cry. Carter had sent two messages to two very special friends on the same day, and the timing was astonishingly accurate both times! Even if you refuse to believe this is possible, what are the odds of this happening?

She continued to tell us the first two were duplicate messages and the next two were new ones. She had wanted to tell us about them, but didn't know if she should. I understood of course, but asked if anything happened again to please tell me.

Happy and excited I asked, "Do you still have them on your phone? Can I see them?" Unfortunately, she had dropped the phone and it broke, but she tried to remember them. I asked her to write down everything she could remember about them for me, when they were sent, if they were sent around special days, or if she was upset when she received them. I was noticing a real correlation to not only what was happening, but also when.

"I don't know why we are being blessed with all these signs. Why is Carter doing all this?"

Cayley said tearfully, "Carter could never stand to see anyone sad or upset while he was here. He always had to do something to help us feel better, and I think he has to help us now just like he always did."

"Wow Cayley, that's perfect—thank you. I never thought of it like that." And I gave her a big hug.

After everyone left, I excitedly told John her story, adding that I thought this was our gift to help get us through Christmas. John said there's no way Carter could have sent the messages, there must be another explanation. He must have sent the new messages before his death but she never received them, and all four messages must have been in the atmosphere and came down randomly. "But that's what I'm trying to tell you; it wasn't random. The first one's timing was absolutely perfect just like Sean's was!"

Once again, I felt John wouldn't even consider what I was thinking. I was fully aware that I sounded crazy, but at least he could think about it. I'm giving him possible evidence that Carter might be trying to help us somehow from somewhere; wouldn't that be better than us thinking he's gone? I tried to stay calm and listen to what John was saying, remembering that I must also be open to others' thoughts even though at the time I wanted to scream out loud in frustration. I didn't believe in any of this either, and I was very skeptical, but I was trying to stay open-minded.

I tried to discuss it further with him. "So you think Carter had sent them while he was alive? If that is correct what are the chances of the perfect timing of the first message and the rest being received monthly all close to the date of the accident? That's not random, is it? The odds become huge."

December 26, 2009:

We struggled through Christmas and then went to Collingwood for a getaway. John and I attended a timeshare talk as part of the trip package. As we were seated with a sales representative, listening to the presentation, I began to feel a vibration under me. I watched to see their reaction to this; especially John because he's often aware of subtle noises and movement, yet neither one of them seemed to notice anything. The vibration grew so strong it felt as if there was a room of massive engines right below us, yet no one acknowledged it and their conversation went on normally. I must have looked confused as the representative asked if I had a question.

I hesitated. "Yes, do either of you feel that?"

"What?" Both she and John asked. By this time, not only could I feel the vibration, I could also hear it and I couldn't believe that they didn't. It continued for ten to fifteen minutes and I couldn't think of anything else while I was experiencing it, then it gradually faded away. I have no idea what it was, but I wondered if it had anything to do with being in the north in the Canadian Shield like our cottage where I had two other similar experiences.

February 2010:

I remembered that Victoria had copied all of Carter's incoming and outgoing text messages from his phone for me. I excitedly searched through them, looking for the two new messages Cayley received in order to find out if John was right or wrong. I will finally know an answer to one of my questions with certainty. The two new messages Cayley received weren't there. This was progress; I discovered Carter hadn't sent them before he died; one question had been answered in my favour.

Later that month, while I was in Carter's room sitting completely still in meditation, I felt the chair cushion sink at my back as if someone had sat down behind me in the chair. I knew I hadn't moved, and with ease, I smiled and said, "Hello, Carter." Whether people believed me or not, I was gaining confidence that he was with me.

The Wings of Love

March 10, 2010:

While driving, I noticed a pink cloud to my right within a completely light-grey cloudy sky. That was odd; I saw the sun behind the clouds on my left, but why were these other clouds pink when everything else was grey? Though most of the clouds in the sky seemed still, the centre of the pink cloud began to change to dark grey while leaving a ring of pink encircling it. As I watched the dark cloud continue to shift, I saw what could possibly be the shape of wings. Yes, it looked like wings in full flight and pulled back. Then I saw a body form, followed by legs in the still shifting cloud. Was it a bird? I checked it over and over again and yes, I thought it was a bird. Next, a beak began to form and got longer and longer when all of a sudden I realized—oh my god, it's a hummingbird. I checked it again: wings pulled back, head, body, long beak. I couldn't believe it, it was a hummingbird! The clouds had now stopped shifting and held as I examined it over and over again. Finally, when I was convinced I silently said, *I see it Carter, I see the hummingbird*. As soon as I acknowledged that, the clouds shifted and the shape was lost.

I was stunned. Was it a sign from Carter, or an odd coincidence? I had so many questions. The pink cloud drew my attention to the sky, but I couldn't see any reason why it would be there. Why did it darken and shift once I noticed it, then hold until I was sure that it looked like a hummingbird? And why, as soon as I said "Carter, I see it," did it disappear? How could this be? It wasn't possible, and even if this was from Carter, how did he do it? I tried to think rationally, yet everything lined up to make me think Carter had given me a third hummingbird. This was not rational thinking! The first hummingbird arrived on the first anniversary of his death, the second in my Thanksgiving meditation, and the third on a day of no importance in the shape of a cloud. Are you using hummingbirds to signal me, Carter?

I backtrack a bit now because it works into the next story. On Nov 30, 2009, Carter's godmother, Maria had brought me to see a medium who told me there was the spirit of a young male present holding up a single flower that was colourful like a mum but shaped like a daisy. This young male spirit said that this flower was significant or special and he wanted me to know that he was showing me THIS flower. She asked me what it meant. I didn't know; it meant nothing to me. She kept questioning me about it as I struggled unsuccessfully to think of anything. I thought she was making it up. I went home feeling disappointed about the reading and forgot about it until March.

March 17, 2010:

I was standing beside John as he turned on the computer. I gasped as a screen came up with the icons of everybody who had an account on that computer. Above Carter's name, I saw an orange daisy-like flower, the exact flower the medium had described.

"John was this always Carter's icon, or has someone changed it?"

He said, "I don't know, I think its Carter's. I didn't change it, why?"

I knew it could upset him to hear the ideas I had and I was aware of how strange I often sounded so I said, "That's okay, it doesn't matter."

I raced downstairs. Breathlessly, I asked, "Olivia, that icon on the computer, was that always Carter's?"

She said that was Carter's.

"Nobody changed it since he died, that was his?" I asked.

"Yes, I always thought it was strange it was not a very Carter thing to have; why?"

"Remember I told you about the flower the medium had told me the young male was holding?" Immediately Olivia's eyes filled with tears, she smiled as she remembered how I'd described it to her.

"That's the flower, Mom. Carter was not really thinking, mentioning the flower to you. He knows you never go on the computer. What was the point of giving you that message, because you're never going to get it?" We laughed happily, and more importantly, I had fit another piece of this puzzle into place. I had doubted the medium but I just hadn't understood the message; maybe it had been Carter.

My doubts were dissolving and I was becoming more confident that I might actually be able to find proof of Carter's continued existence. All the time I had spent gazing vaguely into space seemed to allow my mind to contemplate new ways of thinking. I had become more inquisitive and paid closer attention to things. I was excited by each curious event and saw wonder in their possibilities while I was encouraged by their constant uniqueness and continuous appearance. One thought was leading me to another and I could refer back to connect an older experience with a current event. This was allowing my acceptance to continue to build. As it did when I had checked the texts Victoria saved for me from Carter's phone and I saw that Cayley's new texts had never been sent by him while he was alive. I was gradually trusting my thoughts and forming a few answers I could accept.

My Second Dream Visit

March 23, 2010:

I had a second very special dream that began with me standing in our kitchen as the doorbell rang several times. As I walked toward the door, the bell rang for the third time and the knob began to turn. I was frightened as the door flung open, not knowing who was entering the house. Immediately I saw Carter's face. He was holding the doorknob and leaning his head in past the open door as he said loud and clear with a huge smile, "Hello, Mom."

I screamed, "Carter, oh Carter I've missed you!" And I grabbed him and held him tight. I was beyond happy, thrilled, as we twirled around joyously in circles. I began singing "It's a Long Way to Tipperary" (why I was singing this I have no idea.) Our twirling shifted to dancing and I felt his running shoes resting on top of my feet. No wonder we were moving so smoothly. It occurred to me that I was carrying all his weight on my feet, so why wasn't this hurting me? To check, I looked down through his arms that were holding me and I clearly saw his feet on mine and right then he vanished and I woke up. I could feel pressure on my feet, I couldn't feel it in my dream but I could then, and I started to cry.

I told myself not to be upset because I woke and he was not there, but rather be happy that he had been there. I had wanted another dream; this was a gift. I told myself to hold on to the feeling of pressure on my feet as long as I could and enjoy it. Then somehow I was back into the dream. I don't remember falling back to sleep or even how I could go from being wide awake to sleeping, but somehow as I was thinking *hold on to this feeling,* I was dreaming once again. I was still in the front hall, but this time I faced the stairs with Carter standing on my left side. Olivia had now come downstairs and was standing on the bottom stair, leaning on the railing and beaming with joy to see Carter.

He was bursting with happiness to see her. He smiled, then leaned down, scooping her up with excitement and in his big booming voice said, "LIV!" and our combined joy defies description. At that exact moment, I woke, completely overwhelmed by how vivid the dream was and my feeling of pure joy when I was within it and that I still had felt his feet when I first woke. I tried to be happy that Carter had come to visit me and now, three and a half years later, it still plays as perfectly in my mind as it did that morning.

April 4, 2010:

Both John's and Carter's birthdays are in April and often Easter as well, so it is a difficult month for us now. As Easter approached, I had asked Carter to give us a sign if he could that he was with us. On Easter I had sent thoughts of love to him all day, but sadly, I didn't notice anything that I thought might be a sign. The next day, John asked me if I had come up behind him when I was serving dinner last night. I thought about it then said no.

"I didn't think so," he said. "I looked around and no one was there, but I felt something touch my back."

Without hesitation, I said, "It was Carter. Tell me exactly what happened, what did it feel like?"

John explained when it happened that he'd felt a back and forth movement down his back like a hand lightly touching his shirt. He had looked around, but no one was there. He said it both unnerved him and made him feel good to think Carter was with us and then he had poured himself and my mom a second glass of wine. When he said that, I remembered the moment because it was unusual for him to do this.

He was happily talking about his experience then abruptly stopped and said, "But I can't prove it was Carter."

I said, "Of course you can't prove it, but you know what you immediately felt and thought." I went on to say that this is exactly how it happens to me: I'm not looking for these things to happen, they just happen. I also remembered that after he had poured the wine he started talking about Carter when we hadn't been before. We had laughed and reminisced about how during dessert Carter would try to scoop all the whipped cream from the bowl for himself or he'd spray it from the can right into his mouth and then do the same for Olivia. It's such a nice memory. I was happy to learn Carter was with us at Easter and this time he gave his dad a special experience.

April 8, 2010:

Carter's twenty-first birthday began well. John and I joined Olivia as she won an award at her school's Breakfast of Champions. I was happy for her achievement, but upset by the fact that Carter's death overshadowed every special event. I tried both before and after the breakfast to meditate and feel Carter's presence, but failed; I was too anxious to succeed. Later as I drove to work, I listened to a soothing CD to calm myself, and I noticed how lovely a song sounded. I looked to see the song's number then began to cry as I spoke out loud, "Of course it's six, what else could it be today, Carter?" I kept replaying the song so I could see six on the display screen, and took fleeting glances at the passenger seat as I wondered, *are you here Carter?* I asked him to stay with me as I walked into work, then said, *thanks Carter, I'll be okay now for the day. I love you.*

I know this may sound like wishful thinking to many, but it was giving me hope and it may sound insignificant, but was it? I was upset because it was Carter's birthday when I was drawn to look for the number of a song that I've heard for over a year but never noticed that it just happened to be number six. The odds of these things happening increase with each occurrence, don't they?

April 14, 2010:

A week later while driving on a lovely spring day, I opened the car windows to enjoy the fresh air. My thoughts drifted to Carter and how happy he was. I was optimistic by the myriad of signs lately and decided to send him my love. I visualized a sparkling gold stream of love flowing from my heart and wrapping around him. As I did this, suddenly the car fan came on full blast. I froze and examined whether I had touched something. My hands were both on the wheel and not near any buttons or dials, and I was sitting still so I hadn't bumped anything. I looked over to see the fan dial was in the off position. I felt elated; Carter seemed to be acknowledging the love I was sending to him. This was amazing and again, perfectly timed!

There had been a steady stream of events occurring almost weekly for several months. I tried to examine each as thoroughly as I could. If I was not truthful to myself about every aspect each time, then I minimized the credibility of all events. I needed a body of proof to convince myself, just as a scientist performs numerous experiments to find consistency in the outcome. My search for Carter was never for the purpose of writing a book or to help others. These efforts were only ever meant to help me so I could either believe that Carter's existence continued or that I needed to see these strange occurrences with a different perspective, one that would allow me to accept a unique randomness to the universe.

May 5, 2010:

It was my daughter Victoria's nineteenth birthday. As it came closer, my mind was overcome with worry. Carter's nineteenth birthday had been his last; how could she be nineteen? He never lived to see another birthday; would she? No one could convince me it wouldn't happen, because it already had once before. Victoria was struggling with her own thoughts and had just started her summer job. I didn't want her to be alone on her birthday, so we went to the cottage together. Her friends also came north to surprise her and stayed for a few days. What a gift of friendship they gave her to help her through her day.

I wasn't winning my battle that day to stay on top of my emotions, so I went into Carter's room and I could smell him. Oh, I'd missed that. It hadn't happened since last summer. I sat on his bed and thanked him for being there for me, and I told him that Victoria was nineteen today. I hoped he was listening as I told him about all the thoughts tormenting me and her struggles. On a happy note, I added that I loved it when I could smell him. A few hours later I smelled him again, but only fleetingly. I imagined a big smile on his face as it felt like he was teasing me.

I laughed as I said out loud, "Okay, Carter, very funny." This was just like him.

I now faithfully meditated each day as I worked to increase my focus within that first successful guided meditation. I saw myself walk toward the entrance of the woodland path as I tried to hear and feel the crunch of the gravel under my feet. I enhanced the details of my visuals. When I climbed the rock and asked Carter to join me I usually felt a sensation in my left hand that I believed to be Carter, but in mid-May, 2010, I was surprised when I felt a sensation in my hand much earlier in the meditation.

"Hello, Carter, you're here already. I didn't even call for you yet." I envisioned him beside me as we enjoyed watching the stream, then we continued our walk together.

I believe this was the first time that I was aware of his arrival before I called him. Normally when I was sitting on the rock in the meditation I asked him to join me. I then tried to remember him with as much clarity as I could; the shape of each finger, fingernail, his open palm, and the top of his hand as I saw his hand slipping into mine. It was during this focused concentration that I would normally begin to feel him as I visualized him with every ounce of memory I had.

My Question is Answered

The law of conservation of energy which is a basic law of physics states that energy cannot be created nor destroyed; rather it transforms from one form to another.

As May ended, I was anxiously waiting for my appointment to see medium Sandy Wiltshire who wrote the book, *My Gift of Light*. Though my confidence was growing that these occurrences were signs from Carter, I still couldn't prove it was him.

Every day for weeks prior to my appointment, I asked Carter, "Please give me enough information during this reading to prove that you are still with us. Our family needs to be less worried about me and more positive about you. Also, if you don't come through with enough evidence to convince me, then I have no idea what to do next to prove you're there. I will continue to search, but I feel that I'm at a dead end for ideas once this appointment is complete."

June 2, 2010:

After almost a year of waiting, I went for my reading. My father spoke first through Sandy, and then Carter. The session was better than I could have ever hoped for. They gave so many facts and incredible details, convincing me without any doubt that it was them giving her the information. Carter described the movements of people at the scene of the accident including myself as he witnessed it; Sandy was brought to tears! He gave information about conversations and things that had happened with friends and family since the accident. I was stunned by the sheer profusion of unknowable truths! I was completely astonished to realize all my questioning and searching had not been in vain because today Carter spoke. I came away from this appointment with my question answered with an absolute YES, CARTER, YOU ARE THERE!

For days after, I had trouble focusing on anything but what I had just experienced. How could I think about supper or laundry or any of these meaningless tasks and thoughts? My son could be here with me at any time. As an added gift, for several days most of my grief had evaporated, and for the first time in almost two years I was experiencing pure joy!

I was certain that the family needed to hear the recording of this reading, but I felt it would be too hard for Mom. The next day I hesitantly told her about my appointment. I hadn't told her before because I knew she wouldn't approve. I didn't want to upset her, but now I had messages for her and I felt obliged to deliver them. I played her only the sections of the tape that had messages for her. She became very thoughtful and asked to know more.

After I told her a couple of things she said, "There's no way that woman could have known that."

Relieved, I said, "I know; those are exactly my thoughts."

Then Mom enthusiastically said, "I want to hear the whole tape." I was surprised at her attitude and I told her parts were difficult for me to hear and I thought it would be too much for her. I was worried about her, but she insisted she'd be fine and wanted to hear it with the family.

June 7, 2010:

After four days of being in an emotionally heightened frenzy, I realized that I needed to settle down so I went into Carter's room to meditate.

I spoke to Carter. "At the reading, Sandy said you were a strong energy and a very bright light, much brighter than most spirits that she sees. Can you show me this, Carter?" I closed my eyes and waited, but I felt nothing so I asked again and again. I didn't even know what I was hoping for. I switched to a different approach. "Show me your light, let me see you." Once again I closed my eyes, but still felt nothing and though I was disappointed I continued to ask very earnestly. After several minutes my left arm lifted once, very slightly then again. I told myself to stay calm and breathe as my heart had started pounding. I concentrated on holding my arm very still and steady, though not resisting, while allowing whatever this was to happen. I felt a gentle pressure from under my arm pushing it up and it continued to rise bit by bit. After a few minutes, I opened my eyes and stared in amazement at my arm that was now twelve to sixteen inches above the leg it had been resting on.

Two days later I drove north. Victoria had several days off from her summer job so I was going to bring her home. I was steadfast in the certainty that the family needed to be all together to hear this reading. The next day we would all support each other as we experienced the emotional heartache and thrill of letting Carter give evidence that he was with us.

June 10, 2010:

I gathered everyone in the family room and explained that twice before I had gone to a medium but I had never talked to them about it because I hadn't felt I had heard anything very convincing.

This time I said, "please trust that if I have asked you to listen to this reading, it's because I have confidence in it. Even if you think this is nonsense, don't discount it. Pay attention to what you're hearing and trust it is who they say from the start. Carter and Grandpa will quickly convince you it is them." Excited, but nervous also, I pressed the play button and sat down hoping that they would feel it was as incredible as I did.

My gaze moved to each person for their reactions to certain information. After Dad spoke on the tape at one point, Mom sat forward in her chair and listened with greater attention. I thought she wasn't clear what was said, so I started to clarify what he said. Without moving her eyes from the tape machine, Mom put her hand up to stop me from speaking. She was mesmerized and didn't want to miss a single word. Further into the recording, Carter spoke lovingly to his dad, and feeling it might be too emotional for John to bear I thought he might leave the room, but he too sat transfixed in his chair. For a full hour as we listened the air was charged with emotion though no one moved.

The tape ended and the room fell silent. I didn't want to be the one to speak first, so I waited as everyone needed to catch their breath. Finally, John was the first to break the silence. I had been as worried for him as for my mother. He dealt with Carter's death differently than me and we are often at odds because of this; I didn't know how he would feel.

He dropped his hands from around his face to the arms of the chair and softly said, "Thank you so much for doing this."

What a perfect statement for me to hear. All our clashes and struggles over the last two years washed away for that moment. I felt he wasn't only thanking me for going for the reading, but for everything I'd gone through to get me there.

Victoria spoke next. "What Carter is talking about happened two weeks after his death." Victoria is a practical person like most of us, believing what can be explained.

When she said, "What Carter is," got my immediate attention because she was speaking of Carter in the present and she spoke with confidence that it was Carter speaking. This was immensely helpful for me to hear her say this so frankly. Carter had a message for her that made no sense to me, but when she heard it she knew precisely the night he was talking about and the person mentioned. I was glad I didn't know; I felt that made the message more wonderful for her, knowing it was between them. Also when people said Sandy was reading my mind—which opens a whole other conversation—the fact that this event wasn't in my mind dismissed that argument. This reading was extremely helpful for all of us, and I will be forever thankful.

After a lively discussion we all sat down to dinner where we continued to reminisce. I was aware of how light and happy everyone had become, and the awful burden of sadness was lifted at least for a few hours. Carter and Dad had proved beyond a doubt that it was them and they were continuing to be part of our lives.

Mom continued to add value to the messages when she said, "I knew your Dad would be there for Carter."

During the reading, Dad had said he was at the accident scene and he had lifted Carter out. I realized it was at that exact moment on the tape that Mom had sat forward and had begun listening with greater interest.

"That's why you sat forward; he got your attention."

Mom explained that as we were telling her the awful news about Carter the day after his death, she saw an image of Dad holding Carter in his arms.

"Why didn't you tell me, Mom?" I asked.

"I did tell you. I've always said I'm sure your dad would be there for Carter if he could."

I remember her repeatedly saying this, but at the time I thought, of course, Mom, we all hope Dad was there, but it doesn't really help me.

"You never said you got a vision at that same moment."

This wouldn't have helped me then, anyway. I would have dismissed it with the thought—a vision, that's nonsense; it's just your thoughts creating an image. Now, two years later she had my attention. Today she sat forward when Dad stated what she had seen, and her acceptance of this reading shifted. On that day two years ago, Dad had shown her that he had Carter and was keeping him safe with the hope it would help her through that difficult time. The more I thought of how wonderful that was for her, the more I tried to envision the image. Several days later I had questions for Mom.

"Mom, can you remember what you saw that day?" I asked.

She was happy to talk about it. "I know now your Dad was trying to protect me and let me know Carter was safe, that he was with him and would look after him. He was reassuring me as best he could at the time and I had faith he would do this if it was possible."

"Yes, but can you give me details of the image?" As I continued to ask questions, her memory was still crystal clear and this is the image that emerged. The background was black and she only saw Dad and Carter, nothing else. She didn't see him picking up Carter, just a single image of Carter in Dad's arms. Dad's arms were bent at the elbow facing straight ahead and Carter was resting between his wrist and elbow.

I couldn't imagine Dad being able to lift him, so I asked, "Was it a younger Dad and Carter as a small boy?" I had seen Dad carry Carter many times years before.

"No," she said. "Dad was old; he looked like he did when he left, and Carter was all grown exactly like he was. They both looked the age they were when they died and Carter was fine, he didn't look injured."

For me, hearing this story after the reading allowed me to blend the vision into the reading and add unexpected richness to the information. From separate sources, I fit two more pieces of the puzzle together.

I made copies of the reading for everyone and said they could listen to it or not if they chose, but they didn't have to ask me for it if they ever thought they wanted to hear something again. Several times over the next few months when I visited Mom, I found her listening to the recording. She was the last person I assumed would have any interest in hearing it again. I remarked about it one day when I again walked into her room and heard the recording.

"Mom, I'm surprised that you're so interested in the reading because you were against me doing this."

She smiled and said, "Yes, but there isn't anything said that isn't correct. And there is no way Sandy could have found out some of this information."

I know that was precisely how I felt but added, "I thought it would go against some of the teachings and beliefs in your faith."

"Oh no, it doesn't say anything wrong to me. I just never knew how close they were to us. I believed they went to heaven and we were separated for now, but they are so close it's wonderful. It makes my faith in God even stronger."

We have all come away from that reading relieved of some of the grief and pain. How each person uses that to help them go forward with their life is their choice, but as a wife and mother, I feel that I have truly helped them. My gratitude to Sandy, Carter, and Dad was boundless as some of the weight of not only my pain but my family's had been lifted off my shoulders.

My meeting with Sandy had given me answers, but also many more questions, and I think, more importantly, a new way of seeing my questions. She had begun by saying there were three energies there for me. I had no idea what she meant. I asked her if she meant three spirits, and she said yes. I began to wonder if the vibrations I sometimes felt along my back when I sat or lay down were my father's energy. Sandy had said my dad said he's been at my back supporting me since Carter's accident. If he was at my back, could I feel him there, because she described them as energies? Was that what I felt? My mind swirled with excitement as I repeatedly listened to the recording of my reading with Sandy.

Several days later, Olivia said a woman was speaking at her school about bullying and told a true story that happened a couple of years ago at the local high school. The senior football team saw a boy being bullied, so they began having him sit with them at lunchtime. After this, he was never bullied again because of this thoughtful yet simple act of kindness. Olivia said she had a great big smile while the woman was telling the story because she was certain this was Carter and his friends; it was typical of how they were toward people.

June 11, 2010:

Olivia was sorting her collection of teddy bears before packing them away. She had spread them on the floor around her and then got up to get something.

John was working nearby and said, "Olivia come and see this; you've put the bears in the shape of a six."

Olivia got the camera and took a photo of it then looked up and said, "Carter, did you do that?"

June 25, 2010:

Cayley was coming to visit and I was anxious to see her; I had so many wonderful things to tell her. When I last saw her in December, she said she'd write the other text messages she received from Carter with details for me. Even though the last few days had been emotionally draining for me, I looked forward to her information with hope, and I wasn't disappointed. She told me the second message came in late September 2008, when she was in class at university. Carter had chosen Brock University partly because so many of his friends, including Cayley, were going or were already there starting their second year, and his friends were extremely important to him. So Carter should have been on that campus when Cayley's phone beeped. Once again it said "duplicate message," and then a different message from Carter came up. She said she couldn't move, she had put her head down on her hands on top of the desk and waited for class to end and the room to empty, then she lifted her head and left the classroom in tears. The message she received that day had originally been sent to her on July 28; I know because I referred to the texts Victoria copied from Carter's phone. On his phone, it was sent at 8:22 a.m., just before he went out to teach Olivia to water ski. I find it interesting that the first one she received was the last message he sent to her, and this was the second last message. Was he getting access to the old texts in order?

The third text came one month later, in late October 2008, and this time it was a new message that she'd never received before. She couldn't remember the exact words, but thought it said: "how has your week been, I miss you." Cayley couldn't remember anything specific about that day except that it was her first time back at home from university that year and the previous year Carter had always come to see her whenever she came home from university, which might be the reason he was at home to "meet her."

The fourth message was also a new text that she received toward the end of November 2008, again like the others just prior to the date of his death. Cayley said she didn't remember the circumstances, but she remembers the message perfectly: "I miss you."

I wondered if Carter could only access what was in the phone at first, then he had learned how to send a new message. I also wondered with the second message coming in September at university if he was just checking on his friends or was it that he knew he was supposed to be there and wasn't missing it? I deeply hoped he was feeling part of it and enjoying it somehow while also helping his friends cope with his death.

Cayley also told me that in August, shortly after Carter's accident, she had looked up in the sky and saw two clouds side by side, one looked like a happy face and the other was shaped like a heart. As soon as she saw them, she thought they were sent to her from Carter because it was so perfectly him. She said she took a photo of it with the same phone on which she had received the four texts from Carter, but the phone was now broken. I would have loved to see the messages and photo for myself, but I took strength in the fact that she was so touched that she took a picture of it. This made me believe that she was seeing what she thought she was. His message was clear and precise, floating in the sky, just like my hummingbird in the clouds. Cayley felt a bit silly telling me about the clouds, so I shared my story of the hummingbird forming in the clouds. We were both pleased and relieved to learn of the other's cloud story. We laughed and said maybe he really can do this, but how?

June 27, 2010:

I sensed a tingling movement or energy come and go around my entire body while in meditation. As I "walked by the stream," I sensed it again, and it became stronger between my waist and shoulders. Then I felt an increase of pressure squeeze me around my shoulders and chest for a few moments before releasing. This happened three times, tingling over my entire body, then heavier but even pressure around my chest, back, and sides pushing in on me. I couldn't believe it—Carter was giving me a hug! It was incredible!

When strange things first began to happen a few years ago I had wondered if they were signs from Carter, and I tried to focus and think clearly about each one through my grief-stricken mind. As time went on, when I became aware of sensations, smells, and occurrences that were odd or unexplainable I no longer wondered, I needed to KNOW. For the last year, I believed that if I met with Sandy, and Carter was able to give me enough proof that his life continued, then my quest would end and I'd somehow find a way to go forward and live my life with the reassurance that he was living his.

Well, Sandy definitely proved to me that Carter and Dad were still with us, and I was one thousand percent sure without a doubt, but was that enough for me? Of course it wasn't enough and IT'S NEVER GOING TO BE ENOUGH! So once again I was back to wondering. Somehow Carter, Dad, and Sandy were communicating. How was she doing this? And if she could do this, why couldn't I? My quest, therefore, wasn't finished. My mind wouldn't be allowed to rest; a new phase had just begun. I felt compelled to learn to hear them if I could.

In meditation, I began asking, "Carter, I need your help so I can learn to hear you. Can you have a book fall off the shelf that I need to read, or have somebody or something come into my life that I need to help me reach you? Can you please help me because I have no idea what to do."

As summer 2010 began, I felt much less anguish than last year because I was consumed by my new quest—to learn to communicate with Carter.

July 9, 2010:

John was in the living room at the cottage with me as I meditated when once again I began to feel my arm lift as it had several times over the last few weeks. I knew this looked odd, he's going to think, *what is she doing now?* I hadn't told him that this had been happening.

I said, "John, you might want to come over here and watch what is happening because I'm not doing this."

He watched my arm lift very slowly, then a sudden, larger movement flung my arm over my shoulder, hitting a photo frame on the table and I lost my connection to Carter. John walked away without a word. What could he say?

July 11, 2010:

In meditation, I asked if I would be able to tell the difference between Dad's and Carter's energy. Sandy knew there were three spirits present for me; how did she know there was more than one? I had a sense that they were both with me, so I asked Dad to show me that he was there. I felt a presence in my hand that felt different than usual, little bursts of energy jerking my thumb and finger. Then I feel that presence slip out of my hand and I felt nothing for a moment, followed by the very familiar feeling that I was confident was Carter slipping into my hand. It's a more smooth, even pressure that I actually felt slide into the palm of my hand. Dad came first and then Carter, one right after the other. This was amazing; I was shown what I asked for and they showed me in a way that I could feel the difference between them. From that day on, this is how they let me know which one is coming forward. They taught me to tell them apart.

Throughout the summer of 2010, every day I was aware of Carter's presence with us at the cottage. I smelled him several times a day not only in his bedroom, but also in the hallway between the living room and his bedroom, and I felt that I was walking right through him there. As July progressed, I was increasingly sensing energy all around me that I experienced as a tingling or vibration. It varied in intensity from very delicate to strong or forceful—almost urgent—as if they were trying to get my attention. Whenever this happened I felt I was supposed to do something, but I had no idea what.

A Heavenly Gift

Love you Mom. Rest in the assurance, the knowledge, that we are not apart, you are not without me. It is only a physical separation, you cannot see me. I have every sense of living continued with you all, the life continues, the journey unfolds. As there, our loved ones step in and out of view; daily tasks, places to live, different phases of life there connect us and separate us. Though there may be a physical separation, our love and attachment to that person remains. That is true for our time now, we are in different places with different tasks yet we are not apart, we are connected through the heart. We, you and I and Grandpa, are now working on the same project but we have different jobs to serve the task but it is a united effort and we are in constant contact for the task. No one is ever truly separated from those we love. Love transcends time, space, existences, for remember I am not existing separate from you. I am within the same existence, the only existence. All is within existence and exists for and toward eternal existence within Love. I love you all; let's move ahead with our task Mom xxx. (Carter, writing received July 8, 2012.)

July 26, 2010:

John and I got up at 4 a.m. on Monday. I made him a coffee as he got ready for his drive back to the city. We couldn't sleep as the memories of those final few idyllic days two summers ago were all either of us could think of. A single heartbeat was all that separated happiness from a life of unrelenting pain. Daily I felt robbed of Carter's enthusiasm and his ability to seize life and bring happiness to others, and this had been snatched from me in a split second.

I was wide awake when I returned to bed after John left. As I tried to relax and fall back to sleep, I was pleased to feel Carter's energy in my left hand.

"Oh hi, Carter ..." As I talked to him, I began to feel my hand gently being moved from side to side. My mind was clear and unburdened of thoughts when I got one of those ah-ha moments, and this was the best one I'm sure I've ever had. I was enjoying Carter twisting and moving my hand when I remembered he had lifted my arms on several occasions recently. The thought continued to come to me: *if I held a pen in my hand could he move it?* What a completely bizarre thought, but I was going to try. After all, it was 4:30 in the morning and nobody was there to witness this silliness.

Still lying on my bed, I reached for a piece of paper and a pen on the night table. I positioned my elbows on the mattress, brought the pen down onto the paper, and closed my eyes. I don't know why, but somehow this felt like it was the right thing to do. Then I waited. In less than a minute, I felt my hand begin to move in a straight line up and off the paper. OH MY GOD, what just happened? I hadn't done that! I needed to try again and make sure I didn't move the pen, although I was certain that I hadn't. This time I put the pen in the centre of the page, hoping it wouldn't go off the paper if it happened again. Once again the pen began to move; I was stunned but tried to concentrate on holding the pen still, yet it was moving. This time the motion felt more fluid, adding curves to the movement. Soon I felt what could be an O next a V being shaped on the paper and then abruptly the pen stopped moving. I felt the pen hadn't moved enough to write anything, if that's what was actually happening, so I continued to wait with my eyes closed. I started asking silently, *come on Carter, keep going*, but still, the pen didn't move. Then I remembered Sandy telling me, "your father says he's always with you; he's been at your back since Carter's death." *Dad, if you're here, please help him* I silently pleaded. A moment later the pen began to move again, and when it stopped I hesitated for a few minutes, then nervously opened my eyes and saw: I LOVE YOU ♥ O.

My heart was pounding as I looked at the writing on the paper. Over and over I had to push it away from me and then I'd grab it again to look at it. What I was looking at was emotionally overwhelming, astounding, my feelings defied description. There was nobody available for me to talk to; who would I talk to anyway because this was certifiable craziness now! Yet, the words sat visibly on that page and I was absolutely certain that I hadn't moved that pen. I knew this was Carter writing, and even though it was me that had picked up the pen, this was beyond belief!

Carter couldn't have written anything that mattered more or meant as much to me. If you could speak only once again to someone you have loved and lost what would you say? What truly matters? Exhausted, I rested my head on the pillow and eventually fell asleep, thinking if he never connected to me ever again these words were perfect. When I woke several hours later I reached immediately for the paper to see if this really happened or had it been a dream. There it was on the paper: I love you. I hadn't dreamt it, it was real. The paper existed.

All day I was bursting with frenzied energy as I realized that together Carter, my father, and I had just catapulted into a whole new reality. I felt as if I had been a boulder held securely in the arms of the catapult, but now the time had been right to break down some walls. I had been flung into the fortifications and smashed through to the other side. I felt stunned by the hit; I didn't realize my battle to regroup with Carter and Dad had just begun a major assault.

I felt like I was in an episode of *The Twilight Zone* or a science fiction movie; this was definitely not a reality that I knew. This is apparently called automatic writing, it was mentioned in Sandy's book but I couldn't read about it originally because I thought it was too odd and creepy for me so I skipped over it. At the back of her book was an additional chapter about it that I didn't read either. (Several years after my writing began, I read this chapter for the first time and was amazed by the similarities I experienced. I was happy that I hadn't read about it before so all my experiences were original and unexpected for me as they happened.)

For the past several weeks, I had been asking Carter to help me find my way to him. I realized that he had been showing me a path all along. In fact, it brought a smile to my face as I thought how frustrated he must have been with me. He had been right there saying, "Mom, pay attention, I'm trying to show you," as he was lifting my arms. Thank goodness for John driving home at 4 a.m.

All day I was scattered and distracted. I wanted to try this writing again, but Olivia and her friends were with me, enjoying the lake. When they went to her friend's cottage I seized my opportunity, and on the off chance that this would happen again, I used a lovely journal my friend Lyn had given me, to keep the writing safe. I meditated until I felt an awareness or sensation in the palm of my hand, then I held the pen, allowing it to rest lightly on the page. Almost immediately the pen moved. I knew I was not moving my hand and I felt no pressure on it, but somehow my hand was moving.

The pen stopped, I thought, *keep going Carter, you can do this*, but still no movement. Once again, since this had seemed to help last night, I said, "Dad, please help him." After a brief pause, the pen began to move again. When it stopped I opened my eyes and was thrilled to see written on the page: LOVE X, X, X, X, X, X.

I had to talk to someone before I burst because this had inexplicably happened for the second time. Bewildered, I called Nancy, and as I told her I began to feel a tingling sense of energy all around me and it continued to get stronger. I hung up the phone and wondered, "Carter do you want to say something to me?" It was now 7 p.m. as I attempted this writing for the third time, but I was too excited to concentrate. When the pen stopped, I looked at the paper to find that I couldn't read anything that had been written. This was horrible; if it never happened again, I wouldn't know what Carter's last message was to me.

In a panic, I turned the page, attempted to calm myself, and tried again. Maybe it would help me read the words if I concentrated to feel which letters were being written. I closed my eyes and tried to determine what letters were shaped as the pen moved; I could feel certain letters, but not all. I opened my eyes and I was relieved to be able to read most of this writing, somehow that seemed to make a difference.

I immediately placed the pen back on the paper and the writing continued. I then read all the writings from the first on July 26 and then walked away from the table crying, unable to cope with what Carter seemed to be doing. Mentally and emotionally drained, I collapsed into a chair and stared out the window at the lake, but my rest was brief as I felt tugging on my arm between my elbow and wrist.

"Do you want to say more, Carter?"

The tugging continued. Exhausted, I grabbed a piece of paper, hoping not to move from the chair. Once again it began, and I sensed these might be important words so I moved to where the journal was, and happily, the message continued.

When a thought felt complete I put the pen down, but somehow I seemed to know when he had more to say and each time I placed the pen back onto the page, another message was written. I was having so much difficulty concentrating under these incredible circumstances when again another message came. I was out of my depth. I needed to pay attention because once again I was having a hard time reading what had been written. I fought to find the mental strength to stay focused.

Another message was coming onto the page. *Concentrate, Charmaine, you need to know what he was saying.* This one was much clearer; I could read every word. I didn't know who was improving, me or Carter, probably both. At the end of this message for the first time was a signature, Carter xoo and I put down the pen, exhausted.

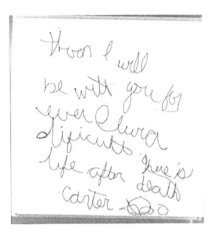

I was shaking and all alone. I had been immersed in this for two hours, trying to hold my emotions in check as I struggled to focus my attention. I needed to calm down. Thankfully, Olivia and Victoria arrived home and time with them helped. I was startled as I realized that I never doubted who it was from the beginning. I knew it was Carter, but I didn't think about this until he signed his name.

At 11:30, when the girls went to sleep, I sat to write again. For the first time, I heard the words in my head before they were written. That wasn't happening before. Carter completed his thought and the writing stopped.

July 27, 2010:

It was after midnight as a second message formed. I felt weak as I heard the word "ghostly" in my mind. The letters *g* and then *h* were written and I thought, *no Carter, don't write that word*—I didn't want to hear it and I didn't want to see it. As I talked to Carter, I got more upset and lost my focus so when the writing stopped I couldn't read the next few words that had been written. I asked Carter, *what does this say?* And he rewrote part of it—gather them around—but it still didn't make sense to me because I had missed some of the other words. I quickly learned that I must let Carter's thoughts come through me and try not to dwell on them while they were being written. When I became distracted by my own thoughts and lost my concentration, it seemed to me that I had less chance of being able to read them.

I got one more message, and at the end of this message, for the first time he calls me *Mom.* I AM TALKING TO **MY SON!!**

them around me
o Mom ,

I was meant arange
for lives to be better
Lives of people I
love your life mom
oXo

I was meant arrange
for lives to be better
Lives of people I
love your life mom
oXo

July 28, 2010:

It was now one day before the second anniversary of Carter's death, and we were all very fragile. I was missing him and grieving his loss, but I also had all that had been happening over the last couple of days swirling in my head. I had no idea what was going on with my life, it felt out of control! Between my sadness, grief, and worrying about everyone else in the family, plus being overwhelmed by this experience with Carter, my mind felt like it was going to explode.

The girls wanted to be at the cottage on the twenty-ninth again, and it was the right thing for them to do, as they must deal with the loss of their brother every day and I would do whatever seemed to help them. When I woke on July 28, I sat trying to process all that was happening when the phone rang at 8:30 a.m. It was John, saying he had just been told by his sister-in-law Barb that his brother had a seizure during dialysis and was on life-support. After talking with the doctors it had been decided to take him off of life-support. This was a horrendous time of year for all of us and now John had to face the painful news that his brother was dying the day before the anniversary of his son's death.

John didn't know anything about what had been happening here since he left two days ago, which is when it all began. How would I even begin to tell this to him? He hadn't experienced or struggled with the hopes and possibilities of what might be as I had. He couldn't see how any of that could happen, so what was I to say about this? I was pleasantly surprised when John said he had told Barb about some of the things I had experienced and that I seemed to be able to feel some awareness of Carter's presence when he was with me. I thought this was great that John was able to tell her this.

John said Barb wondered if I could ask Carter to be there for Joe. As I hung up the phone I also wondered if this was possible. *Carter, if I asked you a question, could you give me an answer using this writing?* After yesterday, I hoped this might be possible. I sat still until I felt him, then I told him Joe was dying and Barb hoped he could be there for him. My hand shook as I put pen to paper and tried to clear my mind, and quickly the writing started.

July 28, 2010
9 a.m

I am there

I pushed the journal away in tears; this was too much for me to deal with. I phoned both John and Barb; I was overcome with emotion and must have sounded very scattered as I felt I couldn't tell either of them what actually just happened. I was hit by another huge new realization that Carter was not just talking to me, but Carter and I were talking to each other. I asked him a question and he answered!

Later that day, John told me about a conversation he had had with Barb. She said earlier that morning Joe, though deeply unconscious, had been trying to speak and his daughter was sure he was saying, "Carter." This happened before Barb called John and before Carter told me he was there. Did Joe know Carter was with him? Hearing this helped validate Carter's words, "I am there" for me. About ten minutes after Carter had replied to me I had walked past his bedroom and I could smell him, so I knew he was with me, but I was confused because he had said he was with Joe. Did this mean he had left him? I don't think so, certainly not when he was dying. Could he be in two places at once?

With the anniversary one day away, I decided to tell Victoria and Olivia that Carter was talking to me, and though I knew this was probably harder for them to believe than all of my strange thoughts combined over the last couple of years, the good thing was that their brother seemed to be fine. I told them in the hope that this would ease their pain the next day, even in the slightest. I hadn't told John, since it had been so sad for him with his brother's death. I was completely exhausted by the emotions of the day and went to bed early but couldn't sleep, so I got up at 11:00 p.m.

The only thing I was certain about was that I didn't know what I was doing, but I was trying my best to figure it out and learn. I did know that once I became very still both mentally and physically I felt a pressure that varied in my left hand and I knew Carter and I had connected somehow. I didn't know if I needed to do this before we wrote, but my concern was that if I just sat and wrote without being secure I felt a connection to him, then it could be me and not Carter writing. I wanted to make sure that it was Carter. So, I waited patiently in meditation to feel our connection, and once I felt what I believed was Carter's energy in my hand I held the pen upright and steady against the paper. Then I concentrated on letting the pen flow, making sure I didn't move it, and I kept my mind clear of my thoughts, which seemed to allow me to hear the words that then formed on the page.

Carter's first words came quickly: "Joe is here." Was he already with them? I don't know what I was expecting, but this surprised me. Carter then wrote: "I think I know Olivia is sad [and she was very sad!] We are here." *Who are we?* I wondered. Is it Carter and Joe? Why would Joe be with me? I asked Carter, who is "we?"

"Grandpa and I."

Oh, it's my father and Carter, that makes more sense to me.

At this point, Olivia came into the room and sat with me since she couldn't sleep, either. When she saw what I was doing she wondered if I could ask Carter through this writing who cooked her French fries at the restaurant that last evening. She said she had ordered them, hoping that he might cook them for her and she was going to ask him when he came home. She became very upset when she said he never came home and she had been wondering for two years whether he cooked her fries or if it was somebody else, but she always hoped that it had been him. So in my thoughts, I asked him the question and hoped for an answer as both our hearts were now breaking. With steely resolve, I knew I had to hold my emotions in check; this was a critical question for Olivia. I made absolutely certain that I did not move the pen at all, and hoped an answer would be given. The next words written were: "I cooked French fries. Love XX"

Olivia was smiling through her tears. She had got her answer after two long years and more importantly, her brother had answered—amazing. I still felt like I was playing a part in a science fiction movie, but how wonderful was this!

July 29, 2010:

Midnight had just past. It was now July 29, and once again this awful day must be endured. Olivia and I had spent an hour getting our messages from Carter. As midnight approached, Kevin had sent me a message and he and I had been texting back and forth. He was very upset also as the day approached and he said Carter's friends were gathering at his house on July 30 and they'd love to see us if we were home. I said we'd love to be with them and was glad they'd be together, but we had decided to stay at the cottage. My thoughts would be with them as they gathered for Carter and I wished I could be in both places.

After I replied to Kevin I had put the phone down and started writing with Carter. While Carter had been answering my question of who cooked Olivia's French fries, my phone beeped with Kevin's reply. Olivia was standing beside me watching as the answer to her question was being written on the page. She automatically picked up the phone and started to read the text message.

I told her, "Leave the phone for now because I need to concentrate. You asked a question and I don't want to lose this connection and not get the answer for you."

Once Carter finished answering her question I picked up the phone and began reading the first of the three-part text, then I stopped before advancing to the second part.

I held up the phone toward the ceiling, looked up and said, "Carter, these are from Kevin. Can you read them?" I finished reading the texts then picked up the pen and waited for his response, if any. The words written were, "friends gather, I'm there."

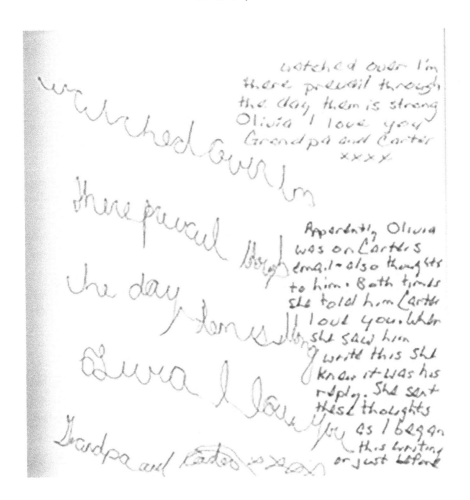

I didn't know what, if anything, I was supposed to do with this information. I asked him if he wanted me to tell somebody this. Carter replied, "tell Kevin." Great, just how do I tell Kevin this? I don't even know how to explain this to myself. My words to Kevin stumbled along something like. "I'm sure Carter will be with you all on that day and try to find some happiness knowing that he's with you." I was glad this was sent through text because I felt my message was vague. I didn't try to explain any of this to him, certainly not in a text. Carter continued speaking to me through the writing as he talked about the family members getting through that day.

While I was concentrating on the writing, Olivia set her computer up on the table across from me and started typing messages to Carter.

She asked me, "If I send him an e-mail, do you think I could get an answer from him?"

After these last few days, I had no idea what was possible so I said, "try it and see what happens, you never know."

Olivia was hoping that he would reply through her computer. So at the same time she was sitting across from me typing messages to him, Carter was continuing his writing through me, talking about us getting through the day. When my writing finished I read it to Olivia, and when I read the part where he said, "Olivia I love you," her eyes popped wide open as she exclaimed, "I wrote on his e-mail, 'Carter I love you'!"

Her eyes danced with life as I said, "well, Olivia, I think you just got your reply." Skeptics might say this is a just a coincidence, but as she was writing he was replying to her through me, and I didn't know what she was writing. Also, though it seems like a generic response, Carter didn't say it to anyone else, myself included, only Olivia.

"He must know you wrote it, because he's answering you back," I said.

It was now only hours short of three days since this writing began, since I first picked up the pen, and now not only was I asking questions but I was getting answers and hearing the words in my mind before they were written. For the second time in two years the world I knew had been shattered by Carter, but this time it was more like an earthquake knocking down barriers and allowing me to see a much greater vision beyond my view. It is the same world, but as some of the secrets were revealed my perception and understanding of it began to shift. Over the next few days, I continued to communicate with Carter while doing my best to support the family through their grief. I was immersed in a very tough game of lost and found where the stakes were high.

Carter and Dad, Their Special Task

Live your life fully

I am with you

I'm not missing anything

I'm here with you

(Carter, writing received July 31, 2010)

I began the day thinking of dad and thanking him for all his help over the last two years that I hadn't been aware of until my reading with Sandy. During these moments of gratitude, I felt an inner warmth begin to stir as I remembered how on many tough days I had heard my father's voice giving me advice, but I had never thought it was actually him. Whenever this happened, I'd tell myself, *yes, I know exactly what Dad would say to me* and I can create the memory of his voice. Today I began to realize I had been hearing him all along; it wasn't just Carter that I could hear. My thoughts evolved: If Dad has been with me and I've heard him, why is it that only Carter has written and Dad hasn't? Maybe Dad can't do this? The more I wondered about this, the more it bothered me. Finally, I thought to ask Carter if my father could also write, or was it just him?

The reply came from Dad: "Hi, Charm."

I was so happy to hear him and I took this opportunity to again say, "thank you so much for being with me since Carter's death. I didn't know you were here helping and supporting me all this time."

He wrote simply: "You're welcome

During a second writing that day Carter wrote:

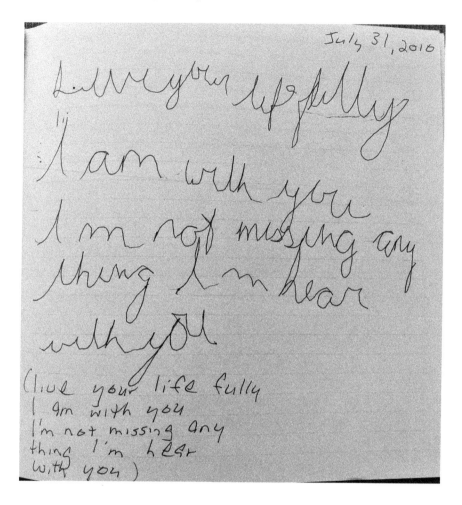

July 31, 2016

Live your life fully
I am with you
I'm not missing any
thing I'm hear
with you

(Live your life fully
I am with you
I'm not missing any
thing I'm hear
with you)

For almost a year now I had been blessed by many signs that were helping guide me through grief. I felt that this was too much for only one person to benefit from these signs I was receiving, they should be used to help others also, but how? Maybe now I could get some answers. I have chosen selections from the writings over the next few days to show how quickly we advanced into a conversation.

CH: Carter, have you been guiding me to learn to reach you?

C: Yes I need to help others.

CH: How can I help you do this?

C: You will find the way.

CH: Will I be able to see your world?

C: Yes when you're ready.

CH: Will you arrange for this to happen?

C: Yes.

CH: How are you moving my hand to write?

C: Can't tell you any answer won't make sense.

C: I am in a better place.

CH: Why is it a better place?

C: I have home, Love, God is near [this is the first time Carter mentions God] I'm back here.

CH: If you are back, were we both there before?

C: Yes we were together here. There's a lot to be done up here to prepare for life there, don't waste it.

CH: Before I came, did I know that when you followed me, I was going to lose my child so young?

C: I mustn't tell you.

CH: Why?

C: You're not to know.

CH: But you know now. (My tone had become stern as I tried to get him to tell me and I was frustrated that he wouldn't. I was aware of how ridiculous I was being, because I was arguing with a dead person and only days ago I would have given anything for any contact at all with him!)

C: Yes.

CH: I am facing your death. Why can't I know if you knew this would be part of my life?

C: So you learn.

CH: What am I to learn by not knowing now? (Learn!! Is he kidding me? There's nothing to learn from this, there's only suffering.)

C: Pain, grief, forgiveness, joy.

CH: (As he spoke, I felt the warmth around me dissolving my barriers of frustration.) This sensation I feel all around me, is it you? Are you doing something so I can feel you?

C: I'm hugging you.

CH: I LOVE that Carter! Every time I feel this now I'll feel so good. Is it always a hug?

C: Always.

CH: With this wonderful news I send you a big hug and kiss good night; I love you.

C: I love you xxo

Carter could see I wasn't ready for these thoughts, but he knew a hug would work magic. I wanted to learn to connect with him to the very best of my ability, but I had no idea how. I believe it had been Carter's effort more than anything I had done that had gotten me this far. Though I acknowledge it was my inability to do most daily tasks that had provided me with a great deal of time in stillness. I knew as I sat and stared blankly it looked like I was doing absolutely nothing, but for me, it had been hard work to learn to be still and to quiet my mind, and from this quiet emerged an inner knowing. On a very positive side, I was seeing a future with Carter in it. It was not the future I wanted, but it was much better than a future without him.

August 16, 2010:

For two very long weeks, I didn't write with Carter while John was on vacation. I certainly hadn't been ready to try to explain this to him yet. Finally, on August 16, I had some time alone to write, but I was worried that I'd lost whatever ability I'd found to connect with Carter. I was relieved when our writing happened easily.

"Hi Mom, how are you?" His greeting was startlingly normal, as if nothing was unusual about our situation at all, only that we hadn't spoken for a while. How am I? Are you serious? I've been driven crazy with worry that I might never be able to speak with him again and that this has all been a crazy fluke. I attempted to compose myself but I was still rattled by how complacent he seemed about it. After more than a year, it was the appropriate time for me to ask him the simpler yet critical question for me—WHY? Why him, why me, why, why, why?

CH: Why are you able to do this? When others die, I don't think this happens, does it? Why is all this happening to me?

C: You and I are meant to help others.

CH: Are we only to help people grieving, or anybody?

C: All people.

CH: I'm happy that you kept reaching out to me until I found you and we will continue to do things together.

C: Love enables all.

CH: I'm always sending you my love. Does it help?

C: Yes it strengthens our connection.

That is an interesting statement. He not only receives my love, but it is helping our connection.

August 17, 2010:

Carter and I must both have been feeling a little more relaxed after yesterday. He said he was too busy to write to me now because he was having fun. Now that sounded like the Carter we know and love! I had begun to notice at my reading that Carter and Dad sounded very much like they did in person. They were both very positive, easygoing, happy people, and I began to contemplate how this might relate to us all. Some people had wonderful personalities and were easy to be with, and others not. We all need to be more aware of our behaviour. Grumpy people might find some enjoyment with being difficult here, but if we carry these traits into the spirit world, does anybody really want to be unhappy for eternity?

August 19, 2010:

Carter and I had a talk that I think was both poignant and rich with information.

CH: Olivia slept in your room again last night. We could both smell you and she's still sleeping well. What did you do all night?

C: I was with Olivia ... I love her.

CH: Do you know why she's sleeping so well?

C: I hugged her.

CH: Were you there all night?

C: I'm still there.

CH: You say you're with Olivia still, but you're also here with me in the dining room area?

C: I can be in more than one place.

CH: How can you do that?

C: I break my soul in two.

CH: Are you aware of what you're doing in both places?

C: Yes.

CH: How do you bring your soul back together?

C: I will it back.

CH: Can everyone do this?

C: I don't think so.

CH: Can Grandpa do this?

C: Yes.

CH: Do you know why you and grandpa can do this?

C: I think we are more advanced; we have been there many times, done well, kind, loving.

WHAT? I am shocked by his words, "been there many times." I can't believe my father would let Carter tell me this because it goes against what he believed. But I must remain focused and not get distracted by his statement. I can think about what he's saying later, let him continue to speak; this is great stuff!

CH: Are you close to God?

C: I can always feel him.

CH: Can you see God?

C: No.

CH: You say you feel God. What are these feelings of God's presence around you?

C: I see beautiful light, I feel his love, joy, I feel so good.

CH: You were always so happy here. Was this just you, or were you able to feel God then also because you say you feel so good now?

C: I knew God on earth.

CH: Were you aware of this as a person, or only now that you can reflect back?

C: I, my soul, knew.

CH: Do we all come down to earth together?

C: Usually.

CH: How does this happen?

C: One decides then the rest of us want to help.

CH: Help with what?

C: Help to enable the person to do well.

CH: Does this help us all advance?

C: If we've done well.

CH: What if some do really well and others don't? Are we separated there? Are we no longer together as those of us that do well advance?

C: There's no separation, those that do better can do more.

CH: What is our goal there?

C: To be one with God.

CH: How does this become possible?

C: We just keep trying to improve.

Wow, he had given me lots to think about here as the conversation flowed into unexpected but interesting areas. Some of it made sense and lots of it was a real stretch for me, but why would Carter tell me anything that wasn't true? It helped that I always believed in the person giving me the information. Whether it was Carter or Dad, I had a deep understanding of their humanity as a person and their genuine love for me while they were here, and I believed this incredible effort they must be making was for good. I don't know if I could have believed in a lot of the information, especially at first, without a complete trust in whom I was speaking to.

I know Carter sincerely wanted to help others, but I was only interested in our being together. I found our daily talks life-sustaining for me and I needed constant reassurance he was with me. I knew he was there yesterday, but I needed him to prove it again to me each day since I was worried that he may disappear again. Reluctantly, I told him we will do what he hopes to do to help others, but I had no idea how to proceed or where his ideas would lead me. Gradually I would accept his ongoing ideas, though always with reluctance and long hesitations while he patiently waited for me to bring my thinking in line with his.

August 26, 2010:

CH: Okay Carter we'll do this together. I'll definitely try to help people with this. I have no idea how I'll do this, but how could I not do this for you?

C: I am glad.

CH: I feel you. (I feel him in both my hands and then around my torso.)

C: Yes, you use me for good.

CH: Carter, can you tell me what you wrote on July 27, 2010? (I then flipped the pages of the journal back to July 27 to show him the page.) This page Carter, what does this say? I can't read it at all, and I have tried many times.

C: You've had a struggle to find me, that's what it says.

Over the next few months, whenever I questioned if this connection to Carter and Dad was real, I would often refer back and examine the page of July 27; he had told me what was written. I had tried many times to figure it out, I even tried to rewrite it copying with the flow he wrote it in to see if I could perhaps feel what letters he was forming to better guess the words, but I could never make any sense of it. This reassured me when doubt crept in that it must be Carter writing this as I was certain that I didn't know what it said.

C: Our lives are still joined.

CH: It has been a living nightmare, Carter, but I had to find out if these signs and feelings were from you. I had to know if it was possible to find out if you were ok.

C: So much pain but you didn't give up. Hugs, do you feel it?

CH: I do! Let me enjoy it for a moment. (I feel him hugging me.) I miss you.

C: I know, but you can always feel me now. Our connection is strong ... Use your instincts they are very strong.

CH: Just mine, or everyone's?

C: You are more open to yours you are doing so well, incredible. I'm writing quicker some days, today our connection is amazing. You're opening your mind to me. I am part of you, we are as one today, it's easy, better, you hear me clearly. I'm with you. I'll guide you; you'll learn a path will come for us together.

CH: I know I want to do this for so many good reasons. But my real reason is that I want to spend time with you.

C: You will, big hug X.

September 3, 2010:

CH: Good morning; who was making my fingers twitch just now in meditation?

DAD: I was, Charm.

CH: Hi, Dad, were you trying to tell me you wanted to talk to me?

DAD: I want you to be patient, to let this happen naturally, your chances will come. I can hear you always; I will help you and Carter, but enjoy each day. Practice meditation to keep your mind open for us, but enjoy each moment there. Use us to keep your focus on what you know to be true and live your life fully with this knowledge. Carter will teach you, guide you. You are our voice to others. This is a special task, live with it with joy and let this joy touch others.

1999 Carter age 10 with his Grandfather John Carter age 87

Their behavior suited each of them perfectly. Carter was always excited for new experiences and was helpful to people. My father was patient, steady, reliable, and was also kind and helpful to people. He didn't worry about the outcome, just in doing your best.

CH: Dad, did Carter know this when he was here?

DAD: He didn't remember but was fantastic, so much growth he's very bright now, is happy.

CH: What does Carter look like to you, Dad?

DAD: He's very bright, whitish, full of joy. Others gather around him, teens mostly. He's teaching them how to advance here to let go of the life that was and BE here, be amazed, learn, reach, grow.

They are home, all return.

CH: Are many there white light?

DAD: No much duller, not white, yellow, often can't do what Carter can do.

CH: Why the different colours?

DAD: The goal is to become whiter and brighter, more vision of all important love. Carter spread this on Earth also his message always strong even now through you. I am helping him.

You are a major project for him, a big task. I am to keep you steady and strong so you can do this. Give you good thoughts. Much easier now that you can hear us. You will be happy if you take this tusk in the end but don't push, follow, the chances will come.

CH: What do you look like, Dad?

DAD: I'm okay, not so white but still white. I lost focus on earth sometimes. Carter more determined, exuberant. Love flowed, always focused on the important, touched many lives, great job. A great effort he now sees rewards. He did as he hoped; many hope but human minds difficult, they fight our good intentions. Follow your instincts you're getting better, relearning. The knowledge we are giving you is to be shared. You and I are connecting for a purpose to ease other's pain, find joy. People need to rethink how they look at things, so many problems where none should be. Be happy. To help one person is as important as helping many. It's that spark of kindness, a light in your soul. All gestures matter, seize each moment, bring joy, find joy, be happy.

CH: You were also a very kind person, Dad.

DAD: We are who we are here or there, advance sometimes. I tried my best.

CH: I am so happy you talked to me today. I love you.

DAD: Me too, I love you all.

CH: Is Carter here?

DAD: No, not here, he's never gone long, will appear. You know Carter, he's having a great time, of course, loves all his freedom. It is so good for kids to see his energy bursting out. Can't contain him, joyous, draws many near him. His energy is wonderful to see working.

CH: This writing was effortless today Dad, it just flowed. It was so easy, it makes it even more difficult to believe.

DAD: It is you, you're accepting me, I am part of you. It's a pleasure~ Love Dad.

Perseverance and Hope

Love you Mom. Life's crush can be like a vice but remember a vice is controllable. Yes, people can feel like they are being crushed, suffocated, pushed in all directions and lose the strength to push back. They try to push the pressure away from them but they can only resist while they have the strength and energy to resist.

When they are depleted, weakened, lose focus, the weight of life's struggles then can come crushing in relentlessly against them and they cannot get free. Life of course is only at times like this—I think life's amazing so I am only trying to give a visual for a more effective mindset through struggles. This was beginning to sound way too DEPRESSING for me! Anyway OK let's continue

People's strength, physical and emotional can't always sustain them during these pushes of difficult times so they need a more effective tactic or approach. You see the sketch—the person isn't going to defeat the vice but if the person can find ease they relax and not LET the vice, and themselves, struggle against each other. Yes, of course they realize they are struggling, in possible peril of struggle but see it not as insurmountable. Ask for help; accept help and the pressure eases, not from you pushing back but from help. Find stillness to try to cope through struggle. Realize it is difficult, but easier dealt with in a calm less emotional mind. "I am not winning this battle, so I need to find a way through it." Place yourself visually within the light of the divine. Walk enhanced from the spiritual strength you can be absorbed into. Find an inner strength for struggle and from the warmth and love begin to feel the vice is still present, you still sit within it, but you have allowed yourself to be helped. You have found a more effective way to cope, you are no longer struggling alone. (Carter, writing received August 17, 2012, for a friend.)

As summer ended, I think I could safely say that this had been the most incredible summer of my life. I now had a personal connection to Carter that was beyond my wildest dreams, but it felt strange being home, and autumn was a struggle for me. Each day, as I tried unsuccessfully, I became increasingly worried that I couldn't connect to Carter and Dad away from our cottage.

I had also not approached John on this topic so that also made it difficult as I tried to find quiet times to practice writing, but there were always interruptions. I had never told anyone that I needed quiet, so what could I expect? I didn't really want to get into this discussion with him, he had not been approachable over the last two years when I was questioning things that were happening and hoping it was Carter. If he wouldn't explore those possibilities, what was he going to think when I told him Carter was writing through my hand? I was shocked by it and I was the one who picked up the pen in the first place.

September 8, 2010:

I wrote with Carter for the first time since coming home four days ago, and though it was very difficult to connect and maintain, we managed to get this writing.

C: Love you, Victoria doing well, watching her with love [she's just begun university]. Like you to keep practicing [this writing], keep this connection, doesn't come easy. Dad can know, he will struggle but you need to practice. You have struggled too hard; our journey must move forward we have a purpose together. This connection takes great effort for you. You need to work each day, it is with constant practice our connection grows stronger, our tasks will come easier but with great focus from you … I need to reach you.

It took me another three days before I told John, but I realized the only way for me to move forward was if he knew what I was trying to learn to do as I was being constantly interrupted. I awkwardly explained, and I was happy that—though shocked—he reacted positively.

September 9, 2010:

This writing stopped me in my tracks. It began with a question then an answer, but when I asked the second casual question the answer was gut-wrenching.

CH: Did you send Sean the text message on his birthday in August 2008?

C: Yes.

CH: You could do this so soon after your death?

C: Yes, I was okay right away, no time lost. I knew what I needed to do; never scared Grandpa got me before I knew what was happening. Grandpa knew I was coming so he got me out before the accident.

CH: *WHAT? NO!!* How can that be? Dad!!!

I was shaking and upset at this information IF it was right; I was hoping that it wasn't right. I criticized my father's actions and I felt deeply wounded by him.

"Dad, why did you take him? Why didn't you leave him? He might have survived and still be here with us. I can't believe you have done this to us."

DAD: We all know when we will return. I took him so there was no pain, no need to suffer. He needed to come home so his path could continue, it was his plan.

CH: I am shaking; I don't know if what you're telling me is good or not right now, Dad.

DAD: You must trust I was waiting; I lifted him out before impact. He knew right away when he saw me it was as we planned. Awful for us to see the suffering, especially hard on Carter, he was trying right away to reach so many. Cayley was right he found it impossible not to help, knows it's for a purpose to grow, strive, to conquer our battles. He's so much happier now that he can talk to you, not all these little distractions [signs from him]. He suffered when he saw everyone's pain. He needs to help, is so happy to be through that part and work toward your path together to reconnect and help.

In the days immediately following this writing, I was crushed. I certainly wasn't helped at all by this information. Stunned by the words, I reread it many times and gradually I saw some good within the knowledge. First and foremost, Carter didn't suffer and this is what both the coroner and Sandy had told us. Carter said, "Grandpa got me before I knew what was happening," so he wouldn't have been frightened in those last few seconds. Ever since the accident, every time I was driving and turned to see a truck coming toward me I panicked, thinking this was his last terrifying sight. But if I put Dad's and Carter's words together, he was gone before knowing what was going to happen, and under these circumstances that would be a good thing. I became increasingly amazed by the bigger picture, not only for Carter, but for others who suffered in their final moments. Over time through quiet contemplation, I was able to move past hurt and anger to gratitude. It was humbling to be allowed to glimpse the capabilities and magnitude of existence.

Throughout the next several months, Dad, Carter, and I struggled to connect as we seemed to have to adapt to whatever circumstances were different between the cottage and home, and this could sometimes be heard in the writing.

September 12, 2010:

CH: Carter, I can feel you but not hear you.

C: Yes, I'm trying hard to connect here today, very difficult.

I concentrated with a greater focus to clear my mind and be open for his thoughts to flow through me.

CH: I can hear you now.

C: Yes incredible effort for us both but yes I am trying to stay in your mind, difficult. You're trying to stay open for us. This is why you need to practice its harder here [in the city], so much harder. The space is not as pure the cottage is, go whenever you can, practice stay confident, we are here.

September 13, 2010:

I thought I was focused and open, but I could neither feel nor hear him. Happily, he managed to get a few words written. Over the years I would learn to realize that these words *were* the message that Carter was trying to teach me.

C: LOVE IS ALL IMPORTANT, ALL ELSE HAS LITTLE IMPORTANCE.

September 16, 2010:

I was so happy, this connection was amazing today!

C: Love you, there is no separation of space we are here with you, we live among you. Our world and yours intermingle. We know this you don't.

CH: Are you always within our space?

C: No our space is boundless but space is space it is all one we have a bigger range.

CH: Do you leave our earth and go into this boundless space?

C: There is no reason to, my connection is here and my purpose continues to be here. I am to help.

CH: I thought you were helping teenagers cross over?

C: Here or there I help souls heal and find joy. They must understand they chose this. They are sometimes confused and need encouragement, guidance. I am able to give them this.

CH: You were doing that here also when people were upset or needed encouragement.

C: I do that here or there, always it is me. I understand in both places.

CH: You and Grandpa have both said you were never confused; you understood as soon as you saw Grandpa. Why weren't you confused if others are?

C: I'm at a different level, have more growth. As we grow in love knowledge also comes. I can step back here, jump right back to where I was before my break. Complete knowledge of how I did, good and bad. Where I failed or could have improved. This knowledge is known within me right away. I have things I want to do right away. Help all of you, reach you Mom. Break the barriers; I don't want our purpose to fail. My time for you reaching out to find me won't last forever. I mustn't lose the chance or our chosen path isn't accomplished and we will have to try again.

Besides still being generally astounded by this whole experience I found some of his information unsettling and beyond belief, quite simply I thought, *this can't be!* Whenever Carter made statements that I couldn't understand I spent a lot of time in thought as I tried to grasp their meaning, but he was describing a world beyond my understanding.

By mid-September, Janice had signed us up for meditation classes that I hoped would help. Though it had only been two weeks since I returned home, the fear that I was going to lose contact with Carter was making me panic. I had lost him once and I couldn't lose him again.

September 17, 2010:

CH: What did you think of the meditation class two days ago, Carter?

C: It's a good idea, will help, don't think that's the one to do though but try the class again. You did better yesterday with our writing, a clearer connection. Stay focused I'd like you to try to absorb nature around you. Complete awareness, all the senses, be in nature silent, bring all your awareness to nature, become part of it, will help meditation and help us. Grandpa stays with you, you feel him reminding you: stay strong we're here, he's behind you. Nature works for you and Grandpa too. You are doing great Mom xxx.

September 18, 2010:

We were at the cottage for the weekend and I was eager to try to connect to Carter and Dad there once again. Carter wrote, "Love you," then the writing ended. I had hoped being immersed within nature would benefit us.

After three or four minutes of concentration to connect I was frustrated, so I spoke to both of them, "Even if you guys have nothing to say, let's practice since I am at the cottage." After a short wait, Dad wrote.

DAD: Love you all. Both of us are here. We want you to know this will come back, just keep practicing. This space is better but without constant effort it is a bit more difficult than in the summer. Keep clearing your mind, ask for clarity of connection, and use your will. Allow your spirit to rise to your consciousness, it connects to us. Meditate above all, use prayer or speak to ask for this connection to strengthen. I will help from our side, stay with you and send you supportive thoughts. If your mind is clear you will receive them. You won't know they're from me, but you will allow a flow of positive thoughts to go through your mind. Stay focused on our task, it will come easier. Your thoughts and mine to you will intermingle as one, we work as a team.

CH: I like that, Dad. (But I have no idea what he's talking about when he says "allow your spirit to rise to your consciousness.)

DAD: I like that too.

September 20, 2010:

Today Carter was guiding me to concentrate back to our basic connection as we both strived to recapture a better connection with each other.

C: Love you, concentrate, feel the energy [I put down the pen after each of his instructions and try to follow his guidance] … concentrate, feel me … keep concentrating, start work in meditation, an awareness of when I'm here. You will know it's me by your instincts. Focus first on feeling me xx … you're not concentrating enough, clear your mind …You did better after meditation class your mind was calm and clear.

CH: I can feel tingling over my whole body. Carter is that you?

C: Yes a big hug, have patience Mom don't get frustrated, stay with it.

I knew I needed to be patient, but I couldn't seem to find a place or time that worked, which brought me more frustration. Then, during a walk with Shannon, she suggested I wake up before anyone else and attempt this when the house was quiet. I liked her idea, but often I couldn't get myself out of bed. Once I realized I had more success at this time of day I became committed to rising early each day. This time spent in meditation followed by my time writing with Carter both stilled and centred me and I got through my days with greater ease. My talks with Carter reassured me daily that he was happy and with me still, and it brought to focus the bigger picture of a life beyond our time on earth, which helped put life's daily issues in a better perspective for me. As time went by, I also began to realize Carter and Dad were a constant and reliable support for me as they witnessed my life and could guide me with wisdom, free of human attitudes and ego.

September 30, 2010:

After almost two weeks, I still couldn't comprehend Dad's instruction from September 18. Finally, I asked what he meant.

CH: Dad, how do I get my spirit to rise to my consciousness?

DAD: Hi Charm, just ask for it to happen, concentrate, won't happen quickly and keep asking. Very subtle change for you, mostly you must believe it is going to happen. You must request daily for your spirit to rise to your consciousness.

I simply trusted him and believed as I repeated the words written on September 18, and I was successful even without understanding their meaning. Gradually over the next few years I learned to understand, but that understanding also continued to change and deepen as I expanded into a greater knowledge of the world beyond form.

October 2, 2010:

Once again as I sat at Carter's desk to write I failed to connect with him and I dropped my hands in my lap in frustration. Within moments, both hands began to lift until they hit the edge of the desk, and even though there were no words written I felt better knowing we had connected.

The Gifts of Autumn

Love you Mom. Let's find purpose together Mom, you and I, mother and son. Let our physical bond and connection through this life effort give you the focus and courage to move forward. My life has not ended; our time together has not been shortened not within our true presence of form for we move forward now in a task of love and hoped for joy. A task that comes through grief, pain, struggle then comfort and hoped for joy as you learn how full and complete all our lives continue to be. We connect through improbable odds within the drive and focus of love. Let's do this well Mom. Be our voice, carry our messages and give people who hunger to hear another voice of truth to hopefully have the chance to hear, Love you. (Carter, writing received September 14, 2012.)

October 3, 2010:

As I transcribed today's writing, my attention was drawn to how lovely a song sounded on the music I had playing. I looked to see what number it was and of course, it was six! I had heard this song dozens of times but had never noticed it before, and as I sat wondering whether Carter had anything to do with me noticing it that day John called to me and said, "Charmaine, you might want to come and see this."

I walked into the den and on John's computer was a photograph that our neighbour at the cottage had taken the day before of mushrooms growing by our stone stairs. John asked me to look at the picture and see if I could see anything. I looked but, saw nothing worth mentioning.

"What am I supposed to be seeing?"

John said, "There's a face. I noticed it right away, can you see it?"

My gaze darted all around the photo, but I didn't see it and asked where should I look. He zoomed in to enlarge the area.

"It's right there. Do you see it now?"

I did see it, and I couldn't believe what I saw. It was not just a face, it was Carter's face! John said he spotted it as soon as he saw the photo but he wasn't sure if he should tell me. I told him to never keep anything from me concerning Carter no matter what it was. I was thrilled that John spotted it and I wondered if Carter helped him see it. Excited beyond words, the answer to that question didn't matter; this was thrilling.

I had never heard of anything like this, a photograph where we could see an image of Carter's face couldn't be anything but what it seemed to be, could it? That Carter was showing himself to us. I was beside myself once again with joy and disbelief. How did Carter do this? John printed a paper copy then I tried to reprint it as a photograph, but the machine wouldn't copy it. I phoned our neighbours and without any further explanation asked them to save the photos until we got to the cottage.

I needed to talk to Carter right away! I returned to his room and without any thought of meditation or preparing my mind to connect I opened the journal to the next blank page, picked up the pen, and asked the question.

CH: Carter, it's unbelievable, your face is on one of the photos taken at the cottage. How did you ever do this?

C: Surprise!! Told you, you would see me. Great for Dad spotting me thought it might be missed. I can't explain how I did it. It has to do with energy and will, clarity of purpose. I'm thrilled with the effort and result. As you can see I'm fine, happy and yes so happy to give this gift to you for Thanksgiving. Enjoy the day try not to be sad, know it is as planned. We will both be there at dinner.

On September 14, 2010, I had realized that I was now able to smell, feel and hear Carter and I had asked him if I would ever be able to see him.

CH: I will be looking for you in every picture now.

C: Only the cottage ones but very difficult to make this happen. Big hug Mom, I know you love pictures, knew this gift would mean so much. Great fun doing this is for all of you. Hugs to Dad he saw me right away on his own no help.

CH: Could many others do this?

C: Not really many, creating image to be seen in clear view to you. You and I have contact in many ways, but all can see me now. Share this; I'm with you, right here. Help prove to people who can't accept because they can't see me, well now they can see me. If it's not me what else could be the explanation, my face clearly on a rock at the cottage. I live, believe. This is good today, no luck for you last couple attempts we'll do it Mom XX.

October 4, 2010:

I was still eluted from yesterday as I drove to work, thinking of all the ways Carter was managing to reach back to me. To blend his thoughts with mine, I inserted the *For Always* CD and pressed six for Carter, which was the song "You Raise Me Up." I knew he and Kevin had lots of fun singing this at the restaurant that last summer and I began to cry as I pictured them and thought of all the fun he was missing. When it finished I was startled to hear the song "Remember Me" begin to play. Why is this song playing? I looked down at the display screen to see the number four. That can't play next, it should be the next song, which is seven, and it wasn't on shuffle. Was Carter trying to help me feel better by reminding me that he was still here? I smiled; it certainly did help, and my thoughts returned to happy thoughts of yesterday.

I was finding life very stressful on a daily basis; I felt both uplifted and drained at the same time as I had all the normal demands of a full life while hiding much of my new experiences. I felt lucky whenever I was able to be at the cottage, because what I experienced there always came easier and was richer in context. A lot of the frustration that I was experiencing was my own doing, as this wasn't something I felt I could share with most people. If I were to say what I was doing either they'd look at me like I had three heads or the explanation would be so long and difficult that I would be exhausted by the time I said it. Explaining this was never a one-sentence statement.

October 16, 2010:

When I returned to the cottage for the weekend my only thought was the photo. The first thing we did was visit our neighbours and learned it was Garn who had taken that photo. I was bursting to tell them, but insecure about showing them what we saw in their photo. Would they be able to see it, or even be open to the possibility of seeing it? I knew they didn't believe in an afterlife and I hesitated before I asked them to bring the photos onto their computer screen. Finally, summoning my courage, I showed them the image Garn had captured in his picture. They were amazed, speechless, but they could both see the image of Carter and they understandably didn't know what to think.

Garn began to go over his memories of the day he took the photo. The mushrooms grew at that time every year around the area, and he really didn't know why he took the pictures on that day. He didn't think anything of it at the time, but now, after seeing what the picture had captured, he couldn't explain why he took it. He said he was there talking with our neighbours when he noticed them. He knew he felt a strong enough urge to take a picture of these mushrooms that he stopped the conversation, went home, and returned with his camera. He had to admit it was odd. They made me a CD with all six photos he took that day, though Carter could only be seen in the one picture.

When I took it to be developed, I could see all six images on the screen, but the one with Carter's image wouldn't print even when I tried different machines. It always said there was a problem with the image although I could clearly see the photo. I asked the technicians for help and they said they had never seen that before. I wondered, *did Carter not want me to print this photo? Could the machine detect something odd within the picture?* Because there absolutely was something very odd, this story just kept getting stranger but I began panicking. I needed a print copy of this image before something happened to it. I was still worried I'd lose my connection to talk with Carter; I needed this evidence to help me feel confident he existed still and was with us and to have trust that our ease of connection would return with diligent efforts by both of us.

C: Love you all. Hi Mom. You need to take my heart and hold it within your mind, that love will flow and strengthen our connection, try that. It's my total love for you within you enabling this to happen, will add an extra level to help this, visualize.

CH: Do I need to keep my eyes closed, or can I try with them open?

C: It doesn't matter if your eyes are open or closed but you may be more distracted by the visual and not be able to hear us as well. If that happens close your eyes again.

I put down the pen, relaxed my hands on my thighs with palms up open to the sky, and let my mind descend into silence. Then with great clarity, I visualized every detail and facet of the image of holding Carter's heart in my mind as he had instructed me to do. I shouldn't have been surprised that by following his directions my connection to him that day was strong and clear. This became one of my working tools, especially during this period of readjustment. I'd had important questions since I saw the rock photo, and today I felt confident that I would get answers.

CH: Carter, Garn says that he took the photo. Did you just happen to be there at the right time, or what happened?

C: I put thoughts in his mind to take some photos. I wanted to see if I could do this, knew it had the best chance to happen at the cottage if it could happen so I was there drawing his attention to things and thoughts of photos I put in his mind. The situation worked for me, lots of things we try for people's attention but their minds are too busy to hear our thoughts. Happy this happened, thank Garn.

CH: Were you actually visible? Could you have been seen then, or were you only visible through the photo?

C: Yes, I could have been seen at that moment but very briefly. Better in a photo and you can go back to it, know I'm there. Use it to focus on what I'm telling you. If you saw me for that moment you would never have absolutely believed, did you see me or not, even you now Mom with your knowledge of us. This I thought was the best way to do it if I could, plus you have a gift from me XX.

A gift from Carter! His thoughtfulness was perfect, and its physical existence is mind-boggling. I'm amazed the answer was clear and precise and that I received it without a struggle. This is such a pleasant change from recent attempts that I don't want today's session to end, but I can't think of anything to ask him.

CH: Our connection is so good this morning at the cottage, but I don't know what to ask. Tell me something wonderful, information that you know that I will find interesting.

C: Love is all important, only thing that really matters. These other things have some importance because these judgments reflect on how you have loved all of God's people and things he created on Earth for us. So really you are not judged by yourself so much on these little things you have done wrong but on how that may have hurt others or things by lack of love given by you. It is love that must flow constantly through your life from you to have gained real growth in your time there. Love is all important; everything else falls away from importance. If you have done something wrong, but with love in your heart you will see the errors you made here but at least you did it for love but you must learn from mistakes and hope to do better the next time. Great suffering sometimes here when even though it was done for love it was also wrong. The soul must reflect and realize why it made such bad judgment, often just not strong enough to battle the mind and other influences. Here love is all important so spread love and joy and you will be so happy with your effort, what else really matters? How was that Mom? You wanted some info. Big hug, you did well with eyes open, at the cottage again.

I had been finding this work with Carter far too time consuming. I needed to find a more efficient method as it was becoming more difficult to carve the needed time out of my days. It took me at least fifteen minutes to meditate and feel Carter connect with me, and writing together often took another thirty to forty-five minutes. I kept my eyes closed throughout the writing to help keep my mind clear for Carter, which meant that I had to also transcribe the writing immediately after while I could still remember and decipher it. If I didn't have time to transcribe for a few days, I struggled and couldn't make out parts of the writing. I knew I couldn't hurry the connection process, so I had been trying to learn to write with my eyes open and eliminate the transcription. As in all of this process, it took patience and a lot of failures but I was determined to persevere and work beyond my current limits. Gradually it became easier, as I learned to use my will to focus and our connection often became almost instant.

An interesting outcome came from this effort. With my eyes open, I was using greater concentration to hear Carter with more clarity, and without being aware of it the writing became a more equal effort between Carter and me, and we wrote quicker. As time went on and I became completely confident in what I heard, we would adapt again. I always waited until I felt Carter in my left hand, then I picked up the pen and he wrote the first few words by guiding my hand. Then when I was confident in our connection because I had also heard the words he had written, I took over and wrote what I continued to hear him tell me. This again shortened the time needed to get his messages written and also helped me grow as I continued to improve; it allowed me to reach new heights and experiences of spiritual connection.

November 11, 2010:

I was in Carter's room at home, struggling to write with him yet again when the phone rang. This wasn't the first time that the phone had rung while I was writing with him, but this was the first time I ever thought, *imagine what it would feel like if I picked up that phone and heard Carter's voice.*

Later, I asked who was on the phone, and Olivia said, "That was really weird, Mom. When the phone rang I picked it up and heard, 'Hi, this is Carter from Anderson Windows.' For a second I thought it WAS Carter until I realized his name was just Carter but they never say their name only the name of the business, like hi, it's Anderson Windows calling." I stared at Olivia momentarily in stunned silence, unable to believe what she had just said.

"Did he sound like Carter?" I asked.

Olivia said no, he sounded like an older guy. My mind began to race once again. Why did I have that thought this time when the phone rang? Odds of it being a person named Carter and saying his name must be huge, and this was the only time I had ever had this thought. Was it a coincidence, or a sign from Carter?

My next few days were hectic and I didn't make time to talk with him, which didn't pass without Carter's notice. His answer to my question that day was unexpected, as was his reminder of my lapses of effort lately.

November 13, 2010:

CH: Carter, two nights ago when we were writing the phone rang, which has happened before, but this time right away I thought, *imagine if I heard Carter's voice on the phone.* Then Olivia said the person on the phone said he was Carter!

C: Yes I did that call; the call was arranged by me. I put our telephone number in that phone of the person whose name was also Carter. Trying to signal you, your intuition knew it was Carter. Learning to accept these thoughts also is part of your growth. It's all developing your mind for our task. You're not working enough on this lately ... you can get so much better at this but with practice only.

How was that possible? That couldn't be right, could it? Whenever I shared these stories, I wasn't surprised when people didn't believe me. I wouldn't believe me, either. Carter's answer brought me many more questions, all beginning with "how." As I have said, it was only because I had such trust and love for the person answering my questions that I would give the answer consideration and thought. In my mind, under any other circumstance, these answers would be fictional at best and too absurd to be believed.

November 22, 2010:

I had a lovely birthday shopping in the USA with Victoria, and when we got home Olivia gave me a message from a friend who called me that day. Instantly, I was covered in goosebumps. Was this Carter's way of acknowledging my birthday because I knew she believed in telepathy? Hearing her message completed my day nicely, but I was tired so I called her the next day.

"Do you know what day yesterday was?" I asked, knowing she didn't. She said no, and when I said it was my birthday, she was amazed.

"Let me think," she said, "you and your family have been on my mind for the last few weeks and yesterday when I woke up I felt I HAD to call you that day!"

Now I was certain that this was my birthday gift from Carter.

November 26, 2010:

CH: Carter did you have anything to do with that call on my birthday?

C: Love you yes I put thoughts of you in her mind.

CH: Why?

C: It's your birthday present from me, my gift to you on your birthday. By her calling you on this day I knew you'd think right away it was me and know I didn't forget your birthday.

CH: Thank you, Carter, it means so much to me and this year I really believed you were with me.

C: I know you did great, much better for me too.

December 1, 2010:

I had joined Janice at her house to do yoga together and during our practice, I had said: "After this let's see if Carter can talk with you." He had asked me several times to try to have him speak to people but I hadn't yet because I wasn't comfortable asking. However, Janice was one of the few people that knew what I was doing. Janice and I were both in a good mindset after yoga and ready to try, but we didn't seriously think anything would happen. This was new for her and I was nervous. I thought I felt Carter in my hand, but my heart was pounding and I wasn't confident that I did.

To my surprise, Janice said, "I can feel him."

I didn't expect that. If she could feel him then I must too, so I put pen to paper. Immediately the pen raced across the page as I repeated what I heard. The pen moved so quickly it was illegible so I dropped the pen. *Slow down, Carter.* He spoke to Janice for himself and for her parents (in spirit). He answered her questions with speed and excitement before she'd finished asking them, and then it stopped as quickly as it started. Janice said that she felt him leave. We looked at each other, stunned by what had happened. Janice said she when felt him arrive, she felt pressure against her chest and similar to what I had described I had felt in the car on September 3, 2009. She said at the time she thought it sounded weird, but that's exactly what she had felt.

December 8, 2010:

From this day forward, Carter began almost all writings with what would become his signature sign-in: I ove you Mom. He had done it for the first time on October 21, 2010, but used it only occasionally until this day, when it became his daily greeting to me

The Gingerbread House

Love you Mom,

CH: I love you Carter, Merry Christmas Eve.

C: Merry Christmas Eve, be not sad by my passing. Today try to rejoice in our connection, a miracle of the strength and determination of our spirits, us three, a very real testament to the power of love and for love. We are honoured to have this opportunity to reach back from our connection, reconnection really of our spirits' true knowledge away from form and to have this opportunity to serve a purpose by sending some of it back through you. You open for our voice; you accept our guidance and words of love. The struggle in form is to find the truth within the confines of that form, that mind and ego. The knowledge known at whatever level is held transparent, unseen, locked within the spirit origin and for spirit to find strength to rise and grow within form. For us to be able to give voice as we have reattached with our knowledge and awareness. We have our whole body of our strived for knowledge within our conscious thoughts now as we have returned to our origin and reconnected with our knowledge and awareness. We through our connection can send this knowledge to form through you. We can help struggles, burdens, and hopefully pain for it is love that is the purpose, joy, reason and struggle. A miracle of love, not just at Christmas but let's let the spiritual presence of mind of many at Christmas enhance and carry within you a true joy for our spiritual journey and true presence during this yearly celebration of spiritual birth in form for goodness and love. Rejoice in our love, our spiritual "rebirth" but with your voice and form. We love you all, Merry Christmas Eve. (Carter, writing received December 24, 2011.)

Christmas Eve

December 24, 2010:

Our family had always made gingerbread houses at Christmas, and for the first time since Carter's death, Victoria and Olivia wanted to try to make one. I bought all the supplies, feeling it was a step forward just to think about it, but I never expected we would be able to build one. I thought I would end up throwing the ingredients out after Christmas, but I believed even voicing the hope to make one again was progress.

Victoria's two Australian friends were spending Christmas with us and they were excited to enjoy Canadian traditions. They had never made a gingerbread house; this was the push we needed, so we'd do it for them. On Christmas Eve, my girls decorated one side and Victoria's friends decorated the other side. I left the room because I couldn't watch it being made without Carter. He loved all our holiday traditions, and by leaving the room I could hear the fun of them making it without having to face Carter's absence.

After a while, although I was reluctant, I felt I should go see how they were doing. The Australians' roof was classic, but my girls' side was very odd. I looked at it again.

Confused, I had to ask, "What are you doing?"

Olivia said, "We're making hockey players."

That was an unexpected answer.

"Oh, that's really different. You've never done anything like that before. Why would you make hockey players on a gingerbread house?"

"Victoria decided."

Victoria said, "We had other ideas, but they weren't working out and Dad had bought some hockey puck candy, so I thought we'd make hockey players."

"Okay," I said, still thinking this was strange. Victoria would never make anything like this, and certainly not on a gingerbread house, and neither would Olivia. I was confused by their choice, but they were all having fun so I returned to the family room.

Olivia was decorating the hockey jerseys and asked, "Dad, what are some of the colours of the NHL jerseys?"

He described the Calgary Flames and the Minnesota Wild.

I went to see the finished product once I heard them cleaning up. On the side of the house my girls decorated, I saw a xox and said, "Victoria you put kiss, hug, and kiss on the house."

"No, we didn't," she said.

"Yes, you did. Look on the side of the house: xox."

She looked up nonchalantly from washing the dishes and said, "Oh yeah, so I did. I didn't notice; I was just decorating the window," and she went back to washing dishes.

I continued to stare at it on the kitchen table, still confused by the whole experience. Then I smiled as I thought, *Carter and Dad, if you're here, the xox is for you from us, Merry Christmas.*

Christmas Day

December 25, 2010:

I was the first person to wake up Christmas morning, and as I came down the hall toward the kitchen I faced the gingerbread house with its two hockey players smiling directly at me and one of them looked as if he were waving. Shocked, I immediately turned and rushed back upstairs thinking, *Oh my god, is the gingerbread house from Dad and Carter?*

I desperately needed to speak with Carter; I entered his room and sat at his desk. My hands were shaking. How could I connect to get his answers in this state? *Talk to me Carter ... is what I'm thinking possible? It can't be, can it? I need you to talk to me! Did you have anything to do with making the gingerbread house?* Incredibly, this is his reply:

C: A kiss Mom, Merry Christmas. A gift for all of you from Grandpa and I, tell Grandma too. Victoria's mind was in a good place and we both gave her our thoughts in the hope she could hear us. Our thoughts flowed through her mind to create this decoration for you. We were giving ideas to Olivia but mainly to Victoria. She took the lead in designing what we wanted. Thanks, Victoria. Grandpa's thanking you both too. We had such a good time once you got started no one gave it a thought. C: Calgary Flames. No, Carter. The goalie's Grandpa when we played road hockey at his house. See it now, so much fun and your Christmas gift from us with all our love to all of you. See the window xox. Victoria didn't even see it, but you did Mom.

CH: I thought I was sending a kiss, hug and kiss to you and Grandpa.

C: No, its Grandpa and I sending you xox for Christmas, make sense now. Tell everyone it is a gift, our pleasure, joy to be able to do this and we were right with you making the gingerbread house just like before. I wouldn't miss these things for the world. Grandpa says him too, big hug Olivia.

(Olivia had been very upset at bedtime. She was crying and saying "It's Christmas. This is not fair that Carter's not here." I agreed completely with her; this wasn't fair to any of us, including Carter. I had told her to ask Carter to stay with her and to believe he was there with her.)

C: I am here, was here with you last night, believe, you only have to ask, I am with you still. Know we're there with you today, feel us if you can. This completes the gift perfectly, our enabling it to happen and letting you know with absolute certainty it's from us with this writing xxxxxxxxxxxxxx Merry Christmas.

Before our guests woke up, I read what Carter had just written to John, Victoria, and Olivia. They were understandably speechless, but in hindsight admitted they couldn't explain why they would ever choose to put hockey players on a gingerbread house roof. Victoria repeated that she wasn't putting hugs and kisses on the side, but agreed that is what's there.

I said, "We have Carter's explanation, and if Grandpa and Carter have made this incredible effort to help us at Christmas and are asking us to please try to enjoy the day as they will be with us all day, then what else can they do to help us? They're trying so hard. If they can guide you to make this, then we have to also believe that they will be with us as they say, and we need to let them see that their efforts are helping us."

Throughout the day as I watched my family and saw them smile and laugh with ease, I realized what a miraculous gift Carter and Dad had given us this Christmas.

It has been unbelievable what Carter had done over the last few months, and on every special occasion, I had received a gift from him to help me get through that day. He seemed to be reinforcing over and over again that he was still with me: the photograph for Thanksgiving, the phone call on my birthday, and now Christmas. This year I was also happy to once again be able to buy a Christmas present for Carter. It was a new journal for our daily talks together and the fact that I could once again include him in my gift giving had helped me enormously at this most difficult time of year. His thank you message when we wrote two days later was perfect.

December 27, 2010:

> C: Love you Mom ... Thanks for the gift, we have both been able to give wonderful gifts to each other. See Mom, I can still be part of your life always but with our greater purpose. Thank you, big hug for my gift it's great.

My Christmas had been so much more enjoyable and happy. Having Victoria's two friends from Australia helped us all; we wanted to share our Christmas traditions with them, and this gave us reason to push past painful hurdles. Time had also helped, as this was the third Christmas since Carter's accident. All of this helped, but I know the magic ingredient was Carter. I had him back in my life and it changed everything; I could breathe again. When my heart ached for him, he consoled me. He had reached out and given life back to me within the palm of my hand. I could hear his voice and his thoughts. I had him in my life once again and my heart sang.

December 28, 2010:

After Christmas, we went to the cottage for several days to enjoy the snow. I had been enjoying a strong connection with Carter once again, so I wasn't as stressed, which allowed me to think about what I'd like to talk about with Carter. That morning I remembered to ask a question I had been meaning to ask for quite a while. I asked it with only the vaguest hope of an answer wondering if he even knew of this event. Over the past two years, I had occasionally wondered how that toy cow got on the toy store order back in August 2008. At the time, we couldn't understand, though Olivia said she knew. She was certain that it was from Carter, meaning he had ordered it for her. Today, two and a half years later, our question was answered. Olivia was right, but the order hadn't been placed by phone or in person; the order had been placed in an unexpected way. I was getting accustomed to unusual answers, but this one caught me by surprise.

CH: Good morning Carter, I love you.

C: Love you Mom.

CH: Carter, did you have anything to do with the toy cow on the invoice with the bunny hutch for Olivia?

C: Yes knew it would startle you Mom, begin to get your mind thinking. Put the seeds of thought in your mind. It was for both of you really, a gift for Olivia, a gift of thought for you. Olivia knew why the cow, I reminded her of our conversation, that WAS why the cow ha, ha LOL.

CH: How did you do it, Carter?

C: Just learning to put thoughts in a person's mind. Bunny hutch was on the order not the cow. As they were writing hutch I put thoughts of that cow, I could see it was there in the store order, knew it would be perfect for Olivia. So, as they wrote bunny hutch I just put that cow vision in their mind and held it there and then without realizing it they added it to the order. That's why when you questioned the cow being held and said that it wasn't ordered the girl picked up the paper and said it was ordered it was on the paper where they were both held. You knew it wasn't ordered, got your mind thinking, didn't it.

CH: Yes, absolutely! You're right; it started to put what I thought were "crazy" thoughts in my head: "Could it be Carter?"

C: I know a long journey to where we are now. So glad you did write it all down. You need to read that again, see the journey unfold. You'll have more questions for me I know, so many attempts, you missed some too and that's okay. See, inside your spirit knew it was me, the person needed to learn. I love you all xxx. Tell Olivia I'm ready to watch the TV show with her.

December 30, 2010:

Over the last two years, I had pushed myself forward relentlessly to keep searching and progressing. My success had far exceeded my hopes, but as I became increasingly confident in the knowledge that Carter was happy, thriving, and he shared our lives with us, still I was losing the urgency to constantly focus on this effort. I was regaining a sense of control and ease within my days and although this was wonderful, I didn't want to drift back to my old ways. I had worked much too hard and now saw life with more meaning and compassion. If I was to become complacent, would I fade back to how I lived before— busy and oblivious to so many of life's experiences? My life had changed in many ways, and I was surprised to admit I felt some of the pain and struggle had made me grow into a person of more substance. I spoke with Carter about my concerns.

C: Love you Mom.

CH: I feel I am losing some of my focus and not making progress. In fact, I'm not connecting or sensing things as well as I was. I'm losing some of the ground I have gained.

C: You must work every day on your own with your mind's development and spend time with us writing. You MUST do this to improve and move forward. It's not bad you feel this way. Acknowledge it yes and make sure you do work hard. Our path, make it happen. Love you xx.

P.S. Expand your knowledge, remember Grandpa is helping guide you, let his thoughts be yours and grow with us.

January 3, 2011:

A new year began with Carter saying, "Look how far you have come." What a great message. After this writing, I glanced back through the journals of events and Carter's writings, spellbound, to see all that had happened in twelve short months. As I read through the pages, the year rewound and I realized how many truly meaningful moments had enriched my life.

C: Love you Mom.

Try hard this year to make this your priority. You didn't practice yesterday, don't let other things come before this, remember. Again great connection at the cottage, but we must keep moving forward. Focus on us and our task. Look how far you have come since we first began to write together, it's a miracle and you're learning so much. Imagine what another year could bring, but you must work hard and steady, as must I, an effort for both of us. Do not let those who are burdened and angry stop you, be filled with joy, this is a joyous task, a great help! Those who cannot or will not hear don't need to hear, or can hear and will choose to take whatever information they choose. We give you this information to help all. Only those ready or open to hear will really benefit from it. Be positive in your thoughts and days; do not be weighed down by others' problems. Keep your mind open and free xxx Carter.

January 12, 2011:

Today as I prepared to write I was struggling with doubts for no apparent reason. *This writing from Carter can't really be happening, can it?* I needed to prove once again that I was not writing these words, so for the first part of this message I made Carter create every movement of the pen with no cooperation from me. Carter was frustrated by my lack of confidence. He and I had worked hard to get past this, and I felt that he was scolding me in the message.

C: Love you Mom.

I will begin to talk, listen to me Mom, your mind knows this is real, now stop letting your mind doubt it, question it. Why do you need to test our writing? Your spirit knows when it is us and not your thoughts. Accept what you know and feel to be true, trust yourself if you think it is us, it is. You have this knowledge and ability within you. Believe in yourself, this is a leap of faith always, you can't keep doubting it and this is real. Each time you wonder is it us or your thoughts, you already know, trust yourself and let this grow don't hold yourself back, be excited, challenge yourself, great potential if you allow it to happen. You're doing great keeping your mind clear, calm, open, and our thoughts are flowing into you daily. This is your biggest improvement now. You think things are slowing down but they are not. It is your state of mind, your daily work on your thoughts, your perspective, your focus on us and what is truth. You are moving forward greatly from what we see but in your view, you are just becoming calmer, more accepting, happier, this is a huge step forward Mom. We know you are making this happen and we are helping you, one enables the other to happen. I know we will do this, one step at a time, great job, fantastic.

Well, I knew for certain that I hadn't written that. Carter had spoken in a tone similar to a parent scolding their child, and he had made his point clear. I felt almost apologetic for making him write. He was frustrated with me, but I liked his thoughts about my progress and once he pointed it out I could see it. I cast my doubts aside yet again and asked him a question, ready to learn.

CH: Of all the things you are doing now, what is the thing you enjoy the most?

C: Love to teach the kids what they can do, you should see them sometimes when they first get here and I work with them and show them some things that they can do now that they couldn't do there. They get all excited, as do I showing them, so much fun, seeing their reaction when I do things and then they try. I love being around this incredible experience. So happy, joyful, exciting, makes me feel so good. Some won't be happy no matter what, so I just keep trying, most come around. I enjoy that like I did there, a great job for me here right now but I am excited for what we will do in future. Love you always and to the rest xxx.

For almost two months I had been trying to learn to write with Carter with my eyes open, and today I finally felt I had succeeded. There were many roadblocks, my confidence in myself definitely being one. Any time vision distracted me I closed my eyes. If I had trouble with clarity or focus, I closed my eyes. It was by continually attempting it that I built up the mental focus to get better. As I made each attempt, I felt no pressure to succeed, because it wasn't necessary, it was just convenient for me. I had made a note for myself at the end of the day's writing to mark my achievement: January 12, "Today's writing is written with my eyes open after the eighth line. I'm happy with this achievement."

The Power of Love

Love you Mom. Let rise the spirit, for it is within spirit that true and meaningful growth is found, struggled toward and achieved. Find joy in each day there and even through struggles and upsets—SMILE. For that struggle, pain, incomprehensible loss or burden is part of any life's purpose and journey. Feel the pain, express it and work through it. But in the midst of the greatest pains, struggles and burdens of that life raise your head. Lift your eyes to the vision—THE EARTH, THE SKY, THE HEAVENS AND BEYOND—and see what you are part of. What you have come from, what you have come into (form). And within the complexity, beauty and struggles, we are a minute, though intricate, part of creation. All hurtling through "time," through "space," though absorbed more usually in the SELF not the WHOLE. All efforts and events BEGIN AND END!! See the effort, the challenge, the GOAL—smile—make the effort. Be AWARE—smile—work through the struggle—smile—be aware—all is DIVINE all is from the DIVINE and toward absolute LOVE AND DIVINITY. The light of God shines on us all and can shine forth from within each and every one of us. Smile and find joy within each effort. All is ultimately toward purpose and hoped-for growth. All of us here love all of you there—my family—our bond holds strong. Spirit steps from form but the fibre of love holds fast and eternal. XXX from us all today. (Carter, writing received Good Friday, March 29, 2013.)

My attention was often now given toward trying to understand consciousness and grasping the power of love. I found time to spend in absolute silence as I tried to understand what I was being told. I struggled a great deal with how and where Carter existed. He says he could still be with us; he knew what was happening in our lives. He communicated his thoughts with me, but his intelligence and perspective was beyond anything he learned here. He seemed to be fully aware, thinking and growing in his wisdom yet where was he? How did he have this presence of mind yet he had no presence? Where were his thoughts coming from? I kept returning to his writings in search of answers. Dad's instruction to me, "allow your spirit to rise to your consciousness, it connects to us," played over and over in my mind. Consciousness seemed to be a key word; it often came up in their writings. If he existed as pure consciousness, and if I had a spirit within me that could connect to my consciousness, did part of me also exist somehow separate but linked to a greater consciousness where Dad and Carter were? Did they exist individually but integrated into a universal consciousness, and somehow did I now link with this field of pure consciousness through my will and focus? I thought my head would explode as I tried to comprehend this.

In January, I had an unexpected chance to spend four days alone at the cottage. I was excited about the opportunity, and it was my intention to use this time with a single-minded focus toward my work with spirit. I would be completely free of distractions, and I hoped to allow my commitment for this work to be aided by this amazing place immersed within nature. My unbending intention to find Carter had brought results. I had to learn to focus my attention on keeping this passion for the work. I hoped to learn to let my spirit take a stronger lead as I went through my days and learn to interact with the realm of spirit within a higher calibre of focus. I intended to work on keeping my attention on the moment while I used this focus to link more easily with that greater consciousness where Carter existed and apparently was our natural home. I was happy with my progress.

During these four days, Roy dropped in to say hi. When I shared what I was hoping to do with my time here, he mentioned that he thought his girlfriend's daughter (she was in her late teens) had "seen" Carter when they were here checking the cottage for us. This was unexpected and exciting news. I needed to meet her, so I asked if he would ask her mom if I could talk to her.

January 15, 2011:

The next day only her mother came to see me. Her daughter Lauren had been having unsettling and frightening experiences with what they understood to be spirit and she was nervous for her. I was startled as she described some of her experiences with spirit.

In my struggle to find Carter I had headed blindly into an unknown world. I really didn't stop to consider any of these types of possibilities. Truthfully, that wouldn't have stopped me as I would have gone into a burning building to find my child, but in hindsight, I probably should have learned more about spirit before entering this realm. In fairness to myself though, I hadn't been convinced spirit even existed and it was that proof I was trying to find. I would now advise anyone to be cautious, informed, and know how to protect themselves. Unforeseen things can happen quickly as you will see, so you need to be prepared.

I read the mom several of Carter's and Dad's writings to show her that I only heard messages of love and happiness from them.

She cried, "It's amazing that you chose those writings, because I needed to hear those thoughts today."

She thought it would be good for her daughter to talk to me, so we arranged to meet the next day. My hope was that if she could see Carter in the room at the same time that I heard and wrote with him, that would be an additional layer of proof for me of his writing. This was my big plan for our meeting and I was really excited for tomorrow to come. Boy was I wrong!

January 16, 2011:

When Lauren arrived, she told me the first time she was in our cottage she had felt that a very happy spirit was there and it filled the cottage with a wonderful feeling, but she said she hadn't seen him. What a disappointment for me, she talked about some of her unpleasant experiences with spirit, and I said I had only experienced good things with Carter, so I couldn't imagine what that would be like. I asked if she'd like to talk to Carter since it was hard for me to find people to practice with, and she was happy to try. This talk quickly changed from a casual chat to one of immediate purpose.

C: Love you Mom. Hi Lauren, nice to meet you. Can you sense me?

L: Yes.

C: What do you feel?

L: It's a little overwhelming but it's a very joyous feeling. [She was shaking.] Where are you? Are you in the living room? [I see her looking around the room for him.]

C: I am with Mom, I am within her essence, we write as one. You should be able to feel my presence within the room. My energy is emitting from Mom. I'm sending it strong so I know you feel me through Mom. Can you feel it?

L: Yes.

C: What does it feel like?

L: It's kind of overwhelming. Umm ... yeah it's kinda like there are light rays around her.

This discussion between Carter and Lauren became startling, to say the least. He began writing with such speed that it was illegible, so I put down the pen and Lauren began recording as I spoke his words to her. We both had the same impression of the meaning of the words and we both understood that at certain points the words were being said with urgency and were addressing what was happening at that very moment.

C: Bring your total awareness to the task you are trying to do, focus, don't be distracted. Absolute awareness on your task, you will gain more ability to sense.

I feel my left hand being moved and tell Lauren he's moving my hand.

"Do you want me to write, Carter?" I pull the paper that I was initially writing on back in front of me. My hand surges forward as he writes, "There Mom you need to keep this."

Once again I drop the pen. I can't do this. I hear him, but this writing is just an unreadable scrawl. "Carter, I can't transcribe this later." I'm unnerved and upset; I can't keep up with him. He says he wants me to write, yet his energy is so strong. He is taking more control of my hand than usual now and pushing it forward. I feel this enhanced energy is strengthening his message, but he seems more focused on whatever he is talking about then allowing this message to flow normally. I don't understand why this feels so different, but I'm aware something is very different than usual. Carter tells Lauren to focus on good energy.

I feel the seriousness and urgency in his voice and I react out loud: "Oh this is not good right now." I hesitate before I continue. I was hearing what he said, but I didn't like what I heard. I remember all the love and help Carter had given me and I dig deep for the faith and courage to trust him, then I repeat exactly what he said. I felt I had to stay detached for Lauren and Carter, so I found the willpower to keep focused on my part of the task somehow."

C: Don't let any negative energy come within your space. Concentrate on letting only good energy in; work on this, bring your awareness to it and learn how to do it. You can block the negative energy and good energy will flow. You must protect yourself. There are bad things out there, unexplainable. If you leave yourself open to these it can control you, we mustn't let this happen.

CH: Oh shit Carter.

I release my feelings here but only for a moment, then I go back to his words. *Concentrate, Charmaine.*

C: You need to learn how to handle this or it can be dangerous to you. You needed to come and hear this today, that's why this is happening [this conversation]. You could be in danger if you don't do this. Listen to me now, you need to learn, FOCUS [Lauren said later just before he said focus she had been distracted]. There are ways you need to do this because this is very important because you are too open. It must be controlled or you are in danger. Can you do this Lauren? I'm not trying to scare you. That's why you were brought here today so you can hear this. You must focus on this task. You can follow this path, it is your choice or not, you must protect yourself but you have this ability [to connect with spirit]. And they're not after you, but the ability to enter your space. You're vulnerable; they're not specifically there for you. They go after vulnerable people and latch on and attach their energy and affect your mind badly. Protect yourself from them at all times. There are many good energies out there. Like on earth, the fight between good and evil goes on in both realms. Do not be scared though, just like in life, don't focus on these things. Try to be happy and joyous and once you learn to control this and protect yourself you will not have this problem.

CH: This is me, not Carter asking you this question, Lauren. Do you get any other sense right now?

L: There's a bad wave of feeling kind of coming up my back. It's not good. It's like they're trying to come up my back, come around my back.

C: Can you feel it on your spine?

L: Yes.

C: Up your spine?

L: Yes.

C: Tingling? Pressure?

L: Feels like burning

CH: Carter says this can be energy you feel.

L: I think it's my main energy point so they can get to me.

C: They will tap your energy, drain you. You will not be happy; they take all the joy out of your life. They feed off your energy. [Lauren told me after that this is exactly how she had been feeling since her problems began.]

CH: Lauren, do you have anything else you would like to ask?

L: I don't think so.

CH: Carter, do you have anything else to say to Lauren?

During the whole time they were discussing the feelings around her back, I felt my upper body vibrating. Lauren told me later that she hadn't seen me vibrating but she saw an incredible light radiating out from me. (We knew when this was, because we both remember what was being said at the time.)

Lauren said, "The light was so bright that I couldn't see the wall or the pictures on the wall behind you." Although she had been frightened, she said kept looking at the light. She knew the light was keeping her safe and protecting her by stopping whatever she was feeling behind her from coming up any farther. She felt safe because of Carter and this light.

C: She is not to worry the task is doable, don't be overwhelmed or frightened. Be confident, happy and joyous. Don't worry, if you're happy and joyous it also helps give you strength. They won't come around somebody joyous.

As the message ended, we both gasped, inundated by our emotions. Lauren always understood clearly what Carter was saying because it was dealing with what she was experiencing at that very moment, but I had no idea what was happening. We went over the messages in great detail together, and when she added her experience to his words they fit together perfectly. We spent time discussing it then tried to de-stress. Lauren and I arranged to meet with her mom the next day so we could share this with her. I would be there to help reassure her mom and voice it from Carter's side and I could also check for myself on how Lauren was doing.

Lauren's mom was relieved to be getting help, and we were all amazed to hear this meeting was apparently arranged to help Lauren. We couldn't argue that the timing and randomness of how it came to happen was odd, but it had served a valuable purpose on a subject they hadn't shared with others.

Over the next several days, both Carter and Dad tried to explain to me what Carter had been trying to guide her through what she was experiencing that day. Carter also gave me important information to pass on to Lauren. When Carter wrote the next day, he gave me information about our meeting with her that really unsettled me, and I began to realize the full scope of what had happened and what Carter apparently did.

January 17, 2011:
7:00 a.m.

CH: Carter, can you explain what was going on yesterday when you spoke to Lauren?

C: Love you Mom.

I know you were getting uneasy, but you kept focused on allowing me to speak. Your concentration and courage were amazing. I can't believe how well you did this. See, I'm telling you we can be great together, you and I, we work so well for each other, you did this for your love of me, to allow me my task. You wouldn't let me down and I won't let you down. Our strength together as we just begin was witnessed yesterday. I am so proud of you and you didn't pull back, or say you weren't doing this. There were no thoughts from you in your mind, just extreme focus.

CH: Thank you, Carter xx. Although the words came much too fast at first, after a few attempts the words were flowing easily and I didn't want to lose the connection to you. What was happening? Can you tell me?

C: Lauren though a nice girl, is surrounded by evil, bad spirits. Not all from human spirits, just a badness that is latching onto her. She is vulnerable; her mind has some abilities for this connection to us. With this ability and her vulnerability these bad spirits, not always spirits but hard to put in other words, seek out people they can access. I could see them, the ones that were around her yesterday. She needs to build strength and also will and determination. They will use any opportunity to use her energies, her life, for their benefit. Her ability to see and sense them makes it worse, they like this. I hope she listens to me; make sure she is protecting herself, Mom.

CH: Lauren saw a bright radiant light coming out from me, all around me and obscuring everything behind me in its strength and brilliance, can you tell me about this?

C: Yes. It is a combination of the light you are calling around you and my essence within your mind as we do this work. When she saw the strongest light I was working very hard to make absolutely sure I had a very strong connection with you. I focused with great will. The presence of bad around her needed to be frightened and stopped at that moment. My light, my presence was a deterrent. It was good versus evil, the classic battle Mom like a video game, but real. I drew all my power like adding the extra weapons, cheats, to blow them away. Wow, hey, but this is unfortunately real so not much fun. It worked though, I held it back. The power of goodness, God's force can always hold back bad. But the trick is to not let bad touch you or be attracted to you here or there. I drew on God's strength and my presence was felt, it worked. I really wasn't expecting to be starting with such a bang but I am really pumped now by what we can do. I'm ready to do more, what do you think Mom?

CH: Well, I hope there are no more experiences like this. [Unlike him I'm definitely not pumped, and in fact I am more unnerved than before.] I hope we have only happier connections from now on.

C: Of course but this was important Mom. You must see this and be strengthened by this to see how important your task is xxx Carter 🐝

I felt so much pride and love for him at that moment, but this was beyond my ability to understand. A short time later, while I was on my way to work, my mind began spinning out of control because of what he had just written. How could this be going on and I didn't know? It couldn't be good for me to be involved with this and not have a clue about what's happening. I began hearing Carter talk to me as he explained further. I tried unsuccessfully to stop him. *Don't talk to me now, tell me all this later. It's important and I want you to write it so I can remember it.* This was one of the few times that Carter had talked to me when we were not writing, and he continued throughout the morning. I could only hope that he would tell me all this again later when I had a pen and paper. It wasn't until late that evening when I found time to write with him.

January 17, 2011:
10:00 p.m.

CH: Carter, this morning you kept talking to me and it was important. Can you tell me again please?

I must trust that he will do this to help me, and he does.

C: Love you Mom.

Okay I will try to repeat it. You are never to be scared or frightened when you and I work together, you were getting upset this morning after I gave you some information of what happened. Then you started thinking about it and of course you are a bit shaken, so that's why I just kept talking to you. You must absolutely know I would never let you be harmed or at risk. I have asked you to do this, I will protect you. Here bad cannot win over true good; goodness and love are more powerful. If this is ever asked of us again, stay steady in your task and stay calm. You should have no sense or awareness of the struggle, I shield you from it. You are the messenger for me and you would be able to sit still and speak no matter what was happening around you and you will have no sense of this energy from both sides. I stop it from getting close to you. Pure goodness or God's love, the purest form of love and good can repel the strongest evil. If I need to I can call for this help. I can be pure goodness and I can be God's love, it is within my knowledge and ability. This is not who I am, but I am able to call on this to whatever extent is needed. The stronger the evil the more of God's strength is needed to be called for. As you can feel me arrive, I could feel it arrive in me and give me strength. I knew I could do what needed to be done. It doesn't frighten me as I know the power of love, but we mustn't be silly or inattentive. Evil or badness will not stay around joy; it is very uncomfortable and cannot exist. See me as a shield that will stand in front of you. My light radiates and repels, my light is coming from within you and nothing would dare approach you. Grandpa too will throw in his skills; he won't just sit back and is always there to help us. Remember Mom, never doubt love's power. Okay—feel a little better now?

Honestly, my answer had to be yes and NO! I went over and over this writing during the following weeks, trying to grasp the magnitude and scale of topics within what he spoke about in such a matter-of-fact fashion. Each time I reread this, I found more to question. I was astounded by how he spoke about love, of calling on and being able to use love's power. This information I now hold as a keystone in my beliefs, and there was one part that did help me feel better as he said it. When he spoke of shielding me and never letting me be harmed or at risk, it brought me immediate relief and I trusted this because of the immense love I had for him. I was able to release my worries and move forward with complete trust that my father and son would help protect me.

At the beginning of this section I advised everyone to learn how to protect themselves, and now you can see how quickly things shifted. I had the benefit of unknown protection, which served me well, but as Carter said, "we mustn't be silly or inattentive." This experience has taught me a valuable lesson, one I won't forget.

January 18, 2011:

CH: Carter, I find all this unbelievable. How much are you capable of?

C: Love you Mom.

The truth is I don't know all I am capable of. I continue to grow in knowledge. My path with you allows me more growth also it is for good and done with love, therefore, I grow in spirit. Your spirit will also grow from the task. You will see and know when you return here. You will be happy, I know we both will.

CH: Do you know what Grandpa was doing when you were talking to Lauren? Was he with me?

C: Of course he was, I was busy and focused on what I was trying to do but know he was right there. He was helping I am sure. Ask him.

CH: Dad, can you tell me what you were doing?

DAD: Hi, Charm, yes I was watching if Carter needed help, but my focus was completely on you, helping you. You were doing amazing though. You're listening to us and your mind is in a good place, but I also helped you hold your focus. My presence there was helping Carter strengthen the force of good, light, but I didn't have to do any more than that for him. He was in control of what was happening, what needed to be done. I watched him with joy. I love him and he loves me. A tribute to his spirit, [the way Carter handled the situation] calm and controlled, he is not often like that here; the joy exudes from him usually. I did help but stayed in the background, he was in control. I've never seen anything like it, not something I think I'd see here or there. I've seen bad things in the war but this was totally different, the feeling was different. Soldiers never felt evil in pure evil. This, you could feel badness, not just bad judgment but real evil in our presence, not what I like to be around, but amazing to see the struggle in spirit. All is possible, think positive; obviously, there are more reasons than what I have been telling you, proud of you both xx Dad.

January 19, 2011:

CH: Carter, I have learned a lot from this event.

C: Love you Mom.

Yes it is all amazing. You have got your focus back haven't you Mom, yes! I know you have been learning so much, lots of reasons for us to teach you more information, a busy last month.

CH: Yes, good and bad, but certainly unbelievable. Every time something big happens I think, *well that has got to be it, Carter could never top this*, like your photo at Thanksgiving. Then you do something like the gingerbread house! You and Dad are truly amazing.

C: Thanks. Some of it is quite fun, we think oh this would be great to do and if we can make it happen we are sometimes amazed too how well it turns out. We often don't know if it will work out or not and some of these tasks we are trying for the first time, so lots of fun, an idea you are excited about. Even better when it can be made to happen. We're both learning so much, many new things; its great keeps us thinking.

CH: I'm trying to figure out how advanced you two are. You are doing so many things for us. Is there an order for advancing? Can you give me some insight into this?

C: Yes, I have a bit more growth then Grandpa but I think we may both be pretty close in abilities. It isn't like there are exact levels like you pass a test or certain task and you are at the next level. It is a very gradual thing and little by little you advance, gain more and brighter light, clear white light but very little at a time. A bit more if you accomplish some huge task, but huge by the standards here, you in form may not see them as big tasks and we just become brighter, stronger, more knowledge and ability within us. We aren't ever looking at ourselves really to see it, see if "oh I did this, what has happened to me." We don't think that. We, all of us are just trying bit by bit to advance. Some aren't making much progress or some not really trying at all for long periods of time but they still know their purpose, their aim is to grow in goodness. Grandpa and I are moving forward and advancing right now. Grandpa is not moving as quickly as I am right now, maybe because I am able to do many tasks and move between one and the other. I have this freedom to do many tasks if I want, and I do. Grandpa has chosen to stay with you now, so that is his real task, his only real job at the moment. He knows his accomplishments won't be as many right now but it doesn't matter. This is what he has chosen to do; it is always our decision completely. He is so happy and content to do this, to spend the rest of your time there with you and I am happy too, without his helping you our work would be much less accomplished. He and I worked this out together we are both so happy with our work and he and I won't be apart, we are united in love, growth won't separate us.

I may help him out more another time then he will grow more than me. There is no rush; it just works out all in time, what's the hurry. I am having fun and so is he.

Finding A Path

Love you Mom. All paths lead home.- You will find your of service on any path. Many paths open and you will see these before you. It will be interesting for you as they divert your trip into unforeseen areas but all paths help your trip. You may get off the main highway at times and take a side trip but getting off the main highway can show you surprising vistas and serve you and others while witnessing the beauty of getting off the main road. We would like you to work on and complete the book. This book can be used as a road map for others. You are acting as a cartographer, mapping your route. Take options that feel right for your heart. You can be helpful in many ways, be open to opportunities. Get on and off the main path for secondary sights and roads but always come back to the main highway. –For you it's the main route to take you home – but ALL routes lead home. Just as the blood is sent out from the heart and returns back again. (Carter, writing received June 3, 2019.)

I had created a new chapter and decided it would be easier to ask Carter to write after giving him the chapter title instead of looking for a suitable writing I already had. I had done this several times lately. This was how easy it was.

CH: Carter, I need a new writing for a new chapter, in our book, titled finding a path.

C: Of course, I'm glad to help

The writing was effortless and suited the title. He ended his writing with –"How's that Mom?" I replied "Thank you, it's perfect and I was shown great visuals too."

In February, Carter asked me to start learning to see auras and instructed me how to begin. I sat on my bed, stared into the mirror, and with focused thought, I repeated the words he told me. Within a couple of minutes, I could see something come in and out of my view but I didn't know what an aura looked like. Carter and I were both very encouraged that I had some success in my first attempt and he said I was to continue to practice this. Unfortunately, this was one of several things they asked me to work on that I rarely found time to do.

February 11, 2011:

C: Love you Mom.

Yes let's begin. I am happy with my life now and my connection to you, our path, purpose together. It is thought life is over when you're dead but that's definitely wrong. We are more alive than anyone can imagine. This, where I am now, is our natural state, where we should be. Your life there is a journey from here. One for purpose, growth of spirit, hopefully and to experience pleasure in form, not just thought but a physical experience of things. We go there with such enthusiasm but it is so often lost as we grow up and cope with life experiences on earth. Our aim for life, our hopes, chances, opportunities to make a difference, that great thrust to achieve good when we leave here is so often diminished by the sheer task of living, but hopefully we achieve some growth and achievement while there. There is usually some. It is easier to achieve growth in form because here we always know the aim is to improve in goodness and love. When we're there this aim, though known within us, is not always so obvious, it's not the focus. The focus of our life there is often success, money, stature, position, power. To let the focus of love fight for top priority over these other naturally occurring priorities is hard. When it happens in life, life is an incredible joy and much growth, but many distractions there.

CH: You always seemed focused on happiness, joy, and love while you were here.

C: Yes, I'm very happy with my life, I was surrounded by love, happiness and good times. So much love surrounded me, I was safe, happy and full of joy and my love and joy flowed and reached out naturally to many. Those I loved and people who just entered my life. I found everything worth enjoying. I lived each moment well. I have given many people the opportunity to witness pure joy in living, letting love flow freely. I hope they remember and want to have that in their life, if they do they will touch many other lives. I am so happy with my life effort. Your love always surrounded me Mom and still does. We give each other great purpose and of course great love. But love, great love was shared by me and with me by many, true pure love. Our spirits were touched and blessed, I send my love to them all and Grandpa's love is also very powerful xox.

My Third Dream Visit

February 19, 2011:

C: Love you Mom.

CH: Carter, last night I dreamt that you, I, and Victoria were in a large auditorium running from a cult-like group. We were running through doorways, halls, and stairs. At first I couldn't see you, but I knew you were there and then as we were running down a hall I saw your arm reach around a corner to get Victoria and me. You then raced with us as you lead us through the maze of hallways until you opened a final door where we saw daylight. We were all sweating and breathless, but we all looked at each other with big smiles, knowing we were safe and free. Weird dream, do you know if it has any meaning?

C: Yes it's a message of course. That with this gift you must know in your own mind what is right. There are many who will want to lead you, many with selfish ideas. You must follow your path; follow me through the unknown, the dark into other areas, the doors. When Victoria hurt her foot you helped her, slowed down but kept following me. Yes at first you were in the lead I was behind you, then in the dark, I rushed past you on the stairs, through the doors and you raced with me with speed. At first you were in the dark trying to find your way, you were leading, your thoughts. Then you'd found me, you "saw" me, I then passed you and took the lead. Now you are to follow me, I am leading you, it's symbolic. Really it's more than just me, Grandpa too and the knowledge of life in spirit. At the end all three of us were outside safe in the light. I was who I've always been, I look healthy, happy, because my spirit is. You were relieved, nervous of the journey that was unsettling but happy to be outside in the light Mom. You brought Victoria; we will keep her with us always too. You knew when you started to run away from this situation Grandma and Grandpa were coming and you wanted to wait but knew you couldn't, that means they will be with you, us, but not down this path for Grandma, it is your path. It symbolizes follow me, I will guide you through the uncertainty to light, knowledge, happiness and together we will be happy. Thanks for letting me explain XX.

Cleansing a Room

February 26, 2011:

Lauren had spoken to me about how there were areas of her bedroom that frightened and unsettled her. I wondered if I sat in her room and focused on bringing in the light of the divine if that might help. Even if this was nonsense I felt it couldn't hurt, as I would just be focusing on love and goodness, and she agreed it was worth a try.

I had asked Carter for guidance and just as he had told me to do, I sat in the room with her. I felt her bedroom, looked at it, and asked her what and where were the areas that bothered her. Then as I had been told to do, I sat on a chair in the middle of the room and faced the corner that bothered her the most. I closed my eyes, asked for protection, and visually drew the light down onto myself. The house was quiet but I was aware of noises, of where I was, and her bunny moving in his cage. I don't think I was ever in a deep meditation, though my visualizations and images were crystal clear. I created some of the visual images but not many. I will now try to describe the visions I had through the cleansing.

1. I saw the room become enclosed in a glass box; a layer of rocks appeared and covered the floor of the box. Next, a layer of crystal clear water flooded over the rocks, followed by another layer of rocks then water, this continued layer after layer until the glass box filled to the top (the ceiling of the room). Then all of the water drained out in a whirlpool through the bottom of the glass. Once the water was gone the rocks also drained away.

2. I now saw the glass box and space within it, which was the bedroom, as gleaming and clean.

3. The inside of the glass box became a very bright sunny meadow with tall grasses, butterflies, and birds. I saw myself standing in the middle of this meadow with Carter on the far left side and Dad on the far right. I watched Carter reach in front of me as he pulled a coloured ribbon from my chest. He then flicked it up and down and the ribbon arched over to Dad, who caught it and placed his end down onto the ground. I watched as they continued to do this, each time Carter pulled out a different coloured ribbon from me and threw it to Dad in an arch and they continued until they had built a rainbow. I sensed a

very happy feeling here with the rainbow reaching from one side of the meadow to the other.

4. The meadow and glass walls disappeared and I began "looking" with my mind's eye at the corner wall by the closet that Lauren said was the worst area. Carter and Dad appeared as radiant orbs. I knew, but don't know why I knew, that Carter was the orb on the left and Dad was the orb on the right. I seemed to understand that they were both looking at the corner, trying to figure out what to do. Carter began to paint both sides of the corner white from top to bottom, then when he was finished he stood back and they both looked at it. Dad did the same but with pink paint. They each did this several times, then I understood them to think, "There, that's good now," as they stood back one last time and looked at the corner before they disappeared.

5. I "saw" very large words begin to appear on the wood panel walls of the room. A single word would span from wall to wall and once it was spelled out, the colour from the letters would drip down the wall. The words HAPPINESS, LAUGHTER, LOVE, JOY, etc. appeared all over the walls and ceiling of the room until it looked like graffiti, then the words disappeared.

6. A long white and pink ribbon with the word LOVE written over and over on it began to wrap itself around the room until the walls, ceiling, and floor were completely covered. I understood that this ribbon was enclosing the room in a soft, gentle love.

7. The two radiating orbs reappeared, and once again I understood them to be Carter on my left and Dad on my right. This time they both reached into my chest, pulling out a radiating orb that I understood to be my spirit. We as three orbs stood together holding "hands" that were radiating points of light and formed a heart shape with me on the bottom.

We then zoomed all over the room, bouncing off every corner, the ceiling, and walls, illuminating every area of the bedroom. Then the orbs disappeared.

8. I sensed that this exercise was ending, so I turned my awareness toward drawing as much light into me as I could and then I sent it out into the room as bright, strong, and intense light. The effort of "cleansing" the room then ended as quickly as it began; my effort and visuals had stopped. Lauren said at the end when I was drawing the light, my body was pulsing in the chair, but I had had no awareness of this. I felt that I wasn't as prepared as I would have liked to be, but I was amazed at the beauty and ease of the visuals that I experienced.

Lauren felt much more at ease and comfortable in her bedroom afterwards, it wasn't one hundred percent better, but it was remarkably improved. I thought the readers would like to know how Lauren was doing now, these are her own words.

"I love life; I seem to have gone from one extreme to the other since then. Having someone come through from the other side to show me the vulnerability I'd left for myself helped. I took the protection bubble concept Carter later gave me and built it out of steel. Charmaine and Carter have helped me while staying true to the values that made me vulnerable in the first place."

March 3, 2011:

Our town's Minor Hockey Association called to tell us they would be presenting the Carter Roud Most Sportsmanlike Player Atom Division award for the first time. I was disappointed that I couldn't be there because Olivia was competing in a figure skating competition at the very same time, but I was happy to hear John say he would present the award. John asked if I had any suggestions on what he might say. I told him I would write down some ideas, but every time I tried my words scattered into fragments of emotional and disjointed thoughts.

In frustration I told Olivia that I didn't know where to begin, and she replied without hesitation, "you know Mom, you can just ask Carter." That natural trust and innocence from my daughter blew me away. The answer had been staring me in the face and I hadn't seen it.

"I never thought of that, what a great idea."

Relieved to take the pressure off myself I asked him the question, "Carter, is there anything you'd like to say when your award is presented?" This was his answer:

Carter's Speech for AMH Most Sportsmanlike Player Award

Thank the Minor Hockey Association for the honour of remembering me with a trophy. Thanks to all the coaches and volunteers who enabled us to play and have fun. I loved to play, and liked to win. I really wanted to win, but more than that I wanted to play. To get on the ice, feel the speed, the strength of my legs, the sound of the skates hitting the ice. The challenge, win or lose, to face our opponents with my friends as a team with purpose, but the added joy was to share the moment and the challenge with friends. It is the time spent together, growing, learning, and having fun. The Most Valuable Player I think must want to win, but more important, the Most Valuable Player gives his heart to the team, his friends, and his coaches. They aren't interested in glory, but the experience to join with others, win or lose, with a good attitude, and leave each season thinking, "that was fun." Please thank Mr. Hulsman, even with his loudness and gruff ways, it was always fun when he was around; he's a great guy. I know he wanted to do this trophy for me. To play with joy is the real prize all players can take away from the games and the season.

As his words flowed without pause onto the page, I was amazed by the quality of the composition and sentiment. I gave it to Olivia to read.

"Wow Carter, if you could have written like that in school, you would have gotten really good marks," she said as she looked up and smiled.

March 6, 2011:

Carter's friend Richard joined John at the awards, and that meant so much to him. I'm sure Carter was pleased to see him supporting his dad on a difficult day. Meanwhile at the competition, while Olivia was warming up off ice with her coaches, I had been sitting in the stands when I sensed energy in my left hand and I knew was Carter telling me he was there with us, and I began sending him thoughts about the day. Within a short time, I began to feel a tingling sense of movement all around me and I sensed an increasing urgency about it. Instinctively I knew this added sense of energy was also Carter, and I felt that he wanted me to tell Olivia that he was there. I left my seat to find her and simply said, "He's here." She smiled and nodded. Her warm-up went well on the ice and she began her solo. I could see that she was relaxed, immersed in the flow of her music and her blades on the ice as she skated flawlessly. She won first place and she told me as we waited for the scores that it helped to know Carter was there and that she had asked him to be there for her. Now I understood why I felt a sense of urgency from him to tell her!

I was thrilled with her skate and her win, and thrilled to know Carter was there and I was happy that he found a way to let her know he was with her. I was confident he was with John also. Carter was such a blessing to us; I immediately sent my thanks to him and the heavens for this gift of love. This had also strengthened my faith in trusting my instincts as he has repeatedly told me to do. Carter wanted her to know he heard her and was answering her request.

To make the weekend even more of an emotional struggle for me, besides my not being able to be in two places at once, the day before was Olivia's birthday. In 2008, Carter had returned from a trip with his friends as he promised to be with Olivia on her birthday. This year he had returned to be with her again and had found a way to let her know. What an amazing birthday gift he had given to her.

When we came home from the competition, both Olivia and Carter were excited about the events of the day and wanted to talk to each other. They had a wonderful conversation that was so helpful for Olivia. Carter was still Carter, how would we have coped if it wasn't for him helping us all? Here is a snippet of their talk:

C: Love you Mom. I want to talk to Olivia.

O: Thank you so much for coming to my competition today.

C: You're welcome Livlou, glad you knew I was there today. You did great, are you happy with your skate?

O: Yes, I'm very happy. I won first place.

C: Yes I know, glad Mom told you I was there; I wanted her to tell you. She did good being intuitive. You looked great on the ice, you know I wouldn't miss these things ever okay Livlou? I'll always be there for the important things or when you call for me, just like I would do it when I was still there. There are no real changes that way okay? Love you and happy birthday and congrats on winning the skating competition.

March 9, 2011:

With all the stresses and emotional struggles over those last few weeks, I'd been having difficulty connecting as I did once again on this day. I was able to feel Carter in my hand, but it took three or four attempts before we managed to write. Once again I worried that maybe was I losing the ability to connect. I then received this lesson from Carter, which made me wonder if my lack of connection lately had been used for this message. I felt that it might have been.

C: Love you Mom XXX.

Patience is something you must also learn to work on for our task, you mustn't be impatient. Sometimes the journey to learn is as important as the task being learned. Take your time, learn to wait calmly, concentrate and let things develop slowly. If they don't work out one time don't force it, try another time. Maybe your mind is not in a good state or can't really concentrate or maybe you need to repeatedly try to learn the skill. Learn the task to be still, calm, patient, and believe truly believe it will happen. While building your trust, your belief in goodness and love and the belief that with faith in what is to be will be. Let your abilities reach to their full potential, a lifelong journey now not with speed and there I've got it. The growth to reach this level, to reach more clearly to us, the belief within your own stillness is in us and you Mom. This patience will then reach into your everyday life there and give you an inner strength to endure struggles, live with joy. To not let meaningless, nothingness issues upset you. You will grow with a peace, calmness, love, and joy, a wonderful thing to behold in form, your lesson for today Mom. I'm hoping to talk to Cayley tonight Mom, I'll try hard from here.

That evening we all enjoyed a wonderful evening with Cayley, then she and I left the dining room to try to talk with Carter. I knew Carter was excited too for the chance, but this was causing a wide range of thoughts and emotions for Cayley, though she was hopeful and didn't doubt what we were attempting.

C: Hi Cay, what's happening?

Cayley: Hi Carter.

Cayley: Will you still be nineteen when I see you again?

C: There is no time here and I'm not nineteen here. I have always been here, what age would that be? I will be as you remember me.

Cayley: How did you send me the text messages?

C: I can alter electronics in gadgets, work within the electrical energy, I can program numbers and messages. We can work with energy, we are energy. I manipulate their energy to my benefit. I did it when you were upset and because that was one of the few ways then people could hear from me. I was trying to help, so much pain and so little I could really do then to help.

Cayley: It did help; I loved it.

C: Yes I know, made me feel good to be able to do something.

Roller Coaster Ride

Love you mom. Life is a roller coaster ride. Roller coasters are in happy places – amuse-ment parks – so let's put life in an amusement park setting. People are there to be happy and enjoy themselves; they share the trip with family and friends. The ride has great highs and frightening lows, but once you're on that coaster you experience the whole ride. Don't close your eyes when you reach the drops and roundabouts. Open your eyes, witness and experience it all - all rides come to an end. So, enjoy each moment, nothing lasts, but to experience life with joy is the best way to ride. Once the ride ends you will feel exhilarated by the experience – good and bad. (Carter, writing received January 30, 2019)

I had told Patricia about my connection with Carter, and she hoped I would help a mother she was counselling who had lost her daughter. I said I would speak with her, but I knew this mother's pain and I didn't want to say anything that would make her feel worse. Prior to the meeting, I asked Carter and Dad to help me find the right things to say to her. Dad wrote that I was ready to do this, and he gave me guidance for the meeting.

March 20, 2011:

The next day I arrived at Patricia's house to meet for the first time with a parent who had also suffered the loss of a child. Anna's daughter died in 2007. She smiled upon meeting me, but her eyes were hollow and she looked shattered.

I was cautious as I spoke, and asked Patricia, "What would you like me to tell her?"

She said, "Start by showing her the first page of the writing."

Anna was spellbound, absorbing every word that I said as I read her several of Carter's writings. She asked me how I learned to do this and did I think she could learn?

"I don't see why not, I think probably anybody can learn. I wasn't trying to do any of these things, because I didn't believe in this or even know any of this might be possible, yet I'm now talking with my son." I told her that I thought the two most crucial things for me was learning to meditate and keeping a journal.

She asked me several times if she could try to talk to her daughter. I told her repeatedly that I didn't have that ability but there were people who did. She was persistent, and reluctantly I said that I was confident that I could connect with Carter, adding, "If you witness this and can believe that it's him writing, then if my son survives so does your daughter." She agreed, but I hadn't expected to be in this position. I was nervous and uncomfortable. I knew she had high hopes that I wouldn't be able to meet.

I tried to still my mind and I quickly felt Carter. He said hello to Patricia, then he said, "I don't know this other lady."

I explained and then he said, "There's a young woman standing right beside her."

I was so startled by what he said I felt I couldn't breathe. Anna's daughter began to speak through Carter. It was extremely emotional and I was totally unprepared for this to happen. I tried to concentrate in order to hold our connection, as by then Anna was crying and also talking to her daughter. So I was hearing Carter and focusing on the automatic writing, also speaking his words while listening to Anna speak to her daughter, all at the same time. It was chaos.

Then Carter said, "Well done, Mom, we've done it," and the writing ended. Anna and Patricia were thrilled as I sat in utter disbelief of what we had been part of. I was exhausted but exhilarated when I got home; I realized that this session was successful but too chaotic for me. I decided that if this ever happened again, I would write until the thought was complete then I would stop and read what was written. I lay awake for hours, trying to remember the details of the experience and was astounded by how, with little help from me, Carter had brought hope to a grieving parent.

March 26, 2011:

It was a test day at the skating club and Olivia was testing for some figure skating levels. The arena was always quiet on test days, and as I relaxed in the stands, watching her on the ice, I enjoyed feeling Carter join me.

Later, as Olivia and I walked past the ice to leave, an arena employee passed us, pushing a trolley full of trophies.

"Olivia, I wonder if Carter's hockey award was on there," I said, since hockey awards day has just passed.

"Yes, it was the big one," she said. I rushed back and stopped the trolley as I quickly searched for the trophy. I had not had a chance to prepare myself for seeing this award, and although I only saw part of Carter's name, my heartbreaking cry broke the arena's silence. Olivia grabbed me to stop me from collapsing. The poor employee, having no idea what was going on, pushed the cart of trophies away as she stared strangely at me. A friend had rushed to me to help, not knowing what had happened. As she held onto me I tried to explain.

She said, "Well, you've faced it now." But I hadn't really seen it. I needed to face it today because of the state I was now in. She kindly arranged to bring the trophy into a room for us to see in private.

The rest of the day was a write-off for me. I felt like I had been punched in the stomach by grief. Later that evening I had recovered at least enough to attempt to connect to Carter.

C: Love you Mom, I'm sorry today was so hard on you Mom.

CH: I wasn't prepared to see your hockey trophy. All I saw was its size and part of your name and I fell apart. I still feel shattered.

C: Yes I know. I'm so sorry, a tough day. I'm glad I was there and you had known I was there already, it's so hard for me to see you suffering for me, I feel so helpless at those times. You can't always stay strong, nobody can. You are doing so well though Mom, really you are. Look at the lady you, we helped this week. You are in a much stronger position and happier place than her and her pain has been going longer than yours. We all have setbacks, even us here. Remember those setbacks always happen. Accept them, recover from them and try again to move forward, even just little steps count. Remember Mom I'm here, I'm with you. I never have and never will leave you. Our love cannot be broken or ended. We are not really even now separated, just you in your world think we are separated, we know we are not. Our journey moves forward through time eternal, a journey of love and growth. This opportunity we share to accomplish is immense, enjoy the possibility and knowledge so many need. For we together are much stronger that either of us alone, even me with my abilities now I am much stronger with you and Grandpa with me. Think positive and with love, when sadness pours through love reach inside you for what is real, the knowledge that I am real. The true reality, what is and was for every person. I'm home; I wait for your return. Until then we have work to do, a magnificent task, we are blessed, honoured to have the chance.

For almost a week I felt shattered and exhausted. I was proud they had named the award in honour of Carter, but sad that this trophy now existed only because he is dead.

Carter's writings to me over the next few days were filled with support and reassurance as he tried to help me. Time and time again in weak moments through the years I read his writings and tell myself: *Listen to his words. They are positive and happy. They are never negative or sad—Carter is happy.* I must keep focusing on this to give me strength.

March 28, 2011:
8:00 p.m.

I note the time here because it wasn't usual for me to speak with him in the evening, but I'd had a very tough day. I reached to him for help, as I did repeatedly over the next several days.

C: Love you Mom.

You know I'm here with you Mom, whenever you need me. Trust in that knowledge and believe. Let your mind's eye see I'm with you, we both are xx.

CH: I still feel so tired and drained.

C: Yes but you were strong this weekend. You did so much and if it wasn't for breaking down seeing the trophy I think your mindset would have been different as it has been. When you discuss me with others it uplifts, energizes you usually. It's just once you were sad, unsettled, thrown off balance and then seeing all the other people's pain, you in a bad state yourself sink lower. You didn't have emotional strength to cope with all the events. It was a major effort like a big physical job but this is emotional. You're tired, exhausted of course you are but what strides Mom. I love you.

CH: I love you Carter, I'm trying.

C: You're doing great Mom, work harder right now in the next few days to let Grandpa do his work [supporting me], you will feel better, work together.

March 29, 2011:
8:30 p.m.

CH: I'm feeling shattered, Carter.

C: Love you Mom. I will give you strength Mom, we both will. Both with our love, our words, our sheer will to help and our connection will help send you the strength and thoughts to help support you through the tough times. Listen for us.

CH: You didn't believe in this Carter, nor did I, but you tried to reach back right away. Why did you do this if you didn't believe?

C: I didn't believe there, didn't think about it at all nor did you. When I returned I had the full knowledge of my spirit again. That awareness, body of wisdom, knowledge was within me as soon as I stepped back. Grandpa spent a little time bringing me back, my awareness of who I am and what I am and that I am back in spirit, back to my true self. It was like I was stunned, confused but for the shortest of times. As soon as I saw Grandpa really I knew, I understood. He just kind of needed to give me a shake, a nudge I got you, your back. I was a bit stunned but I knew that the larger body of knowledge I have in spirit than I was conscious of on Earth was within my reach, my thoughts. I knew we could make contact I just had to reach back any way I could to get your attention and of course my skills are greater now than when I left xxxx.

March 30, 2011:
8:30 pm

C: Love you Mom.

CH: Do you think it will be by continuing to use our ability to write together that we will find a way to help people?

C: Yes I think so for now, our connection is strong and so far I have been able speak directly to others. We have also had luck I think with the circumstances and the people we have chosen. I know and love most of them. Lauren was completely different but a challenge, a purpose that has to be met the stakes are too high for her. I have to help her, we have to help her and my will is there to do it. But I'm sure we won't always succeed even this way just as sometimes we have trouble connecting. You're tired, can't focus or negative energy is around us. These types of things can affect our connection and always the mindset of the person we try to talk to also. But eventually Mom you may be able to reach and hear loved ones on this side for others on your own, but not now.

CH: I want to do this with you, not on my own; I want to be together with you. This work keeps me close to you and purposeful and helps me immensely cope with my pain of losing you.

C: Yes Mom but remember I'll never leave you and you and I are to always talk each day, try not to miss, even just to connect to touch base with each other. Our hearts touch and connect each day but this other possibility—and I'm not saying it will happen but that it could happen—and if it does, remember it will be because you're working hard to achieve this. This is not an innate ability that just happened for you, it is through work. If you hadn't worked so hard and diligently we wouldn't be together in this conversation right now, something to think about. You must continue your work to even just strengthen and continue your connection to us and with your ability to connect grows in ways to connect to us and eventually possibly others, it is a journey. It is a happy one, you are growing in spirit with every step you take with us, as are we, though we are separated by you in form and by us in different worlds, what a miracle. We through this separation of existences are together, us three are joining and reaching out and are all growing in spirit through this amazing part of our journey together. Think of it Mom, when you are here we grow together, help each other. When we are both there we journey together, grow together in our time there together. Now for the first time during our time of separation through different existences we are still journeying together and growing together, amazing.

I know Carter was trying to be encouraging, but I couldn't believe he would suggest that I might learn to bring messages on my own for others. I wouldn't even consider doing this without him. Why would I? Everything I had done so far had only ever been to be with him again. I didn't want to continue to improve if there was any chance of me having less contact with him. Our personalities were running true to form once again. Carter had always been enthusiastic and happy to have new experiences. On the other hand, I am hesitant to change and need to come to terms with things gradually, if ever.

The next day, Carter attempted to wash away the unintended lingering consequences of what he thought had been a positive statement. With patience and understanding, he spoke directly to my state of mind, which was still lost in the idea of moving forward without him. Once again he skillfully guided my thoughts back to the basics. He didn't connect long enough for me to speak to him, knowing any conversation would only allow my human thoughts to gather strength and weaken me. He knew it would be futile and counterproductive to discuss this any further at this time. Carter's goal was always to support me as my skills continued to expand, and to do this he needed me to accept my growth and be willing to carve a path I could follow. He would allow this idea to wait.

As you read this next message, try to feel boundless love and patience flowing within his words; that is how I received them.

March 31, 2011:

C: Love you Mom.

Good morning, step back and pause. Find strength, recovery, feed your spiritual stillness and love to fill your body and soul. We are with you, we are happy, we love you all. Work on finding and using your will, find your inner strength, your spirit is strong in both worlds. Learn to use its strength and wisdom, it is within you Mom, reach for it, be still and find it. You will get through spring and my birthday easier if your love is centred. Believe in yourself xxxxxx.

After this writing, I remained seated and meditated on his words with focused intention. I was learning to trust the wisdom in his thoughts and after a brief time my mind settled and I felt calmer.

My second journal of Carter's writing was almost full. I asked Olivia if she wanted to come with me to buy a new journal.

She looked hesitant, eventually saying, "I was planning to buy one for you as a Mother's Day gift from Carter and me."

I smiled, feeling my entire body melt into heartfelt gratitude. "I love that idea. Can you buy it for me early?"

She smiled and nodded.

I was riding that roller coaster of emotions again, having plunged down for twenty-four hours, and now soaring on the wings of angels. Olivia had given me just what I needed by including Carter in her Mother's Day plans. She had allowed me to see he was still part of our lives. By doing her part in the purchasing of the gift, Carter could do his part in the writing, reminding me that I don't need to fear having less contact with him. She made her choice of journals at the bookstore, and then we bought ourselves a treat to celebrate the gift. I ordered a Frappuccino because Carter loved to get them when he and his friends got together to play cards. I wanted to continue to include him with us today, but I must admit I wasn't a fan of that coffee. Otherwise, I was happy and content and my emotions were settled for the moment.

April 1, 2011:
5:00 p.m.

C: Love you Mom, today was a bit better again for you. See you are recovering from your setback. You have been calmer, more peaceful.

CH: Yes, I have.

C: Good, spend time trying to see your aura. Use your time at the yoga convention [which I will be going to on April 15] as a source to find different, thought-provoking learning tools. Things you probably wouldn't see elsewhere. I can't believe you didn't like the Frappuccino the other day; they are amazing I loved them.

CH: Maybe I need to try them in the warmer weather; I thought you liked them, that is why I ordered it.

C: That's okay it was as much the occasion that made them great, being there with my friends was an amazing time always. I guess back then everything also seemed great to me, so much fun, our tradition.

CH: You were there with Olivia and me? (I must admit hearing this made me smile.)

C: Yes I was worried about you after the day before; you got so upset seeing the trophy. I needed to stay close for my sake as much as yours, to support you, send you my love. I was seeing how you coped with the day, it was difficult for you but of course you did it and you really were trying, though shattered to your core. You tried hard to be steady, be strong and think of me, my life. You did well, a hard but valiant effort Mom. You're trying so hard we know, we feel it from you. We're fighting for it with you and you know. It helps you.

Carter was absolutely correct in his last statement. Many days I didn't know how I'd find the strength to continually struggle through grief; I was always desperately missing Carter. Knowing he and Dad were fighting for me far exceeded any help I could be given on this earth. Most days, in meditation, I asked to receive their support and guidance as I visualized their love flowing into my heart. I might have been struggling every day, but I also knew that when I pictured Carter with me that this was not imagined or wished for, this was true. I needed him to be able to see that he was helping me learn to cope with this grief. The only way I could truly thank both Carter and Dad was to show them that I was fighting my way through this with their help. I did this for them, my family, and to share what they had given me with others who haven't been as blessed as I have through one of life's greatest struggles, the loss of a child.

Love is the Answer

Love you Mom. Yes love is the greatest of gifts to us as individuals and as a whole. The strength immeasurable, its purpose great and eternal, its kindness gentle and far reaching, its purpose what is and will be. Let your days flow within and for its presence. A kinder, gentler journey no matter what is faced if time is not spent within the prison of anger, jealousy, judgment, possessions and ego. Hold these with little value or the emotions totally abandon. Life there can be journeyed with greater ease, peace and true pleasure in all that holds great pleasure but can never be owned, possessed or controlled. You are a single unit amongst countless units of existence; all has value, purpose and deserves respect. All things are free as themselves not to be truly anything but admired, enjoyed, respected and appreciated within their life. Respect your life and everyone there existing within that current existence. Each helps serve and complete the journey to the growth toward a true and eternal love. (Carter, writing received January 28, 2012.)

April 2, 2011:

Olivia wanted to talk with Carter to tell him about the Mother's Day gift she bought from both of them. I wrote his response to her. He loved the idea and thanked her, saying he was with us at the bookstore and liked the book that she chose best also. They had a funny yet very touching talk.

At the end, Olivia said, "I wish that I could write with him like you do. I would have gotten him to write you a card."

I was thrilled with this idea and said, "I like that, let's ask him." I picked up a pen and he wrote something both silly and lovely, but perfectly him.

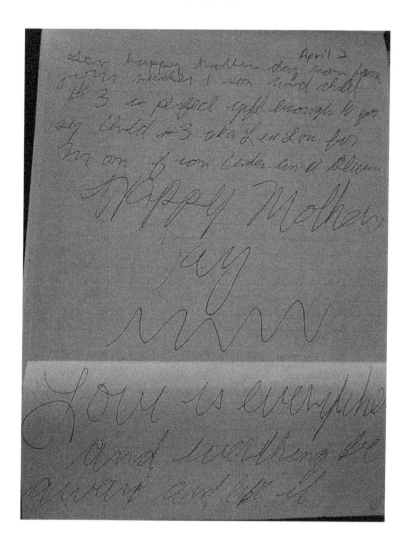

Love, happy Mother's Day Mom from your number 1 son and child #3, a perfect gift brought to you by child #3

aka Liv Lou for Mom from Carter and Olivia.

Happy Mother's Day

xxxxxx

Love is everywhere and everything, be aware and live it.

April 3, 2011:

As Carter and I were writing the first entry in my new journal I "knew" that it was a special Mother's Day card from him. His words had so much more meaning than any card ever could. (This writing can be found on mother's day May 8, 2011.)

Carter's First Message On His Birthday

April 8, 2011:

As we faced Carter's birthday again, this year I received help within the gift of his thoughts in words that were loving and supportive. The previous year on his birthday, I had still been struggling to find a way to prove his existence. If I could have seen one year into the future, there is no way I would have believed what I saw. I knew how blessed I'd been over this past year, but even with all I had accomplished, his birthday was still hard to endure.

CH: Happy twenty-second birthday Carter, we all love you xxx.

C: Love you Mom—love you all.

Try to get through this day now knowing I am safe and home. Happy and purposeful, joyous in my connection and voice back for all to hear and share. A much happier birthday for us Mom, you and I in our reconnection. We didn't have this last year on my birthday and I could only watch all of you and try hard to help. This year you must find the strength to be happy for us Mom, our reconnecting. You truly finding and believing in me, my life now and our purpose, job together to help others. What an amazing journey we can have together, not apart, together as we both want to be you and I. My best birthday gift our connection of love, your absolute pure love for me finding me again through unimaginable odds and against what your mind said. To let your spirit and mine rejoin after really a very brief separation. I spend my birthday with you truly this year. Be happy in what has unfolded within the last year and look ahead with me in what is to come. What we may do together in love and faith in each other. Remember Mom this is your gift of love to me. I accept and acknowledge it today to mark it as a gift from you, I can picture you writing this on a birthday card to add to the gift—with all my love to Carter, happy birthday xox.

CH: (Tears have been streaming down my face throughout this writing.) Thank you Carter, that helps. What a beautiful thought, to think that my effort and success in finding you is a gift from me. Your words always help me. They guide me and give me strength. I love you xox.

C: I know Mom, we're always there for each other, you were always there for me I knew that.

I put down the pen and felt a quality of happiness within me that I never thought I would feel again. Over the last few days I had received a Mother's Day gift from Carter and given him a birthday gift! When Carter died, I never imagined I would give or receive anything from him ever again. I continually returned to today's writing, astounded by many of Carter's thoughts within this message. I had always believed Carter constantly gave evidence, if only briefly, to keep me questioning if he was still with me so I wouldn't lose hope when all seemed lost. This birthday message gave me a wonderful example of how I could move forward, connecting him currently and into the future with all of us. His words were a beautifully wrapped gift of hope given to me from his outstretched hands.

Carter's acceptance of my effort as a birthday gift to him put all of my work to find him into a different perspective that I hadn't considered. Although my struggle to find him, and later reconnect with him, had always been driven as much by my desire to help me as myself, I had never seen it as a gift to him. What a wonderful, happy thought. I felt privileged to have been given the vision of seeing myself accepting from Carter a glittering gold box wrapped with a large gold satin bow. I will never be able to thank him enough for his immense and constant help, but isn't this true of human nature? After all that we have accomplished, I will never feel that I have enough contact with Carter. His acknowledgment of my effort as my gift to him was enhanced when he added, "look ahead with me in what is to come ..." and I saw a vision of him holding my hand as he walked me through a meadow of wildflowers leading into our future, and I felt awash with the love he sent me. This was a well-timed message; he was not sad about the past or the present, and this was definitely something for me to hold on to.

Two days later, Olivia said a belated happy birthday to Carter, what a gift for her to be able to talk to him. Olivia had been in another skating competition on his birthday, and this had been a good distraction for her. Carter said he was there: "Nice it was on my birthday, a special event for the day."

April 10, 2011:

I rose early and began the day with a long meditation. I was feeling less fragile, but it had been another long hard struggle. The lows were so difficult to live through and took such strength to recover from that I wanted to hold what ground I'd gained back. I've discovered the greater the efforts I make to disconnect from my awareness of the physical world in meditation and connect to the wisdom of spirit, the greater my ability to deal with the physical world became. Learning to connect to my spirit in meditation was helping me deal with my grief. I had also noticed when I started feeling better and didn't meditate for a few days I could feel myself becoming less balanced. I felt edgy, my emotions became raw and fragile, and anything could unsettle me. I had learned what an important tool meditation was for me, and though I didn't understand it I could feel the positive changes it made in me.

C: Love you Mom, hope you are feeling a bit better today.

CH: I am feeling a bit better today. I also have this quality time now with you, which I needed.

C: Yes it is much needed especially for the tough times, you are lucky to have this way for support and guidance. It is a way to be given peace within your moments of solitude within yourself, a real focus on time for you, for your spirit to rise. Learn and grow within these moments of solitude we share together. This is a connection very real of our hearts, our spirits, the real us. The us that exists beyond time and form and the life in physical space of time.

Olivia has come into Carters room and asked if she could to talk with him.

O: Hi Carter, Happy Birthday.

C: Hey Liv, yeah thanks, okay you're like two days late.

O: I wasn't around when Mom was talking to you.

C: Yeah I know I'm just kidding. You wished me happy birthday in your thoughts to me. You were talking to me by yourself, I heard you, I always hear you so I knew you remembered my birthday.

O: Thank you for coming to my skating competition on Friday.

C: That's okay, anytime. You know I want to be there so don't forget to tell me.

O: When I was sorting my Briarberry Bears, I got up and left. Dad called me back and said look they are put out in the shape of a six. [This happened on June 11, 2010.]

C: Ha ha did you like that? You were just making a mess sorting them so I thought I'd be creative. I worked it all around you encircling you within the number six. It was me surrounding you like a big hug, My lucky number six and you sitting right within it and the tall part of the six is me reaching back to you and enclosing me around you, surrounding you, holding all of me around you xxxx.

O: Thank you I love it.

C: Thanks for asking me. I know it made you both, all feel good to see it, you thought it was from me. Now I get a chance to let you know beyond what you would or could imagine what a message of love it was meant to be. I'm okay Liv, remember I'm with you, I'll never leave you and I'm okay.

April 15, 2011:

Once again Nancy and I went to the yoga conference. While looking for interesting reading as Carter had asked me to do, I picked up a book called Remember Zen that caught my eye and I felt a definite "buzz" of energy all around me that stopped when I put the book down. I picked up other books and felt nothing, but when I picked up the original book I felt the same sensation again. I did this several times, always with the same results. How odd, it must mean something. I didn't want this book though there were others that interested me, so I decided to wait until tomorrow to choose a book.

The next morning Dad—not Carter—wrote to me, saying that it was him signaling me to buy that first book the day before. It had been his energy I felt; I hadn't thought of that. I told him I would go back and buy that book even though I didn't want that one.

When I read the message to Nancy, she shared with me an experience she'd had recently. A woman had come into her work with a little boy wearing shorts and rain boots that made her think of Carter. She was reminded of a day years ago when Carter and her son were young and playing together because Carter had been wearing an outfit just like this little boy. She couldn't take her eyes off this boy, so she asked the mother what his name was. The mom said his name was Carter. Nancy said that she was so startled she could barely keep her composure.

She wondered if Carter had anything to do with this and asked if I could ask Carter about it sometime. I suggested we ask him now. Carter said yes he arranged this, because he knew I had a lot to tell Nancy and he felt if she had an experience of her own from him then what I had to tell her might be easier for her to accept! The answer brought us both to tears.

April 28, 2011:

Olivia joined me at my second reading with Sandy. In Carter's messages he said that he was at Olivia's birthday and skating competition and he spoke of seeing her on the podium winning the competition. This validated my need to tell Olivia that he was there that day, and the messages from him echoed what he had written with me. This was important to me because it helped me feel more confident in what I had been receiving from spirit. The spirit of a young girl was also present at the reading. I couldn't think of anyone that I knew who had lost a daughter, but Olivia guessed it was my mother's sister. They were extremely close but she had died eighty-four years ago at age seven; at this reading she brought information about Mom's health and said she was watching over her.

Two days later, still basking in the excitement I felt from our reading, Carter expanded on the importance of that day. He added to the richness of the experience by giving his sisters something special to hold on to through the long years of separation from him.

April 30, 2011:

C: Love you Mom.

Let me say how happy I was that Olivia went with you. It is important that she knows how real this is and what connections are possible. Her mind can be a great gift to her also in the future; our connection is and should stay strong. I was very glad Grandma's sister was there, it is the same connection as Olivia and I only decades longer in the time of physical separation, but she is still there for Grandma. Her sister is with her as I will be for Olivia and all of you while your life in form continues, Olivia knew right away, thought of Grandma's sister. It was Olivia that said it to you, you didn't think of her, the possibility of her. You were thinking of the now in time, your lifetime but there is no lifetime here, no time. The connection of spirit stays until reconnection after life in form. Her sister was happy and playful; the length of time she has been out of form doesn't matter. She is who she is, her love for Grandma and the love they share between them keeps them connected, this is and will be the same for me. Olivia was there to not just hear on tape of the connection but see the message come through Sandy and have Olivia make the connection to Grandma. It is a sister to sister with love just as it will be for Olivia and I. Even if she lives to Grandma's age she can now hold on to the knowledge I will be with her and happily watch over her, filled with the love we share. Time there will not separate us. I am in her life still now at any moment, she just has to call me, focus on her love for me. Then know, truly believe I am there with her because I absolutely am, have her visualize me there. This is true for Victoria and Dad too and of course you know this Mom. The importance for Olivia was that it was a young sister, two siblings and their continued connection. Grandma just never really knew, Olivia has the opportunity to be helped by this knowledge throughout her life and it can help guide her forward with a little more ease in her pain. I am so happy Olivia came, thank you Mom xxx.

What an unexpected lesson for Olivia. My girls had often heard my mother speak of her sister and how close they were. They knew how much she loved and missed her sister over a long lifetime without her. My mother had a strong Christian faith, so she believed her sister Marjorie was safe in heaven, but I'm not sure how as an eight-year-old child she dealt with her loss. If my girls could absorb this lesson now, what a gift to their lives it could be. It helped us see life in a bigger picture that now included Marjorie and Carter and could strengthen our belief in the information Carter shares with us.

With no time wasted, I brought the tape of this reading to Mom and listened to it with her. I witnessed her face light up with joy when she heard her sister, and afterward, Mom and I sent lots of love to Marjorie. Our family had been helped from an unexpected source, and we couldn't thank her enough. Mom's sister told her she was not only still with her, but was now stepping into view to help Mom's grandchildren through a horrendous ordeal. An ordeal they both knew only too well.

May 5, 2011:

It was Victoria's twentieth birthday and it was a devastating one for her to face. Her struggle began months before, when she said to me, "How can I be happy to be twenty when Carter never lived to have his twentieth birthday?" She was also unbearably sad to be older than her older brother. She said this will be the worst birthday of her entire life. Her friends wanted to celebrate with her, but she couldn't celebrate while facing the reality of this day. She just wanted to get away from everything and decided that she was going to the cottage.

My heart ached for her and for us all, and there was nothing I could do or say to help, but I did know that she wasn't going to be alone. We spent the day together and once again the cottage gave her comfort in a tough time. Carter had been hoping to talk with her if she thought it might help, and on her twentieth birthday Victoria talked to Carter for the first time through me. At first it was lighthearted and they had fun bantering back and forth, then Carter spoke to her with love and support about their connection throughout time remaining constant and strong. This was a special gift for her birthday. She had his words of encouragement to help her go forward and live her life with joy, knowing he was happy and with her always.

May 6, 2011:

Carter gave me one of my early visual images of a rope to reinforce this lesson while he was writing his message. I didn't realize it at the time, but as this continued to happen, I hoped that either I had acquired a new skill or Carter felt ready for me to take a step forward on my journey. Whichever was the truth, the images added clarity to his words and allowed me to easily remember the message as I could recall these images and therefore his thoughts.

C: Love you Mom.

Thanks Mom so glad I had the chance to talk to Victoria, I hope it helps her. It is time for you to concentrate on balancing both sides of your life. Completely different worlds, tasks, mind-sets but they must be blended harmoniously within each day. Take the peace from our world into each of your days. Find time for our tasks and your tasks and enjoyment there. Let it become one within your life. Not two ends with you being pulled in two directions by each but one. Flow from one end to the other without friction or pressure, a beginning and end each day within a life, your life blended and wrapping both worlds around each other to flow smoothly from beginning to end. It sounds wonderful and can be achieved; you have the time now, work on bringing this into your life. It will make everything so much easier, less struggle, more pleasant. We love you xxx.

A Love Without Limit

Love you mom. Life is joyous when lived well. Whether we struggle, have pain, or have a seemingly easy life, it is all for a purpose that is unseen and can be hard to understand when there. It is once you return home that you will understand the purposes of the events of your life and how your choices of how you dealt with them served your purposes when you left here to live that life. Did you do well or not? Mostly it is of course a mixture of results. Remember simple kindnesses matter, you don't have to dedicate your life to a grand purpose or think only of others. It is also important to be kind to yourself, love yourself, allow yourself to laugh, have fun. There are always big problems in the world. You can make a big difference in a small way or to a few people. Remember yourself, try not to be upset at your faults, failures, mistakes, but try to acknowledge to yourself at least your mistakes and try to sometimes learn from them and try to do better. Don't worry what others think, know and understand yourself and grow and improve within the confines of your personality and traits. One who is quiet and shy won't lead crowds or fight for rights but they can be kind, loving and oh so helpful. It's just as good. Love you Mom for you, always be yourself and enjoy the spirit within, it is you. (Carter, writing received May 7, 2011)

I feel this message is a great lesson for us all to learn. It puts so much of life into a better perspective. Carter wrote this with ease and joy, giving a laid back feeling to the message. He was hoping that I would learn to be easier on myself as I faced life's struggles. As quite often happened I received some of the most meaningful writings while at the cottage as was the case with this one.

Mother's Day

May 8, 2011:

I'd been trying to prepare myself to face this day after the series of events that put me into an emotional free fall last year on Mother's Day. I held onto my daughters tight, never wanting to let them go as they hugged me good morning. They put all their love into their hugs, knowing it would be a tough day for me, but I needed that third hug. Aching for a hug from my son, I went to Carter's bedroom and folded my arms around my new journal, holding it close to my heart as I visualized all the love contained within these messages flowing from him into my heart. The journals had been created through love, and this was as close to his hug as I could get. I asked Carter and Dad to be with us on Mother's Day and give us a sign that they're with us if they could. Repeatedly throughout the day I read the first entry in my new journal, my Mother's Day card, to remind myself that I was not imagining this; he was with me. I was so fortunate to be able to see and read his words; they gave me that continual validation especially when I was feeling fragile.

This is my Mother's Day card from Carter:

C: Love you Mom.

CH: I love you Carter.

C: xxx Enjoy your early Mother's Day gift. Each day you write in it with me it continues to be an expansion of my gift to you. And of course I couldn't have done this without Olivia thinking of it for me, giving it from me, us, her and I. I love you both so much.

CH: And you know how much we love you!

C: Yes enough to search the heavens for me, enough to fight through your pain, your grief to reach step by step, deepening your belief that I was trying to reach you. It is a love that endured all that but fought through the pain, the unbearable existence without me to find me once again. A love that has no limits and reached into the darkness of the unknown, clearing the confusion of the mind but ultimately, successfully finding where I am so we can be together still. A love that endures all to succeed, to once again be one as we need to be for us to go forward. The endless journey we continue to take together. You continue to grow for me mainly to reach and spend time with me but ultimately our connection though a gift at the time of this during crises for us emotionally will bring gifts of love and knowledge for many. Our gift of reconnecting for us will be shared and reach so much farther than you and I xxx.

CH: That is absolutely beautiful. Thank you so much Carter, I love you.

As tears poured down my cheeks, I held my shaking left hand to my heart, then reached up toward Carter and the sky as I sent every ounce of love I had to him.

I would also like to take this moment to address what I'm sure many of you are thinking. Yes Carter's writings are amazing and almost unbelievably beautiful at times. They aren't all like this, but on the occasions when they are I sit in awe of his skill and precision of thought that has flowed onto the paper with ease and without hesitation. As I write my story, I don't try to match his skills, and please, never compare my writing to his. This book would never be completed if I did. His writing is quite simply heaven-sent, and since I know this is true I accept this as the explanation to the question I am often asked: "how does he write like that?"

I could feel all the love and happiness within the walls of our home as Victoria and Olivia worked together preparing a very special Mother's Day tea for Mom and me. During tea, I tried to immerse myself in the moment, in my family's smiles and laughter. I watched, aware that we were all consciously capturing each moment to hold in our memories. We were all very aware how precious the day was, especially this year, for next spring Victoria would be studying in England and Mom would be ninety-three years old. The pain of not having Carter here was unbearable for us all, but we also knew we must celebrate and enjoy this day together. There was every possibility we would never have a Mother's Day together again (and we didn't).

The tea was wonderful; we gathered around the dining room table that had been elegantly set with the family china and silverware, and enjoyed the delicious food the girls had prepared. The weight of emotional burden was very heavy, and it wasn't easy, but I thought we were managing to win the day's battle. In the middle of the festivities the phone rang, "Hi Mrs. Roud, its Cam," I was so happy to hear his voice. It instantly transported me back to the days when the voices of Carter and his friends filled the house, and for a moment I was not missing the sound of Carter's voice. We had a quick chat and arranged to meet in a couple of days so Cam could hear the message Carter had for him during my recent visit to the medium last month. I put down the phone and somehow I felt better. Later I realized how well timed Cam's call was. The five of us were gathered at the table and were all trying so hard without Carter with us on Mother's Day. I wondered, *was Carter letting me know he was with us as I'd asked him and Dad to be?*

May 11, 2011:

Cam had a big smile as he listened to Carter's message for him on the tape that included "I'll be seeing Cam soon," and here he was only twelve days later and I hadn't seen him for quite a while. Astonished, Cam said he was going to visit or phone several times before the April 28 reading, but never did. Then on Mother's Day he felt he HAD to call me. This is the second message I've given to him from Carter. There was a message for Cam during my first reading with Sandy that held great importance in convincing me it had to be Carter speaking through her, and therefore it was extremely important for me to keep finding the strength and stamina to continue my search.

While at university in 2008, shortly after Carter's death, Cam had gotten a tattoo of Carter's initials between his shoulder blades to honour Carter. Both boys had been so excited about the approaching September; they were going to be roommates at university. Just days before Carter's death, Cam had sent him a message: "one month to go." One month later Cam had to cope with being at university with all the new and exciting experiences that they were planning to share but without Carter. Cam was determined he would experience university for both of them and he was keeping Carter with him symbolically with the tattoo.

At my first reading, Sandy said Carter was mentioning the first letters of friends' names and she listed several letters. I couldn't place most of the initials and I was becoming quite upset as they didn't make sense to me. Later, she said Carter wanted to talk about a person with a B name like Bruce or Brian. Once again, I had absolutely no idea whom he was referring to. How could this be? I knew his friends. Then she said it's the person with a tattoo on his back in his honour. Oh yes, now I know; Carter had been using last names, no wonder I couldn't figure them out! (Carter what are you thinking? You're making this more difficult than it already is.)

"Carter's saying the tattoo is between his shoulder blades and that it's for him. Carter says he was with him when he got it and he's honoured!" Sandy said.

She has to be talking to Carter; she couldn't know this. This statement was one of the more important of many that day that was the proof I needed to convince myself that Carter was still with us. This propelled me into a journey that has enriched my life beyond words.

May 16, 2011:

I met with Patricia and Anna to lead them through a meditation as I had promised. It was no surprise to me when Anna asked if we could talk to her daughter again, I would have done the same thing. For the second time, Carter brought through her daughter's words that made perfect sense to her. Carter ended by saying there were other spirits in the room and he would like to try this again another day. I put on my coat and left to meet John, who was picking me up at a prearranged time. When he wasn't there, I phoned him and was surprised to hear he was still at his office and wouldn't be able to pick me up for another hour. This was unusual; he's always on time. I went back into Patricia's house where they were still sitting at the table, discussing the reading.

I said, "Well, I have another hour, Patricia; how would you like to talk to Carter?"

She jumped at the chance. "Oh yes, please!"

Carter began more playfully this time, "Okay Patricia, are you ready? Let's go! There are two ladies here, and they're yours!"

It was Patricia's mother and sister. Patricia was speechless as her mom gave messages to help her deal with a family problem that she had been struggling with, unknown to me.

May 18, 2011:

The high school sports banquet was coming up in June, and Carter's Team Player Award was to be presented for the third time. The award was a gift from our cottage neighbours to honour Carter, and on it is a painting of the view from our dock. It was won the first time in 2009 by Carter's friend, Andrew's sister. Later when Kevin congratulated her, she questioned him about the meaning of the picture. He happily explained how special this place was to Carter. When Kevin told me this I realized we should include with the award a written explanation of the picture, I felt strongly that this writing shouldn't come from me, but from Carter's friends who understood it with the same youthful exuberance as Carter. I asked Carter's friends Kevin and Richard, who had spent the most time with Carter at the cottage, if they would write this for me. I knew this was a lot to ask of them since they would have to open their emotions and replay those special memories that held such great joy, but sadly now also the pain of loss. What an incredibly difficult and emotional task I was asking of them, but they didn't hesitate to say yes. They each wrote beautiful descriptions of what this view meant to Carter, and we gave it out with the award beginning in 2010.

A lot had changed during the past two years, and as the 2011 award banquet approached I had wondered if I should now add my thoughts of what this place meant to Carter, but how could I capture in words the feeling of the perfection he felt there? Each of my attempts to write was too emotional and scattered. The more I tried and failed the more important this became for me, and I was becoming too anxious to focus on anything else. I asked Olivia if she had any thoughts that I might add. She looked at me with concern as she could see the state I was working myself into. Olivia reminded me that Carter had written his thoughts for the hockey award that year.

"Ask Carter, Mom. You have to get better at thinking of this." She spoke with confidence and natural acceptance that was simply profound to me. I talked with him every day; I don't know why I didn't think of it. I went directly to his room, opened our journal, and asked if he would like to explain in his words what this view on his award meant to him. I was amazed at how effortless and well written his response was. All my hard work and frustration wasn't necessary at all. Olivia was right. I included it with both Kevin and Richard's writing after John rephrased it slightly so it read like Carter wrote it while he was alive; the truth was too difficult to explain at this time!

This is Carter's original speech for the award before John reworked some of the wording.

Carter's Speech for the AHS Team Player Award

This view from my dock, my most happy place, this view of contentment, joy, peace, energy, fun, pleasure and family time together, one with nature surrounded by water, my favorite element. I would wake and fall asleep to the sound of the water hitting the shoreline.

I would open my eyes to the sun down the lake as I see it here on the plaque; well it was usually higher in the sky.

I couldn't wait each year as summer approached for that first dive into the lake. I knew it would be freezing, but still, it was tremendous. I was in the water; summer had begun in my mind.

When in the water, the sound of the water around me, the feel on my skin, the fun to play in it, jump, splash, dive, ride, boat, it was an endless playground that also kept me cool, refreshed and invigorated. And this view, this place of beauty, to look up from whatever I was doing: swimming, sunning, sleeping, talking, to raise my eyes to this horizon, to see this view and be filled with a refueled sense of joy, wonder, happiness for that moment, that first glance every time I saw it. My body, my spirit felt even better even if I already was happy and having fun.

I would even at a glance see it and my soul, my core was enriched with the simple knowledge, yes I was here in this space, isn't it perfect at almost every level.

It is still my favourite place as I know you have already guessed, Mom.

The view is perfection, to me the beauty, the meaning of the place, the time allowed for friends, family, your inner self, your spirit to find strength, renewal and focus on what now I see to be so important—the moment and the joy, peace and beauty encapsulated within this painting. I am so happy with this choice. A meaning of more than just sport but life and the richness that can be found and enjoyed within the beauty of God's gift of all life that surrounds you.

How is that Mom? I hope it's okay; I lived up to my current standards, ha ha!

CH: Thank you Carter, I think it will be perfect. You certainly have a way with words now.

C: Yes, I think it just comes with this job.

Later that same day, Patricia called me. As soon as I said hello she began to cry. She apologized, saying she was still so overcome by what Carter and I gave to her two days ago (her mother's words of advice) that as soon as she heard my voice the emotions came flooding back. She told me that I couldn't imagine how grateful she was to both of us. She told me she had struggled so much with those issues that her mother spoke of, and her mother's messages guided her thoughts in new and helpful ways. Her reaction to my voice and her words of thanks helped inspire me to see how much good this work could do for others.

June 12, 2011:

I had begun to read the book Dad had told me to buy at the yoga conference. Within the first few pages I read things that Carter and Dad had already told me and sometimes they were written with the same words and unusual phrasing that I had never seen until Carter had written them. How odd. This raised many new questions for me, so on this day I asked in meditation to speak with Dad instead of Carter, and trusted he would come forward.

CH: Hi Dad, can I talk to you?

DAD: Hi Charm, I love you.

With the first movement of the pen I knew it was Dad. He moved the pen in short quick bursts with less flow than Carter, which fascinates me. Carter's writing through me was nothing like his writing looked when he was alive. On the other hand, Dad's writing through me was almost identical to his writing when he was alive. Not only did it look the same, but the pen moved just as it did when he had held it. Every time he began to write, I clearly saw a moving image of his physical handwriting, and I wondered if there was a reason for this difference. Maybe someday I'd ask them, but today I had a more important question.

CH: Dad, you know that book that you signalled me to get at the yoga conference and then again the next morning in your writing you said you wanted me to get it (**Remember Zen**)? I've started reading it, and I'm startled how its saying things you both have told me: words, thoughts, mindsets, even phrases—it's shocking!

DAD: Yes, that is why I wanted you to buy that one. I knew it would reinforce what we're saying, that gets your attention. Another layer of belief for you in us, that it is us and the knowledge, wisdom we are giving you. It also will give you faith in other things within the book, things untold by us to you so far. But you will still want to believe because of the connection from us. It was the best book there. The only one that was important for me to have you read.

CH: Alright now here's the question: How do you know what is written within that book, and how do you know that I needed to read it?

DAD: Well yes that's a good question of course and you're beginning to read it, thinking yes; yes this is what they're telling me. The thoughts, words, process to connect and who we are. I know that first part connects directly to our teachings to you. Well, we know here at our level. We have that information. It is important for us, Carter and me to know this; we can reach back with this information. We are given the knowledge to know when things are put on paper to advance the human soul. This is perfect for you now, not last year when you wouldn't have even begun to grasp it. It is only now, at this place in your growth, having received our thoughts so far and reached a new level of thinking. This is the right book for you now. In ten years you may have read it and enjoyed it, but it is your yearning to learn, reach for this knowledge, now is the moment for this book. I understand what is in it without reading it or seeing it written, it is just the knowledge to be given to you—THAT'S the book, as simple as that. I knew it was right and you're seeing that it is. We are allowed this information within us to help you for our journey, your journey. Have faith; believe when these feelings come that it is me guiding you.

CH: So you didn't know what was in the book?

DAD: Yes, I did, but the bigger picture was encapsulated within a thought to me. So when you picked it up, I was able to signal you like an instinct or gut feeling but with the added knowledge of the body of knowledge within the book. The knowing it is for you now. I love you, enjoy it and take your time with it. It is important for you.

If I didn't believe that this was my father speaking, I wouldn't waste a moment on this answer. It was so farfetched and confusing to me; I was hoping to get an answer from Dad that I could understand. I would need to allow myself time to read it again and again, and try to allow my thoughts to open and expand into a way of thinking that was beyond my natural boundaries. I began to realize how expansive the world of spirit must be and that some questions couldn't be clearly answered for me because I didn't have the scope of vision or wisdom to understand the answers. Astounded by this information, I needed to ask myself a bigger question that I knew I couldn't answer. How, and within what natural laws, was what Dad was describing able to happen?

Later that morning Kevin came to talk with Carter for the first time. As he settled into the comfortable chair in Carter's room, he picked up Carter's iPod and smiled.

"Look at these songs. One really happy song after the other—it's amazing now to see them." He was reminded of how Carter created a buzz of happiness around him.

Carter immediately connected with me, excited to speak with his friend, but Kevin was doubtful and didn't know what to say or ask, which was perfectly understandable. Carter began to write, kidding and joking around with Kevin, just as he would have done to try to prompt him to talk. Kevin responded automatically, and their banter was as natural as ever. Kevin had been caught off guard and was talking back to Carter before he realized.

After a few moments, he began to ask questions and was surprised to get answers he said were right. One question he asked Carter was what he thought of LeBron James being traded from the Cleveland Cavaliers to the Miami Heat. At one point Carter said, "He was the team" (his old team). Kevin said later that's exactly what Carter had always said, which made me feel good also; I had never heard this.

It was a very warm and light conversation, but it was a lot for Kevin to cope with. Later Kevin said he wanted it to be Carter, but there was no proof it was him. I couldn't argue with that thought. I was once in the same place, and Carter had to work long and hard for enough proof to convince me. I decided to show him Carter's photo from October 2010 to try to help, but Kevin had trouble seeing his image. His reluctance probably didn't help him.

Expanding My View

Love you Mom. We are really having quite a trip together now hey Mom? Many surround themselves with beauty of place but they need to have the "eyes" to see and within these vistas appreciate where they are then placed but also bring awareness within self of the grandeur of existence and how exquisitely perfect they too have been created. Yet their perfection is miniscule within the total scale of earth's perfection. In this awareness of their individual scale maybe they can begin to let wash away their focus on their seen importance of THEIR life and desire to revolve that life around them and let them maybe begin to see their importance but within the totality of existence. Let their life begin to revolve as the earth revolves, holding within its gravity all current existence upon it. Let people revolve as the earth, being part of totality and realizing they are only part but intrinsic within "the view." They must revolve their lives within existence of form and to enhance not only themselves but all they are part of. The focus toward self should be shed, be pulled off and invigorate you when you allow your awareness to see that we are rotating, all gloriously held as one upon one, floating, unbelievably heavy yet somehow held within the "nothingness" of eternal space, it is "magic" yet very real. See the journey, the path, the purpose for all to journey, float, rotate and be part of this miracle that floats and is laden with life and journey. For space is not empty, for it to hold these celestial orbs takes an energy, power, creation and presence of a knowledge, strength and purpose beyond understood or understandable wisdom. The growth of understanding does move forward but so does purpose of journey. We journey toward knowledge but it ultimately will be understood within love. The energy of all that is to be found ultimately through the energy of love, the most complete and all-encompassing of energies. (Carter, writing received May 18, 2012.)

I felt a new door had been opened for me as summer 2011 began. This allowed my awakening to continue into an ever expanding perspective as Carter and Dad began teaching me of universal oneness and our eternal journey. When I connected with them now to write, I felt a heightened sense of serenity and love as their goodness and love flowed to me; while I remained alert and fully aware of both my thoughts and theirs, I received their guidance. I was astounded by some of their writings and equally astounded that I could understand and find logic in these complex and advanced concepts. The words said only a fraction of what I was experiencing, as I seemed to receive them infused with a richness of feelings, emotions, imagery, and wisdom that was held in heightened illumination as the words flowed to paper. I received a deeper, more complete understanding and awareness than the words alone gave, that defied description and brought me greater clarity and capacity to understand. I felt they were giving me more advanced thoughts than previously as they expanded my view of the world. I was encouraged by this, believing they must see growth within me as I strived to learn.

I noticed when people asked Carter questions; they were often answered with thoughts and turns of phrase that I could only wish I had thought of. Friends often said they didn't want me to feel bad, but they knew I couldn't have thought of that even though they had watched as I wrote the words. Another comment they frequently said to me when they saw how quickly the messages were written usually without a pause was that I couldn't have written anything so lovely without working at it. This was true and didn't make me feel bad because that was exactly what I thought: *what an amazing answer; I didn't know that!*

I have chosen some of my favourite writings from summer 2011 that helped guide me into a more advanced knowledge. I now understand the writings as they are written, but for me to continue to grow and grasp deeper wisdom I often reread them, then sat peacefully, looking out at the world and exploring the thoughts within these writings. It continues to be very important to allow myself time and stillness, for it is within this time of ease that my mind can absorb these challenging lessons and my understanding evolves. The more I understood the bigger concepts, the easier life became for me on a day-to-day basis, as it gave a new perspective on life. I began to see how nothing in existence was separate; we were all truly connected to everything that existed. Yes, we were separate beings, but part of one greater existence, and I was learning to appreciate the purpose and beauty of life within all its effort.

I arrived at the cottage as summer began, excitedly anticipating my spiritual growth in this special place, but I knew in my heart that nothing would ever match last summer. I was also weakened by months of struggling with my own roller coaster ride of emotional highs and lows, while at the same time coping with the emotions of others and trying to help them. One unexpected consequence I was experiencing after learning to connect to spirit was that I had developed a hypersensitivity to the emotions of others. I needed to learn to shield myself from this or be dragged down with them when people around me were feeling angry, sad, or negative.

My own emotional state had been heightened since Carter's death, and within any conversation I could cry and laugh. I had accepted this behaviour as part of who I now am. I felt they were honest emotions, and I try to no longer say I'm sorry to people when I cry. Apologies had been my instant response early on, but one day I was given a piece of advice that I took to heart. As I spoke of Carter to a friend of Nancy's, I began to cry, and of course, said sorry as I wiped the tears from my eyes. She said, "don't ever feel you need to apologize to anyone." I replied that I felt bad because I know how uncomfortable it can make people feel, and I don't mean to do that to others. She thought that it wasn't healthy for people to shield themselves from emotions or difficult circumstances. "It can be good for them to see your pain and face their feelings, don't try to shield others, it's natural for you to express your emotions. Don't bottle them up inside; that's not healthy for you."

John, Olivia, and I arrived to join Victoria at the lake on June 24. This was the third summer we faced without Carter, but emotions still ran rampant. Everyone deals with grief and expresses their feelings differently, this was especially true on that day as emotions erupted unexpectedly. In the midst of all the chaos, I realized that I didn't see the journals as we unpacked. I began to panic. "I can't find the journals, will everyone please help me find Carter's journals." My heart was pounding and I couldn't breathe. I remembered packing them and what the bag looked like that I had put them in. I thought that I was going to be sick; where were they? Every message I had from Carter was in them, they're irreplaceable. We ripped apart everything we had brought from home, but they were not there. Since this writing began last summer, I had not gone anywhere without them. When I only had one journal it was easy, the journal fit in a large purse, but it was getting more difficult now that there were three journals and I always carried all three of them from home to the cottage and back.

Our friend Shannon was watching the house for the summer, and John suggested I ask her to check the house. She knew how important these journals were to me and she went right to the house. My mind was racing, if they're not there, then I'd somehow lost them. How could I be so careless with what is undoubtedly now my most precious possession?

Five or ten very long minutes later, Shannon called. "They're here, Charmaine. They're safe, you can relax."

"Where were they?" I asked. "I can't believe that I lost track of them."

"You left them in the upstairs hall," she told me.

My need to speak with Carter every day overrode all else, so the next morning, with more effort and emotional burden than I care to admit, I temporarily relinquished my need to write only in the journals and picked up a loose piece of paper. I needed to calm down to be able to connect with Carter in the hope that he could encourage me to see my life now in a more positive light and advise me where I should focus my effort this summer. This is our third full summer without him, and even with all the help he gives me, the physical loss of him could still feel as raw as if it happened yesterday.

June 30, 2011:

C: Love you Mom.

CH: Carter, should I continue to do what I've been doing or is there anything else I should try to do this summer to develop my ability to reach toward you and Dad with more skill?

C: You are of course to continue meditation, working always on the thoughts you're processing, a good clear positive state of mind. Don't let others' negativity, anger, judgments touch you or upset you. These are not yours to take on. Your path within this journey is different. Your goals, gifts for others and purpose takes your focus away from daily trivialities of worry. You must believe and hold strong to this belief that it is for the good of many human souls if you're on the right path. There are things of course you still need to do for yourself, family, home, job, but within these demands walk through the tasks with joy and stillness of soul to maintain strength and time for our task. Your ability to stay open, focused and peaceful in life must be maintained. Everyone has things important to their life there, this is yours, allow it to happen.

I was hoping for a more clear direction on what to do. In hindsight it was excellent advice for me, and much harder to do than I realized. I reread his answer. Yes, he had given me something to work on, but it didn't answer my question the way I had hoped. I asked the question again, hoping for a more concrete answer.

CH: Carter, could you tell me something more specific that I should work on this summer?

C: Awareness of everything within nature really and the stillness of self and the earth and skies. I am here, reach to me with a greater awareness of all that is here, practice being aware with your eyes, your body, your smell. Listen. Knowledge and ability will come. Focus on the details, the minutiae of the awareness. Daily try to bring vision into your ability.

I'm sorry I asked! I had no idea what to do with this answer. I must admit, I asked my next question with attitude and frustration.

CH: How am I supposed to do this?

I immediately sensed a powerful writing was being given, but I found this writing very difficult to understand, so don't be stopped by it. I struggled with the words and found it hard to comprehend the bigger picture, but little by little I could understand sections. I paused after the first paragraph and tried to concentrate on his words, and by holding his words in steady concentration within my mind, I did have some limited success to see beyond my natural field of vision. I then returned to our writing.

C: As with the auras open your eyes and your mind's eye to an awareness of space, the nothingness of any space. It is filled with more than air, it can be alive with the energy of existence. Try to focus on the nothingness beyond and within the space to see what may or may not be there, bring awareness within the air of existences beyond the human eye. Open your spiritual eye to bring your focus outside of your reality to our reality. Try to see within the unseen of what exists past your reality, focus past it to us. Expand your thoughts, read Grandpa's book and absorb the vastness of existence and within the vastness try to begin to witness within your mind's capability the oneness of it all. It can beat as one heartbeat.

All things exist to feed the existence of all other things. We are all part of the same body so to speak. It is vast beyond any comprehension, yet it is one and all within it are part of this one. The importance people put on things, achievements and their life is so unbelievably small, less than a speck of sand. It is nothingness within the desert. It is the desert that is seen. The sand moves within the desert, blown with the wind, walked on, carried by others but the speck of sand has no importance except for the fact that without all the specks of sand there would be no desert. Each speck is needed to form the whole. It is all the sand together that makes it a successful desert. It is everything within existence that works toward the continued existence of what exists.

It is our movement like the sand, our behaviour, kindness, love we give as we move through existence that counts and creates a greater reality or desert. If all the grains of sand move as one the ripples within that desert would be breathtaking, as we learn to move more as one than struggling for our oneness individually, the ripples and harmonies within all existence will be glorious.

The power and visual beauty I felt and saw as this second part of the writing flowed through me was beyond description. As Carter's thoughts ended I put the pen down, but my eyes stayed riveted on his words. I was in complete awe of what I had just received. It was one of the moments within my journey where within a few words the universe let me see it in all its majesty, and within these few sentences I felt I was enriched beyond anything that I had ever learned! Over the next few days, my thoughts were seldom off these images and words, and they brought me not only peace, but gratitude to have been given such insight from the heavens.

This writing inspired me to strive for greater visual details. In meditation, or as I walked, I began to stop and look not only at the trees, but the bark of a tree, or I would go closer and examine the details of a single leaf. I felt it, noticed the veins and the edges, how it connected to the twig, etc. I replayed the message in my mind in the hope it would help me to concentrate. "Focus on the details, the minutiae of the awareness." During the first week of summer, I spent my days motivated and happily working to improve my skills with his direction.

July 1, 2011:

Less than a week after forgetting the journals, I returned home alone. I couldn't relax until I got them. I arrived at the house, rushed upstairs, and grabbed the bag to check that all the journals were there. One, two, three journals, what a relief. I scooped the current working journal into my hand and continued directly into Carter's room. As I went through his doorway, I could smell him, and I smiled as I opened the journal to write.

CH: I'm in your room and I can smell you. (I quiet myself and wait for a reply)

C: Yes a gift from me to you.

CH: Thank you, I love it.

C: I know you do Mom.

A heavy exhale came from deep within me as the stress of being separated from these journals came to an end. I used this unexpected trip home to spend lots of time with Mom and for quiet meditation. This time alone allowed me to examine and reflect on any awareness of spirit I received during meditation, knowing there was nothing that would disturb the silence.

After only two days I was really missing my family, so, after one last meditation, during which I sent my gratitude for this opportunity of time, I returned to the cottage in a much better state of mind. I knew I had grown from being separated from the journals, and discovered I could still cope. I happily walked into the cottage not as consumed by the pain of Carter not being there but comforted by those that were there. This time I was ready to face the summer in a much more positive frame of mind.

July 6, 2011:

Only days later, as I settled into my morning meditation, the phone rang and I was jolted back to the reoccurring struggles of this life once again as I heard the voice of one of Mom's favourite nurses in her residence.

"Charmaine, your mom has had two COPD [Chronic Obstructive Pulmonary Disease] spells this morning at breakfast. She recovered quickly from the first, but not the second. She is resting comfortably back in her room, but this one seemed more severe; she's still not really coherent yet, but we are all with her and her vital signs are returning to normal range."

I had already grabbed my purse and shoes and told the family its Mom while I was still on the phone.

"I'm leaving right now, but it will take me two and a half hours; I'm at the cottage."

Once again I had to drive toward the unknown, and my emotions overflowed into tears. My mother gave me a love and understanding from our wonderful, life-long bond that couldn't be matched. She had also been able to transcend her frailty and fight with us with her love and inner strength for my family's survival after Carter's death. An hour later, Mom had recovered enough to call the cottage to tell me that she was okay and I shouldn't worry about her, just enjoy my day. Victoria had answered her call and told her I was almost there and would be with her soon.

I rushed to her room. I was so relieved to see her sitting up in bed, weakened, but her lovely self. We hugged each other for a long time, knowing how blessed we were to be able to hold each other once again, and love flowed from us in a great wave of relief. After a short visit, I told her I'd be back in an hour to see her so she could rest. I returned to our house and once again I went directly to Carter's room. I felt physically, emotionally, and mentally depleted. What an awful ordeal this morning had been. Carter, I really need you to once again prove you haven't left me. Do you know what happened? I need you to help me today. I tried to still myself so I could connect with Carter, but I didn't have the mental focus or emotional strength, yet somehow his connection to me was made.

C: Love you Mom, bad start to your day hey.

CH: Yes, it was an upsetting start to the day. I got a call from Mom's long-term care home saying she had collapsed twice this morning. I immediately drove home from the cottage to be with her.

C: Yes your mind was quickly overcome; try to settle back down for your sake. Remember we are here with all of you.

CH: Yes I tried to hold tight to that knowledge.

C: Grandma will be okay no matter what happens there and her time will come to leave form at some point.

CH: Yes, but I really don't want to face another death.

I began to cry at the mention of her leaving. I wanted her to be able to enjoy her life and I certainly didn't want her to suffer, but the selfish part of me didn't want her to leave me, either. I had lost too many I loved within a few years. I think I could have accepted the inevitability of her death if I hadn't suffered the loss of my child.

C: Nobody ever does but it must be faced.

I was frustrated; Carter wasn't saying anything that was helping me. I was in tears again and feeling more upset than before we began to speak. I wanted him to stop talking about Mom so I changed the topic.

CH: Carter, can you help me feel better with some happy knowledge of yours?

C: It is with the passage of your time our hearts hold even stronger to your spiritual heart. Sometimes near the end of a long life or struggle even those there who really don't believe can be witness to our existence. It is usually visually within their mind's eye. An actual visual to see us in spirit as we, often many, draw close to them and want to greet them, bring them home. Many there, doctors and such think they are delirious or dreaming but the reality is that sometimes as their soul prepares to leave form and return, the soul though still in form can begin to reconnect to life in spirit. Its focus on that life is ending, it is pulling its effort and attention away from that physical life because really its effort there is complete and it begins to bring its awareness and focus back to life in spirit. It is the spirit within reconnecting with its natural state, but since it is still in the physical body the human mind has this reality brought into their awareness. It is an unasked for and sometimes startling awareness of their loved ones from there and also here. A gift as it often is at the end of their life of the realm they return to. A continued healthy, vibrant life shed of the struggles of the physical body. The spiritual awareness reawakening before the final sleep so to speak, sometimes both sides are so ready to reunite before release in form.

CH: Thank you, that is nice. I love you both xxx (I was speaking to Dad and Carter).

These words drew my focus into the beauty of his message and away from my emotions of the last few hours. As always, he had helped me, and I sat for a while and tried to absorb the natural continuity of our lives beyond what we see and understand as I reread this message. Through luck or a wiser source of intelligence, the path Carter and I had found to communicate was probably better than any other way to serve my healing from grief. I often opened the journals and read old writings, or referred back to them as I had new questions or thoughts, and realized he had already given me the answers. I could spend hours searching for certain writings without frustration because I was enthralled with each message. I became captured by the beauty and flow of the writings as I remembered how each writing had helped me see with a better perspective on whatever issues I was struggling with that day.

Once again I returned to the cottage after spending several days at home with Mom. I felt that I was never completely where I should be. I needed to tear myself into pieces so part of me was with my family at the cottage, part of me with Mom, and part with Carter. Peace did come to me at times, often occurring without effort as I became captured by a smile, a moment of enjoyment, or seeing the beauty within the natural world that surrounds us. I have come to realize how wonderful life would be if we could let most of our burdens go, but for now, I would try to enjoy these moments as they happened.

That summer I often wondered what people thought as they saw me break into a big smile for no apparent reason. There was a very good reason to me though; I could smell Carter. This happened all summer long, several times a day in the cottage. Of course I smiled; he was letting me know he was with us, as we all knew he should be, reinforcing the strong bond we all have to the cottage. Nowhere else did I feel his loss so profoundly while still receiving the strongest reassurances that he was with us. I smiled in instant recognition of his gift with every occurrence. I couldn't hug him, but I walked through that smell and felt I passed right through him.

July 26, 2011:

It was one year ago on this day I experienced a personal miracle that has changed my life yet again. If this past year was a dream, please don't ever wake me up unless we can travel back in time before the accident and return to the lives we had. On this day I spent a lot of time reviewing the last year, and I was astounded by the experiences and growth I had achieved, and I wanted to talk to Carter about this.

CH: I love you Carter, this is the anniversary of the first time we connected through writing.

C: And I love you Mom, ditto. It has been quite a year for you, hasn't it? A whole range of emotions, experiences, emotional struggles, good, bad, earth shaking and solemn and this is true for us to a certain extent, but nothing like what you have endured and coped with. Your life has more than shifted and the focus and logic in life has changed. It is an understatement; words really can't do it justice or explain the depth of change from everything. Beginning with how you walk through each day and your thought process, to your awareness, tolerance and patience toward life. Then at the extreme end of the change is Grandpa and me. We sit within your constant focus like two stone statues, unmovable yet unbelievable in our absolute presence. Though we are not in sight we are now a constant within your sight and that awareness that we are walking through your life with you, guiding you, loving you, supporting you so you can learn to reach beyond the beliefs you held as truth.

To a certain truth, your life as you lived is shattered and being put back together with a different shape or look than before. It is still your life, all the pieces of the broken glass are ALL still there but they are being put back together complete yet very different. We are still part of the view you look out at your life through, that hasn't changed has it Mom. The composure of the view has changed though.

While we were writing this last paragraph I was given images of a stained glass window being rebuilt with all the original pieces of vivid and lucid glass. It is a lovely image for me to call on to remind me that Carter and Dad are still with me, but their position from the original picture has shifted.

CH: Do you remember your first writing to me, what you were thinking, feeling? If you can remember it I would like to know.

C: Yes of course I remember it. It is a huge event I won't forget. We had been hoping to lead you to me, us. You were growing so accepting of my continued life and becoming so much more aware of us around you. You were asking for more connection. I tried so hard to make you think correctly as I was moving your arms and hands, my presence felt within your hand. I always focused more on awareness within your left hand. I brought you other awareness's of me also but it was in your left hand steadily in the hope at some point you would pick up a pen and try. [I had never thought of this. I had always thought it was because the left hand has a closer connection to the heart, but I am left-handed.]

The anniversary of the accident was fast approaching. Yes, 4:30 a.m. was the perfect time; your mind was between awake and sleep. My thoughts and Grandpa's pouring into you in the hope of some of them being accepted into your thoughts. Come on Mom, I would think when moving your arms and hand, COME ON MOM think, pay attention AND THINK! Finally in the quiet rest of mid evening our thoughts and yours collided I would say and then of course I needed to try to write. A new experience and a difficult one really for both of us but love and willpower drove us forward to success and at this point what spectacular success. We all look forward to the future we go into together with love and joy. I love you, Grandpa loves you all too xxxx.

This was wonderful; we had never talked about that night, how incredible to hear his perspective. Apparently, he had been as challenged and excited as I was. To revisit that evening with the only other people who experienced it was joyful, bringing me back and enriching each moment as I blended their thoughts with mine. I could never convey in words how I felt when I told people how this writing first happened, and now for the first time I was able to share my experience with all the thrills and wonder that it held for me. This sense of happiness carried me to the heights of the emotional roller coaster, but like all coaster rides, the drop was coming, and it was three days away.

As the third anniversary of Carter's death approached, I thought I was better prepared to face it, strengthened by a year of Carter's writings to me, but my human condition kept getting in my way. I was totally confident that what I had learned and experienced was true, and most importantly that my son lived and was with me, yet somehow doubt still crept into my mind and I questioned the validity of what I was doing. *How can any of this be real? I must be making it all up*. Once again, my grief was hard to contain as I felt my family's pain and sorrow, and I struggled to choose the right words and actions to try to help them.

Over the past three years, I had come to realize that each person dealt with grief differently. At first, I couldn't believe that others wouldn't be as excited as I was with each tidbit of hope I found. Nor could I understand how these thoughts made some people feel much worse. How could the possibility that Carter might be letting us know that he was okay make anyone feel worse? But it did. I struggled with this for years, but for the sake of my relationships and sanity I had to learn to accept each person's differences; it didn't help anybody, especially myself, if I was hurt by others' opinions of what I thought. I couldn't see anything but good coming from what I was experiencing, but I had to learn it didn't mean that would be how others would see it. I had come to accept that there wasn't a right or wrong way to cope with grief but I do feel it's important that each family member was allowed to meet their own needs through the process. Grief is very hard work and people need to do what is right for them as long as it's considerate and not harmful. I do believe over time that Carter's strength and love will help each of us in our own way.

I tried to focus on good thoughts to carry me through difficult times, which others can find upsetting. I felt Carter had faithfully made an immense effort to help us: "we can't change what's happened, so let's try to find some peace in the blessings we've been given," but it once again became an impossible state of mind to retain through the anniversary of his death, and the day became an awful ordeal for us all.

As soon as I woke on July 29 I sat to write, and both Dad and Carter spoke in a unified voice on this very difficult day. Dad was still as he always was, sure and steady. He didn't speak often, so it carried a lot of value for me when he did. Their message spoke of meaning for not only the time we had together, but also for our time now and into the future. Over the next few days, Carter's writings to me felt like letters from home to a soldier on the front lines. He wrote them with an emotional resolve to span the distance between us that gave me strength and fortitude to continue to face the battle.

The Spirit Within

Love you mom. You need to stay focused on us, the importance of each day there. Let your spirit guide you, don't be lost within the human mind, the physical mind. See yourself in spirit today as you walk through the day. See the day through the spiritual vision; try to work on tolerance and peace. Remember others' issues, problems, attitudes, and reflect them away from you. Try to protect your physical body from them, it will pull you down. You must keep strong within spirit; the physical doesn't have the endurance that spirit can find. Think positive, cocoon yourself within the goodness of the light and ease the struggles and burdens of the day. Visually put our love around and within you let us give you strength, we are here to help you. (Carter, writing received August 1, 2011)

Though I was emotionally weakened, this writing three days later began with a helpful reminder to get me through the day, it also added to my growing chest of tools for the "job." I closed my eyes and spent the next few minutes focusing on these ideas. It was amazing to see how they worked to serve their intended purpose, and I opened my eyes with renewed vigour for the day ahead. Feeling energetic, I put forward a question for Carter. I was not expecting this much content in the answer to what I thought was a simple question, and by the end, I was tired from holding my focus for so long.

CH: Carter, Garn has given me another question to ask you. "Is love what we call the spirit in us?"

C: No, love can fill the spirit, lift and carry it but they are very different things. The spirit or soul, the essence of you in a form of energy, a living energy that exists and cannot be destroyed, is like a source spark that gives us the ability, drive and sustenance for what is needed by us. Love is separate from our energy of essence but still a force also created by the creator for our journey and to help and enable our process of journey. It is a guide and tool, a processor, enabler, strengthener and focus to lead us to our ultimate goal of oneness to the source. All energy has flowed outward from the source and will flow back to the source. All water flows constantly, is unstoppable, unending its existence, can change as ours can change. It can be water, change to vapours, steam, clouds, fog, ice, water but within any form it is still the same. Visually to the human eye it looks completely different. Is unrecognizable really, who could with only your visual see the cloud in the sky and the water in the lake are identical in their core essence. Their creation of form, the molecules $H2O$, like a chameleon it changes completely, unrecognizably. Yet it is really exactly the same, its essence, that which makes it, it is still exactly the same. Hold this visual now in the understanding of us, you the human being, the form within your world of spirit. Visually we look completely different in body than only in spirit. We are unrecognizably changed, altered differently to the human eye. Those who don't believe or are not interested, they see what they see, the human body, and see that to be the truth, but it is that same component of core essence. We are still there exactly as we always have been and will be. We change absolutely visibly to you, yet we are truly unchangeable. The form takes on a different look, water to clouds yet our composition is still there completely and unalterably intact, unchangeable. Sorry Garn, I got away from the question but still an important awareness of this understanding. No love is not you, love helps you, guides you, encourages you, drives you forward, fills existence with purpose and happiness but it is not your spirit. You can and should fill your spirit with love. But the essence of you, your spirit the energy which carries your existence is different but affected by love.

If at this point before our ultimate unification in oneness if we were love, if our spirit was love and our entire being filled with and consisting of true love, if the spirit was now that, then that would mean every living person, since they are all spirit within form would be love. Think about this. Mom is seeing and knowing this understanding now before it is put to pen! Yes Mom?

CH: Yes. (I feel our "minds" are linked today at some different level than usual. This answer comes to me in an instant and complete thought before the physical message comes onto the page.)

C: If our spirit in you WAS love there would be no need to strive where I am because we in spirit would already be filled and exist in pure love. There would be no need to come into form for growth, our growth would be complete. And if we were love but still came to form, your world would be a very different and perfect place. Because if a spirit within each form was love they would not argue, fight, steal, judge, kill, be cruel, fight wars, be territorial or hurtful. If we now were love and came into earth's existence none of this would be, because a person filled with love couldn't or wouldn't exist the way so many in form do. If we were love [our spirit] within form we would live our days with joy, happiness and understanding for each moment, person and thing within our existence. Life there is far from that but within our purpose this is the aim. Love will bring us toward our ultimate goal. And when our spirits are filled with and become love all moments of all life will be beyond belief. It is for people to understand as they progress of this bigger picture, this knowledge of understanding of the real truth, the true reality. Step away from your individual daily petty problems and see us within a framework of one. The drive, the focus changes in your life. But people must grow in their spirit and be more open to this reality. Knowledge is being brought to you all by many others, not just me through Mom. But many others also in different ways are touched by spirit because for many reasons they are open to us. Humans need to close their thoughts and focus to THEIR thoughts and be open-minded, still and peaceful. Many, many could then become aware of life's true meaning and the knowledge that surpasses that life. Bit of a sermon I feel today but this is truly SO IMPORTANT. People need to be loving, happy, kind even without any knowledge or acceptance of my world, our continued existence. To live like this would propel us all forward.

I agree this message was a bit of a sermon. I hope you find it easy to comprehend, and step away from it changed, if only ever so slightly, in your thoughts. I was thankful that Garn asked questions I wouldn't think to ask. Each time he asked a question, I thought I knew the answer, but boy, was I wrong. I had a lot to learn!

Living once again through the pain of July 29 had taken a big toll emotionally on my family. I needed to put aside the journals for a while and concentrate on our recovery. One long week later I reconnected with Carter, it was obvious to me by his reply that he knew how worried and frustrated I had been because I hadn't found time to talk with him.

August 7, 2011:
7:00 a.m.

C: Love you Mom.

CH: I'm sorry I haven't been able to write with you for a few days.

C: That's okay Mom our connection is strong. What is most important on those days is for you to try to stay focused on keeping your mind calm and undisturbed. Allow it to stay restful during that work and do the task then it is easier to step back to this. It is when your mind is burdened this connection becomes harder. Don't worry Mom; keep focused that we're with you through it all every day. We're right beside you when you want us always, take strength in that. Picture us with you; these words aren't necessary each day.

That was exactly what I needed to hear. I felt more at ease than I had for weeks, reassured once again as I continued our writing that day with a question for Carter from my friend. It was such a pleasure to be less guarded about what I said when talking with the few people I had told about the connection between Carter and me. To my delight, my friends seemed to be getting more comfortable with this and they had begun to ask questions, hoping Carter would answer them. What was most thrilling to me was their acknowledgment through these questions of his continued existence. I was able to speak to these people of not only my girls, but all three of my children again in the present. I had regained (with only a few people for now) what I thought I had lost forever.

CH: Carter, Shari has a question for you. The morning after your accident, she heard on the TV news that a boy from our town had been killed in a car crash. Instantly she felt she had to come over to our cottage; she said it was like she was propelled, there was not a moment's hesitation on her part. Her husband and Mom told her not to go, that it might not be Carter. She told them she had to leave right now; she knew it was urgent for her to come to us. Now in hindsight, she was wondering if this was her reaction or did you have something to do with it?

C: No not me Mom.

The pen dropped from my hand. This wasn't the answer I was expecting. Especially because Shari knew how she felt at the time, and with all I had shared with her about Carter, she was now really questioning it. I sat motionless, confused and surprised by his answer. She felt very strongly that it must have been Carter but he says no. Could there be another answer? I didn't know what to think. I tried to open my mind, then suddenly I thought—if it wasn't Carter, could it have been my father? I didn't even consider that Dad might not be with me at that moment, I simply assumed he was with me as I picked up the pen and asked.

CH: Dad, did you do this?

DAD: Yes, I did Charmie, it was me. I needed to help Mary [my mom], I couldn't risk her being all alone and hearing this. Your thoughts in the car at the accident scene were to call Shari, to let her get the best help at the hospital for Carter. It was your thoughts toward Shari that brought that connection to my thoughts. This was the person who could reach out to Mary possibly. These thoughts are well within Shari's knowledge. I gave her a bit of a nudge when she got there to make sure she did think of it, but she probably would have anyway. It wasn't within your capabilities of thought at that time and I couldn't have reached you probably. So, of course, I knew she was the person best suited for the task.

CH: How did you get her to come over to our cottage?

DAD: Well really her reaction would be to come to you all. What I did was give her a big boost, put the thoughts—go NOW. NOW!! GO! Very simple, easy thoughts repeatedly into her mind and I kept reinforcing them so others couldn't dissuade her. She knew she wanted to go; I gave her the drive, the commitment beyond caution to GO. So in a way she propelled herself with the strength of my direction. So it was your focus toward Shari that brought her to my thoughts to protect Mary. You were together but she is too frail to hear this alone. These are impossible hurdles at the very least. Thank Shari please for me Charm.

CH: At this point, with all I am learning, Shari and I thought it might have been Carter.

DAD: No, he was okay and with me, but at the crash scene I was supporting and loving him and able to also focus on you. It took him a little bit to readjust, but he was aware, a little confused for a little bit not long, was up and functioning quickly.

My gaze rose from the written page to the lake and its distant shore. Far beyond questions, my mind was transfixed on that moment and awestruck by the power of love.

August 7, 2011.
5:00 p.m.

I spent the rest of the day getting very little accomplished, as my thoughts were transfixed on the morning's writing. I felt I needed to connect with them again, late in the afternoon, while in meditation before writing, I saw images of the three of us (Dad, Carter and myself) merging together as close as we could into one single beam of light. Enhanced by this feeling of togetherness I sat to write with Carter.

C: Love you Mom.

Let us focus on conviction, strength and unity. Visually join all three of us as one within your space, our space, let all three energies join and merge. Let your energy of source rise above and around your body and ask for your energy to merge with ours. Stop and practice this, feel this experience.

I stopped writing and attempted this; it was almost what I had been doing in meditation prior to writing, so I believed they put those thoughts in my head!

C: It is a great visual for our united energy and this would be good to do when you need a greater effort for success.

August 8, 2011:

Once again today they patiently tried to encourage me to help others.

C and DAD: Love you Mom, Hi Charm.

CH: It's BOTH of you today, how wonderful; good morning, I love you both.

C and DAD: We love you.

CH: I felt Dad in my left hand and then you Carter, so I didn't know who was going to write today.

C and DAD: Yes we are both here, of course you know Grandpa is always with you right Mom?

CH: Yes. (I feel it is both Carter and Dads thoughts but spoken by Carter.)

C: Let us start with a nudge toward the path, the written words, share them and guide others. It is a sometimes slower journey of time and acceptance. Sometimes an instant belief is only for those in such pain or if they have already been struggling toward us. For others without the urgent needs in this life's struggles to reach to this truth they need time and space to let it sink in, question, process and hopefully ultimately believe the truth you can give. But time and thought will allow for a true acceptance if it comes. Be patient, kind and open for others, you are doing a good job with this but you want them to believe you, of course Mom. This won't always happen or may take time. Remember there is no rush ultimately whatever growth people have is just part of a very long process. So be open and available for people and our path but also make sure you also enjoy your time within that life. You are blessed to be eased of your pain, your burden, enjoy each day and others around you will be absorbed into your enjoyment.

CH: Carter, that last part describes you and how others loved to be with you!

C: Yes it is that pleasure in the moment, the event, the time on your own or shared the realization that all moments can be special. Follow your heart, think positive happy thoughts. Your smile brings a smile to another person's face they are given joy of that moment of your smile. Any burden is diminished even for a moment. To make another person smile brings joy back to you, another reason for another smile. Your joy sent out through a simple smile or laugh is returned to you in the form of a smile also, which gives you happiness and your smile continues and broadens a thing of really extreme simplicity that gives a truly big gift to others and is returned to you. You do not need greatness or to do great things to find greatness in that human existence. Greatness is as simple and perfect as a smile. Don't worry or push too hard, this path will unfold. We believe in your focus and will for our purpose. Work on enjoying each day, it is a gift to you if you enjoy it and glow outward it is all part of your journey.

Their advice was great, but even after years of acceptance and growth on my part; I struggled with doubts, especially about myself. How would I ever find a way to accomplish even a fraction of what they hoped for? I benefited at these times of doubt by reading their writings again. I'm also thankful for the infinite trust and patience they showed me in my continual lack of confidence and my reluctance to attempt most of what they guided me to do to help others.

August 13, 2011:

By now I spent a lot of my time trying to figure out how I could turn what I was learning into a meaningful future for myself and others, but I felt I wasn't making any real progress. I knew grief was an awkward subject, and many people didn't know what to say to me so they avoided any talk of death, but Carter's loss was in my life every moment of every day. Death was always part of my life now; I wanted to talk about it and I wanted to talk past death to the life beyond. I worried constantly about what I should say to whom about my experiences with Carter, while the myriad of others' issues added to my stress. This was compounded by my all-consuming desire to find a way forward, and my lack of time to do so. I must have been wasting a lot of time and emotions on this lately because that morning Carter was trying to reign in my thoughts.

C: Love you Mom. Love you all.

It is the journey each day we step through; see it as a unit, the struggle, the journey of that life seen only through that day. Try not to worry about what may or may not ever happen. This day exists, this moment counts, flow through the day, allow its path to shift and alter constantly as the day progresses. Be kind, helpful, loving, touch others' days. Try to relax away from the trivial daily issues of form and rise to experience each day for the gift it is. It will begin, it will end, that is certain in one way or another, make it count in ways that truly matter. All other pursuits of the day fall behind this in importance for both you as you give and allow yourself to have joy in the day and to the others you touch with joy and love xxx.

August 18, 2011:

Sometimes the information Carter and Dad gave me was so unexpected that it wasn't till days later I could begin to absorb what they had said, and my questions were not thought of until much later. It is wonderful to be able to go back to the subjects and continue the conversations with them.

C: Love you Mom.

I knew that I had connected with Carter, but something had been on my mind from my last talk with Dad and I hoped he would step forward. Once again, without thinking, I spoke to him, taking for granted that he was with me and could hear me.

CH: Dad, I have a question for you. In your writing on August 7, 2011, you said that it was my thoughts of Shari that brought her to your thoughts. But how did you find her? How were you able to find out where she was so you could get to her and have her come over to us?

DAD: Hi Charm, I love you

CH: Hi Dad, I love you.

DAD: Ok it's really quite simple, your thoughts towards Shari, of Shari helping you, those thoughts in your mind I can easily access and know. It was the need to help and our love that gives me this ability to know those thoughts of yours and really to find Shari. As you there see it, I only had to focus and put my thoughts toward Shari. The Shari I knew you were thinking of for help. I put my thoughts to go to be where this Shari is. It is as simple as that. My thought was to bring me to Shari to help you and I am there. I don't have to search her out or find her. I would have no time for this. The need to do this is for others' good, to help, and I am where I need to be. As you may be able to imagine the frantic (in your world's description) pace during these events we must work through. Luckily, I am able to be in numerous places doing various tasks at once, and in this case, it was essential. Trying to do what I can to help my loved ones there and Carter here. He, of course, was my biggest focus for a while, but I also had to reach back to all of you. It is very tiring and would be difficult at my level to maintain for great lengths of time, but of course, you push yourself to do the very best you can in difficult circumstances. So really once I was aware of your thoughts of Shari, I just brought my thought to be with Shari and I was. We go where we want to be, a thought and we're there. The more difficult task was the urgency to be with many under such agonizing, emotional pain and try to reach out to them and also be completely aware of Carter's needs and support him. It was a very difficult struggle on both sides during difficult times. I tried my best for all of you.

CH: Thank you Dad, though I can't imagine all you did, I'm sure it was wonderful and done with pure love from you. Thank you for being there for Carter, when I heard you say for the first time through the medium that "you lifted him out," it gave me such comfort to know he was never alone, frightened, or confused. You were right there with him to help and support him and explain what was happening.

DAD: Yes, of course. Don't worry about that, he wasn't alone ever, even for a moment. Others were here too, but it was my task to take the lead and get and guide him. We love you all.

I don't think the words exist to capture how that last statement from Dad made me feel. As a bereaved parent I had ached to know this. No matter the circumstances of death, I'm sure we all struggle with the same unknowns; were our loved ones frightened or alone? These questions could haunt us for years. My search had not only given me the answer to my original question of whether my son still existed. My search had given me answers to questions that couldn't be answered by anyone here. I felt blessed; my journey had erased a worry I believed would weigh me down for the rest of my life.

August 19, 2011:
C: Love you Mom.

CH: I love you xx. Garn has a question. (Garn is sitting right beside me, so I instruct him to ask Carter the question himself and he does this out loud.)

GARN: Carter, would you give me two or three things that I should do before I come to visit you?

C: Okay well first you won't be coming to visit me, you will be returning home after your visit within form. There is nothing there that has to be done really. Try to enjoy the moments within each day and the people who you encounter in a good way. Let them know they matter to you and let them leave you feeling upbeat, lifted, better for having spent time in your presence than before they were with you. They don't even have to be aware of it really but you will have shared that time with them in a way that matters for all of you, and be ready at any moment—not just as you get older—to step away from that life. So much that seems to matter there has no importance once you step away from it. Even your sense of your own importance in your achievements, abilities, status, you see how meaningless, trivial that so much thought, judgment of others' lives against your own has been a waste of time and energy. For we are not different, we are all one, to judge others is to ultimately judge yourself as we are all part of the same oneness. As others falter, struggle, it slows the growth of the all to reach purity and joy. So all you need to do whatever your personal struggles or goals, is within your personal choices and days go through them with love, kindness and joy for yourself and others.

Garn was sincerely asking the question, as health issues and age was drawing his attention to completing his life. The answer was an important message we could all learn from, no matter what our beliefs or lives are like. I think it puts all our egos in check, and although this was not normally how we thought, I couldn't disagree with the wisdom, can you?

Shari had spoken to me about a concern she had for Olivia. She said she saw how distressed Olivia had looked the day before as she watched her friend play with her brothers, and told me Olivia might want to talk about it. I was thankful for the heads up; you always want to do what's best for your children, but hearing this story first from Olivia would have brought me to tears, and therefore I would have been little help to her. As it turned out I had it easy, she told me what she was feeling when she saw her friend with her brothers, but she didn't want my thoughts, Olivia wanted to talk to Carter about it! A bit startled by that I said we should see what he says.

O: Hi Carter, good morning!

C: Hey LivLou, how's it going?

O: It's been really hard lately. I really miss it; miss you, brother and sister playing. It's hard for me to see that with others and not be sad.

C: I know Liv it is hard, I see, know your struggles all of them. This pain I can't take away, I wish I could. It makes what we shared precious and no one can take it away from either of us. We had so many wonderful shared times there. Some never within a very long life have a fraction of what you and I had, our love bond stays strong. Now when this is happening and you struggle, focus on your love for me and call for me within this love. Then know, REALLY KNOW WITH ABSOLUTE CERTAINTY I am standing right with you. Try to feel my love and if you picture in your mind's eye us two together, then try to smile as I will be smiling to be with you. Try to see it as not such a sad thing but see it maybe as a reminder of us and our moments of joy playing and hope they can feel the same happiness we felt in our times together. Wish them well in their journey together there and try to focus on the fact that our journey hasn't ended, we are together and share a love that is eternal and know I walk through your life always and I enjoy every moment of joy you have. It is not easy but let our shared love help carry you over your hurdles xxx.

O: I love you Carter (Olivia does her handshake with Carter).

C: Nice Liv Lou, you too.

I was deeply moved; there was nothing I could have said that could come close to this. Olivia's pain was centred on her loss of being with Carter, but he put himself right beside her in the present and on into her future. The words he chose the flow and imagery within his writing that she can replay in her mind as often as needed, and with this knowledge know he is there whenever she asks for him I was so touched by how it instantly helped her state of mind and I thanked him in our writing the next day.

August 20, 2011

C: Love you Mom, good morning.

CH: Thank you for helping Olivia yesterday. Your words are wonderful and so helpful; it gives her something to hold onto.

C: Yes I love to talk to Olivia, would like her to think of it more often, then it would be as it is for you, a reinforcement of my presence in your lives daily, a moment that gives a continued purpose, gift of life. To imbed in her mind we are still going through this part of our journey together, absolutely still together with love, just different. As life continues to change and shift there also, people grow, change, move into different paths and purposes through their lives but the bond of love is still there, same as it is now with me. When I was in Arizona working or Florida playing, both times with my friends and both times with different people, but I was having a great time, wonderful experiences away from Olivia. But my love and enjoyment of her didn't diminish or stop during those separations until I returned and it began again. No, my love and thoughts were still there during those brief separations. When I'd talk to her on the phone or the computer it was wonderful. Through only words without our physical bodies being together, it was the connection of words that brought her and me joy in that connection. Love flowed, our hearts were lifted to join only in the mind but though she missed me she always knew I'd be back soon. The words through voice or letters made her happy and she happily went through her day.

Try both of you (all really) to see this put into this separation of ours. Yes, we are physically separated but not permanently, never will we together end. Though it is probably a very much longer separation in your world than the trips were, it is still only a separation with us reuniting again in the future. You have the miraculous ability to speak to me every day. You have my voice, my words we share within words, our thoughts, joys, moments and struggles. It can be thought of as the same as my trip and really very much is but I know not to all of you. Though I am with others experiencing different things in my life than you, our bond still holds strong. Hold tight to our connection in words and see the journey beyond this life span to the eternal view of our journey the time of separation takes on a very different look. And remember the path we three can walk down can help and reach to many for goodness and love. Help send your love to strengthen our spirit to reach these goals. You can still help me also. The strength of all your love given to Grandpa and me will help lift our spirits with joy. We still need each other and remember the written word, my voice, my love to you all. Let's enjoy our time together; it's just a temporary physical break, a longer road trip for me this time. You're still with the family waiting and receiving my calls and messages xxxx.

I had begun by thanking him, and instead of the obligatory "you're welcome," he had given us both a gift of healing within his loving perspective. Carter had always been great at putting a good spin on things. He explained things with a positive outlook and endlessly found resources to teach me lessons within the simple everyday occurrences of life. I kept thinking his wealth of wisdom would dry up, but it hadn't so far.

August 21, 2011:

For the third day in a row, Carter continued to expand on the same thought. He must have felt that it was very important for us to really understand and believe this; he rarely carried a talk on for this long.

C: Love you Mom.

Let's begin today with a focus on yesterday's words.

CH: Yes, alright.

C: Try to hold strong to this information, this truth. See us not as separate but together, we still are. I have not left any of you and continue to share times and events with you all, KNOW that I do. I am giving you information on a lot of important subjects, knowledge so important of the view I now hold and see. The knowledge within me that was not known by you before is now known and I am just giving you a way to think, to keep it within your conscious thoughts. So if you believe the info, and I know you do, then learn to believe and have an absolute belief beyond doubt or question that we are not apart, try to see as we do on the greater view. See our journey continue and see yourself as spirit within this temporary body. See yourself step in and out of it as you can Mom. It is only a temporary place of residence, a home to shelter you and provide for that time there but when you step outside that home it is still you as you walk out the front door, you are only outside that place of shelter. It must be looked after, maintained, enjoyed, it is very special and makes you feel good but ultimately it is only a place you live in for a while. It is not who you are. You existed separate from this home before you lived in this house, it is your place of shelter and comfort when within it, a place to enjoy friends, growth, rest and struggles but essentially not the true you. Learn to see this truth, enjoy and grow in your time there but let your mind hold its thoughts of our journey, all of us continual and together. Try not to be so sad by our physical separation. Learn and reach through the pain to the joy beyond. Rejoice in our reconnection, the joining of two different realities to your gift of knowledge of the one true reality. We together Mom, what we can do is miraculous. Be happy for all in what even little steps we may be able to take for the good of the all toward one. See it from your view of your essence, how wonderful this can be even though it is through great sadness xxx.

This was one of the many writings I often returned to when grief drained my strength to face life without him. I tried not to let myself spiral too far down into sadness. I tried to stay positive and cheerful for myself and others. I used the words I knew were from him to reinforce my courage and will to move forward. He had become my most meaningful teacher, and the lessons he had taught me far outshone anything I had learned so far. He was giving me a way to face anything life threw at me, and trust its purpose. Growth and love could always be found if I looked for them.

I often pictured him right beside me, as he had repeatedly taught me to do. At any time, whether they were special moments or not, I would focus on all the love I had for him, and then pictured him with me. The more love I sent to him and the greater the detail I remembered him with, the stronger I could actually feel his presence with me. With great success, I used the ideas he gave me to strengthen my connection with the realm he now lived in, and I reminded myself to have faith in all I had learned. I also often reminded myself that I had worked as thoroughly and methodically as I knew how to convince myself of this. Carter continued to teach me things I didn't know, and when I tried them, they worked. If this knowledge wasn't coming from spirit, then where was it coming from? I must believe as he said in the above writing that he was with me because all avenues of discovery had repeatedly brought me to trust that this was true. I admit some of this was always going to need an element of faith, not blind faith, but faith in what I had conclusively found to be true and faith that the components he spoke of that I had yet to prove to myself would also be true. Faith is believing in what you can't prove.

All summers end too soon. This was a statement I never thought I would ever feel again, but it was surprisingly how I felt this year. I had unrealistically high hopes for this summer, but in my defense, after last summer I don't see how I couldn't! Not once this summer did I feel my head was going to explode. I'd settled down during the past year and this summer was more serene, but in hindsight, growth did occur for me. I was still optimistic about one or two startling occurrences though, so I asked Carter to help me make strides in the short time that remained for me at the lake.

August 22, 2011:

C: Love you Mom.

CH: I love you Carter xx. What should I work on in my remaining time at the cottage?

C: It is up to you, of course, do make sure you also enjoy being there, be still, quiet, and at peace. Truly bring your thoughts to this place, you being here, its beauty and vitality, let it strengthen you in body, mind, and spirit. Let others also find this peace and enjoyment within this time. Hold tight to the time of unencumbered days enjoyed together. Seize each moment and carry the moments forward with you. You are progressing Mom, Grandpa and I are very happy with your progress. Remember to blend each world into your day with joy and peace, we love you all xxx.

His answer was, of course, perfect for me, but it wasn't to my satisfaction. I knew what type of answer I wanted to hear, but he gave me what I needed to hear. I had to reread it several times before I finally let go of my ideas so I could be open to hear his. He wanted me to enjoy and embrace the cottage, family, and friends, and find strength and peace. To be present and at ease in the days remaining, and he wanted me to know this was what they were hoping for. The pressure to achieve that I put on myself and Carter finally eased as I accepted I had worked to task with heartfelt purpose for myself and others all summer and now they wanted me to enjoy the time that was left. By relinquishing my expectations, I was able to look back and see how much I had learned, but as you can see by the date of the next writing, it took me over a week to truly let my hopes go.

August 29, 2011:

C: Love you Mom.

CH: I love you both. Though I had hoped for more growth this summer, unfortunately, I didn't have the time I would have liked to spend trying to improve my development. I think the most important thing that I will take with me from this summer at the cottage are the powerful and unbelievable writings from both of you and the clarity of mind to have received them.

C: Yes, hold onto them and continue to reread them. The knowledge and picture being painted for you all is important. You are doing well hearing us and walking forward with a continual heightened awareness of the impermanence and importance of your life there but also on the permanence of all, of us being with you, our continued existence and life. A life of substance, joy, advancement, friendship, love, and richness, a richness in the true meaning of what that word can mean. Our life now is richer than any experience in form but remember that life too can be much richer when lived with love, joy, kindness, and awareness of life's purpose. Those that truly enjoy life there will enjoy it more here and vice versa. Let it flow, bumpy roads or smooth, nothing lasts, you drive beyond it into the horizon where the glow of morning's sunrise warms and envelops you. Walk through your days viewing

Grandpa, you and me together, not apart. Our love and presence, our shared joy of being together in a truly wondrous task and journey, our spirits, us three walking together with combined strength of purpose xxx.

August 30, 2011:

Today I asked a question I had been meaning to ask for a while.

C: Love you Mom.

CH: I love you xx. On Mother's Day when Cam called to thank me for the book we gave him on your birthday, was this timing just a coincidence or did you have something to do with it? The timing of that phone call was perfect for me. I was so glad to hear one of your friends' voices, because I was missing you so much.

C: Yes that was me. It was my message, my signal to you on Mother's Day. Yes, I was with you all, we both were (Grandpa and I) but most importantly for you on Mother's Day. I was there at the dining room table with you sending, giving you all my love and for Grandma too, my love to the mothers there and to share in the joy of the day and event with the family, my loved ones. Your family was complete and sharing the day with you. I had been with Camy Boi a bit, knew his mom had been telling him to call you and of course Cam wanted to call you, but I had been putting thoughts in his head or distracting thoughts. Thought I might be able to use that call that was going to happen to suit my purposes also. Thanks Cam, thanks man, good one. Thumbs up for helping me out, read this to Cam Mom. It was timed perfectly, my gift to you from me brought to you by my buddy Cam. Happy Mother's Day Mom, I'm right here—told you.

See when the timing is so right with me anyway you can just about count on it now not being a coincidence. Love you Mom xx.

Soaring on the Wings of Angels

Love you Mom [I love you Carter]. Yes the love that holds us together like "Superheroes," our link is forged in the iron steel of love and time; space or place of being shall not separate us from our forged link. Okay so now we're being so "Hollywood," so "Superheroes" today. But in these created worlds of fantasy that is the battle of good and evil and shows how maybe one person can make a difference. Okay so people don't have these amazing skills—they can't fly or have x-ray vision etc., but one person within their effort can make a difference. And the truth is—that is the march through time, one person, each and every one will rise to goodness. To become better to "see" with greater vision, "hear" with super clarity, have the inner strength (not physical) of a Superman. People can reach into themselves and find the POWER to be greater than they are daily seen to be. Daily they are mild-mannered Clark Kent's but take off the cloak of average person—change and let their spirit be their attire and their focus—and their ability and selflessness comes to be seen by others. We are all "Clark Kent's," we can all be SUPERMEN! Comic book heroes are fun, enter-taining and often seen as childish reading but as human beings striving to reach beyond how we go through our days they are trying to help with strengths not usually visible. We all have such strengths, such compassion and selflessness that we could reach and learn to use as our superpowers. A tiny spark can ignite a great flame, our spirit is the spark of life that we eternally exist within—ignite it while in form and see the great flame. Your spirit is your superpower, let it be seen and appreciated and watch what YOU CAN DO! (Carter, writing received December 30, 2012.)

As my last day at the cottage that summer began I decided to enjoy the fresh air, so I sat outside on the deck to write with Carter, which I rarely did. To my delight, I received an unexpected gift from Carter, with nature's help.

August 31, 2011:

CH: I love you both; our summer here at the cottage has ended. We are picking up Victoria from her summer job and going home today. As I began to write this to you, a hummingbird hovered about a foot above the deck railing, only ten or twelve inches away from my face. Startled, I watched as it lingered for quite a while!

C: Love you Mom, I am right beside you. Yes, the hummingbird was my end of summer gift to you. A gift not of anything ended, my life with you, the summer at the cottage it doesn't truly end, these people and places of importance to the joy and completeness of your life. The hummingbird flies to you as you sit to begin to write with me for the last summer writing at the lake. You haven't had a hummingbird fly this close to you all summer, have you Mom?

CH: No, nowhere near me at all actually!

C: So you know again it is the event and the timing, like our talk yesterday, these are gifts from me. This gift is from Grandpa and me today. We haven't left you, we are very much right with you. The cottage you never truly leave it, yes you may be physically apart as we are physically apart, but you carry us and our lake within your heart. That love, contentment, peace, and joy how it enriches your life, you carry with you out into the busy world. What you have learned this summer, our lessons, your growth and awareness has advanced through the summer in very important ways. You now are grasping not just that our lives continue past form, not just that we have purpose and strive for love and goodness. Your mind during this summer has heard and absorbed our lessons of oneness, unity, of how we are one but within the greater one. This is the important progress you made this summer, a clearer awareness, another awakening to the importance and truth of all journeys.

Hold the visual of the hummingbird above the edge of the railing as we sit to write at the end of summer. I can reach into the mind of this fragile, beautiful creature; I am guiding its movements to help you. I am right here Mom, we can guide others over difficult days with purpose and goodness.

The hummingbird brings my gift of love, our gift of love, a physical gift of our, my continued presence and journey in your life. We love you all.

What a perfect way to end the summer under these less than perfect circumstances. I felt the warmth of the sun, looked out to the beauty of the lake, and felt a sense of tranquility encompass me. I had been frustrated with my lack of effort and growth this summer. I began with such enthusiasm after last summer. All year I had told myself through any setbacks or lack of focus, *wait until you get to the cottage and see what can happen there!* I didn't have the tumultuous events that took my breath away like last year, and I was disappointed. Like many of us, we often expect too much. As my mind lingered on Carter's overview of my summer, I saw the layer of richness they had added to my knowledge and life. I felt more content knowing Carter and Dad were happy with my growth that summer. I believed they had opened a new door for me and smiled as they watched me walk through it as they continued to broaden my horizons.

I returned to the city and all the demands that it brought back into my life, but I wouldn't torture myself with worry like I did last September. My view of life was radically different and worry vanished when I saw it from the perspective of universal oneness. Carter's writings to me over my first four days home were filled with reminders to keep my summer lessons front and centre in my mind and focus on what was important as I readjusted to the pace of city life.

Then on the fifth day, my dad spoke, and his message was infinitely more important to me than the words alone conveyed. He was acknowledging my years of unspeakable anguish and my effort in spite of this to find Carter. As a father, he had watched his child suffering and waited to see what, if anything, I was able to do with the knowledge that I had inherited through my loss of Carter. Could I gain clarity through grief's enforced stillness to open to a new way of thinking that wasn't possible in my old patterns of thought and behaviour? Could my progress into grief wake me up enough to crystallize my way of seeing, my way of being, to shift me away from old ideas to real insights into life? Could he and Carter help steer me to be more attentive so I could truly wake up to the interconnectedness of everything? Could my broken heart find a greater reason to strive and serve others with a greater reach through this expanded belief of love? Dad had been a constant source of love and strength for me, and he was proud of my effort and outcome. This gift of connecting to spirit through my search for Carter kept enriching my life in ways I could never have imagined! Below, I share Dad's message to me.

September 5, 2011:

C and DAD: Love you Mom, Hi Charm, love you too.

CH: Morning Carter, morning Dad, I love you both.

DAD: Let me say how happy and honoured I am to walk down this path with both you and Carter, and I am amazed, jubilant really, with the determination you showed, especially earlier on in fighting to reach toward us. To examine events, concentrate, and try to process thoughts that were beyond processing and accepting. To not let them go and release the possibility, but to hold tight to each piece and begin to put the puzzle together. To ardently hold onto each little, sometimes insignificant, piece until it too could be placed into the puzzle. You really don't much like puzzles usually, do you Charm? But you wouldn't be defeated by this one, or just release the process unfinished. Gradually, as each piece was fit to another, you began to be able to see what was being shown to you. A picture began to take shape. This picture HAD to be wrong, yet the pieces were coming together to without doubt form this picture. The pieces fit, it didn't make sense, this picture shouldn't be what is forming, but it absolutely was. Now you sit with the centre part of the puzzle complete, Carter and me in it and enlightened by light. This puzzle will never within your time there ever be completely finished. It will expand beyond your grasp within that life no matter how hard you work, but that is of no concern for you. With diligence and determination, you have and are doing an amazing job, keep it up xxxx.

September 10, 2011:

I was excited to return to the cottage for the weekend. On the first morning, our writing connection was strong, and it made me feel good all day. After dinner, I took the opportunity to write with Carter again. Here, surrounded by nature, the subtle energies of spirit and the solid world I live in blend more easily. As I began to meditate, I instantly felt Carter's energy in my hand; which was a really pleasant surprise as I connected to him effortlessly. I talked with him joyfully for the second time today, simply because I could. It was often still unbelievable to me that I was able to speak to Carter once again. They say that nobody beats death, which is true, but death hadn't beaten us either!

CH: Hi Carter you were here quick. I feel that as soon as I thought of you—you grabbed my hand.

C: Hi Mom, love you. Yes, amazing sometimes, so easy especially there [at the cottage] more than other places.

CH: What have you been doing lately? (At this moment I don't have any questions or worries, I'm just happy to be able to talk with him.)

C: I have lots to do, don't worry about me. Focusing a bit more on other tasks, enjoy being with those transitioning, bringing them forward into their readjustment of returning. This life here is and can be very full and rewarding without many of the daily struggles there. You can truly feel the love and joy, feel it within you, surrounding you, it is so much more evident not that love and joy don't truly exist there also but it is more subdued, not so wham!! in your face evident. Those of us who draw this love there and grow with it take this joy and are absorbed within it, the feeling is unbelievable. It lifts you, thrusts you forward with such true happiness. Yes in form I lived with joy with love with happiness and often was aware of and invigorated, lifted by the joy, love I felt but it is overshadowed, dwarfed completely by the joy you can feel here. You feel it within every part of your being—bliss! Learn to truly find and feel happiness and joy there, experience it and throw it back out to the world. Be in that state of mind, then when you arrive back here that feeling will be amplified to unbelievable levels. We, Grandpa and I are enjoying our time here very much; of course this is so helped by our connection to you and our helping ease your struggle of my parting xxx.

I could feel Carter's excitement as he wrote. Carter's enthusiasm helped me embrace the importance of this message. I had never heard a better reason to be happy. When Carter's heart stopped beating, my life lost most of its meaning, but I saw now it was then I could learn to live my life with more meaning. Grief had forged an immeasurable strength within me. Carter, like a phoenix rising from the ashes, allowed my life to rebloom. My spirit had soared and I felt more expansive, my life was meaningful and easier to negotiate now. I had needed to truly believe Carter did rise from the ashes of destruction before I could trust and understand what we as people have yet to prove.

For several weeks, I reminded myself daily of that writing, which helped me see problems in a better light. I was confronted about an issue at work one day that became much more heated than it should have been. I was able to state my thoughts while remaining calm and unemotional. I don't like conflict, so I was surprised that I spoke up for myself, yet wasn't upset by it. Carter was referring to this when we spoke the next day.

September 14, 2011:

C: Love you Mom.

Good work on your presence of mind. See, when issues arise at work like yesterday, within this state of mind you rise above it and float over it. You are not absorbed within its creation and tension, touched by all the silly negativity. In this state of mind Mom, you speak up for yourself yet you are unencumbered by it. It doesn't have any hold on you emotionally. This is so healthy for you, both for your physical form and your mental clarity for us together. You don't sit silent and say nothing yet the way you are handling these issues now Mom it is an amazing transformation in you. You see it, feel it, don't you?

CH: Yes, I truly do.

C: Good, it is because you are trying so hard to be mindful. To hold your mind clear and unburdened and see your life in form in a truer view. You listen to us so well; you are constantly thinking, progressing and reinforcing our words, pictures. It will become easier as it already is beginning to for you. It will become you, your beliefs and your awareness. Push out your light and let it shine outward, reach out with this love, it protects and energizes you and brings good energy to others within your presence. They can be touched unknowingly by it.

I could see the difference focusing on the bigger picture made, but like all of us and even with all my help from spirit, my human mind and ego wanted their way and won many battles. This was a challenge I would continue to work on, the more natural my connection to spirit becomes and the easier it is to tame my restless mind.

October 5, 2011:

Like all workplaces, the issues continued, and two days later my superior was upset during her lunch break as we sat together. Carter must have been at work with me because he knew of our conversation and wrote his message for her by name the next morning. I read it to her and then gave her the writing to keep. She thanked Carter, and couldn't believe that he would take the time to help her. It was wonderful for me to see him not be slowed by my failure to see opportunities and seize the chance to help others; he had done this several times recently. Today I thanked him, and his response was both selfless and self-serving: spirit thinks as "we," not "I." It is an altruistic answer, yet simple enough to understand—what we do for others can help them but ultimately also helps ourselves.

C: Love you Mom.

CH: I love you Carter, you're being so kind by helping others.

C: It's what we are meant to do and truly must do for us as a whole to progress. We must move forward with less focus on the one, the self, and focus on all, for we are all created by one, are part of the one in totality and must ultimately return to one. We are the sum and the pieces complete within ourselves but never totally complete until we reunite within one to become one with God and creation. Less individual units moving separately, but one unit moving in precision as one and seeing each of us and all things as one. We struggle against this and see our lives and struggles individually. We need to banish ego and understand true happiness without wanting, needing, outdoing others. Within contentment and love comes understanding and bliss. I am part of you; we do this for good and joined effort through love.

Our family had received an invitation to attend a special mass on All Souls' Day at the church where Carter's funeral had been held. We had been invited to this service for the last four year but had never attended. I was certain from the start there was no way I could be in a church full of grieving people. I would have been crushed under the weight of sadness. A church filled by people feeling all that sadness would have crippled me for days the first few years after Carter's death.

My life had radically changed over the past year, and I now felt ready to attend. Though we were not members of this church, they had been immensely supportive to us at the time and I wanted to think of a way to thank them.

One night while walking with Shannon I said, "I wonder if Carter could write something for the church service."

Right away Shannon said, "You can do this Charmaine, I know you can. Ask Carter, I'm sure the two of you can get something."

It was late and I was tired when I got home, but I felt there was no sense in putting this off. I went directly up to Carter's room, sat at his desk, and spoke to him about what I was thinking.

October 18, 2011:
10:00 p.m.

CH: Carter, the church where your funeral was is holding a special memorial mass on All Souls' Day. The church will be filled with people who have lost loved ones. I thought it would be nice to give them a writing of hope and encouragement. It would be given as a gift of thanks from our family for the church's kindness to us. Could you write something for me that they could read during the mass to touch those attending in a positive way?

His response was a prayer that flowed onto the page in one seamless thought, without pause. I knew as soon as it began with "let us pray," that my father was helping Carter create it for me. The prayer is meant to help those of us still in this earthly life, and is positive and uplifting. I have mentioned how some of the writings are created with a heavenly infusion within the knowledge; this prayer is a wonderful example of spirit's words and phrasing coalescing into perfection. Since I know the words are from those who have passed through death and now live in a spiritual realm, I believe the information about their loved ones are truth.

Prayer For All Souls' Day

Let us pray for our family members, friends, and loved ones whose human journey has ended. Pray for their spiritual growth to continue and be enhanced by the strength and love sent from within our prayers. Let them receive these prayers from our life and be lifted with joy for the love that transcends the life we see and understand and reaches with absolute surety to those who now live beyond this physical realm. Let us all here find the strength beyond our grief and sadness to truly believe that our loved ones have not left us, they have merely stepped out of our view. We are very much still in their view and journey. They do not leave us, but follow us still with love, support, and guidance, for love is the unending force that cannot be shattered or ended, and will hold all our loved ones close to us through life's struggles and joys. We haven't lost them; love, that greatest of God's gifts, connects us all still, a force beyond our human concept. Love flows from heaven to earth, and we send our love from earth to heaven. A river that never ends, it slows, it surges, it tumbles over rocks, crashes over waterfalls, and winds and bends. But our love here and there is unending. It can be the source and strength we need to let our grief open to the reality of all our loved ones' continued life and connection to us through love. Let us smile now as we remember the life, the moments shared with them, remember every moment counts, every smile and happy memory brings joy, and never doubt the power of love. Believe in the miracle of love.

October 26, 2011:

A few days later, I went to the church to offer them the prayer. I read it for the receptionist so she could understand my writing and type it. As I finished the reading, I raised my head to see tears in her eyes; she could only utter "WOW!" It took a few minutes for her to speak again and then she asked if I had written that. Not being completely honest, I told her that I had. It wasn't a lie because I did write the prayer; it just wasn't created by me. I chose to be selective in what I said because I didn't want to turn people off or challenge their beliefs. I simply wanted this prayer read to their congregation as a gift for their kindness. Unfortunately, the pastor said the order of service was set. I was disappointed, but I told him that it was a gift to his church and I hoped he would find a time to use it in the future. After feeling elated by the writing and thinking I had found a unique and valuable way to use what I could do now to help, I was now feeling lost once again. This prayer was eventually first read at my mother's funeral at the church my parents loved, supported, and were active members in, surrounded by family and loved ones. It turned out to be the perfect place for my father's voice to be heard once again. The next morning, I was glad to be able to talk more freely with Carter about the writing.

CH: I was invigorated by the church receptionist's reaction to your prayer. I looked up after reading it and tears filled her eyes as she sat momentarily speechless then said, WOW!

C: Yes that is good it was well received I'm glad. It is also the pace and pauses of your reading, the way you're framing the thoughts which is why I hope you get to say it at the service.

CH: When you give me the words, I seemed to understand very deeply the bigger thought and picture, and knew the paces and pauses to speak them, is this true?

C: It is probably the way my thoughts that you receive with the writing flow into your mind. The writing is mostly a constant flow if you're holding a clear mind for me, but the thoughts may be received with the emotional thrusts, pauses, and phrases I would like them said with. That is the way you're reading it. Though you're receiving it as thought from me, a single thought, I give it dual transference from there. You receive it, "hear it" in your mind to give this writing ease and fluidity, and I connect through your spirit as it sits within your conscious mind. Then I also help guide your hands, your hands don't tire quickly as they normally would as I also take the effort into me, the energy motion is also mine through you. So I give you both the thought and guide the motion of the writing. But now it is truly a joint effort and my struggle to bring these words to form is eased by our co-operation to use your form and mind and hand. I use your hand and mind for these gifts of thought.

Weight of the Burden

Love you Mom.

CH: Morning Carter, do you see how high the lake is this spring? The dock is underwater.

C: Yes, amazing visual Mom. I'm sure I could be having a lot of fun with that. Of course I'd end up wet and cold but it would be fun nonetheless!

CH: Yes, I'm sure you would.

Anyway Mom the submerged dock and the flooding along the land, this is the time of year when rains and melting snow pour into the lakes and rivers. There are times in all life cycles where so much is "dumped" onto us to deal with. We as humans are overpowered by life's issues, pressures, and emotions. They keep flowing at us, issue after issue until it is more than we can hold and we overflow our banks. You have unfortunately had years like this Mom. You were as our dock now visually sits, totally submerged by life, but you are still there; you see the dock visually present below the water. The pressures lower and change to release the dock back to the surface, to breathe freely once again, feel the air once again, to be released from the weight of the world on its chest and once again sit in the warmth of the light. Today the water is perfectly still though bearing down on the submerged dock. Yet the dock sits serenely still waiting to be released into the light. All journeys have pressures; all at some point re-emerge into the sun. Watch the water lower—see the dock rise and be of service once again—solid in its new foundations of steel just as you sit also—strong, steady, rising from the weight. Love you. (Carter, writing received May 3, 2013.)

November 1, 2011:

As I drove to work, I got a call from John saying he and Olivia had been in a car accident; he quickly assured me they were both fine before he passed the phone to Olivia. As soon as she heard my voice, she broke down in tears.

"I'm coming," I said, turning the car around. Panic overcame me; I couldn't believe that I was once again driving toward another accident scene involving my family. I struggled to take a breath as I approached the flashing lights and I was catapulted back to my worst nightmare, but within moments I saw them both standing outside the car, looking unharmed. Olivia ran to me and I breathed a sigh of relief. As we held tight to each other, I was sure I could feel Carter's arms wrap around us both. The vehicle was a write-off, and we were all horribly shaken as we were thrown back to the night of Carter's crash and all that hell poured into us once again. I felt totally helpless, realizing that there was nothing I could do to protect them. I couldn't always be with them to keep them safe and my guilt about not being there to protect Carter burst to the surface.

John and I had worked hard for me to be able to stay home once our children were born. I felt blessed that I could focus all my love and attention to my family. I believed all our lives were richer for this and I knew I nurtured and protected them, keeping my children safe and happy as they grew. I had returned to work after nineteen years, when Carter was in grade 12. It was a part-time job during the school season so our summers at the cottage wouldn't be affected. When Carter died, I felt that I had kept him safe for all those years, but I wasn't there to protect him when he needed me.

Once again the grief of losing Carter became raw and debilitating and I felt my family could all be gone and I had no control of this. Carter's writing during this time to me was supportive and encouraging as he struggled to help me recover mentally. I was grief-stricken not only because of the hell of always facing his death, but also the grief of losing my ability to protect those most precious to me. I now know that this is unrealistic thinking since any number of things can happen that we can't control.

We waited until John and Olivia were checked by the doctors and we could compose ourselves enough to tell Victoria and Mom. We didn't need them to struggle emotionally any more than could be helped. We were relieved that they could see both John and Olivia were okay as we told them.

For several weeks I felt that I was drowning, being dragged down by my out-of-control emotions and grief, but I was fortunate to be able to hear the support from Carter and Dad in spirit, and I will be eternally grateful. As you read the messages I have chosen during this time, I hope it can give you a glimpse of the loving help and guidance they gave me.

November 5, 2011:

C and DAD: Love you Mom xxxxx. Love you Charm xxx.

CH: I love both of you; I've had such a hard week! (This is an understatement, I am barely functioning.)

C: Yes of course you have, we know and have tried to help you but you can see the difference, the effort of struggles overcoming your mind and the difficulties that gives in our support reaching into you, the effects are diminished. We're glad you could physically still feel us. Of course Mom I was glad you knew, felt my presence when hugging Olivia. That was nice, helpful, full of love to both of you, but don't be afraid of life or lose your interest in it. This is just a bit of a setback for you and a scare for all of you, but Dad and Olivia are well. Life moves forward with hills and valleys, you need to rebuild your strength and focus for the trip, the view is to be enjoyed, the moments cherished.

I felt I must try to get something accomplished, so I reached back to yesterday's visit with a friend. She had asked me a question I couldn't answer, so I asked Carter. My heart wasn't really interested, I was so consumed by my sadness, but Carter's answer caught my attention and I found myself immersed in the written answer. It was a good distraction.

CH: My friend wondered if the closeness that you and I have is normal. Do you know if all our loved ones in spirit are so close to us?

C: Well the connection varies of course as it does within that life in form. Some loved ones go off beyond your realm, very unconnected. They may have much to heal from or learn from the life effort made there depending on the struggles, failures and burdens of that life. They can recover, refocus, this effort takes time. Others without the true strength of love connecting them or given from them may return here without so many attachments to those in form, they can do as they choose really. It is sometimes even just the fact they are so happy to be back, rejoice and enjoy this existence, they let life there just pretty much continue until those in form return home here. But love can always link spirits. Many loved ones follow you there, not constantly, but do follow your struggles and joyful events with happiness to help or just be part of those special moments. In struggles they will send love, try to send support and guidance and hope the love at least is received within you. It is the thread that binds beyond life and time. Also, the skills, drive, levels of spiritual ability and the focus to stay with you and "live" with you is different for all. My connection, my reach back into your world and Grandpa's also is stronger, more focused, more constant and with our ability more able to be received, but this is also because of you working diligently with us now and toward us before connection was truly known by you. Our chosen task, Grandpa and I, links us absolutely to the world you still remain in. Our connection is really so much more than usual, to serve our purpose to help ease pain and give life's knowledge of purpose and continuity. But tell your friend that her loved ones see her, follow her, share her life still with her. They have only left the human form, the spirit and the energy of essence remains and exists unaltered; they are still true to who they are. We in spirit hear them talking to us through the connection of love. We know when they struggle or need us even without them calling for us through the connection of love. Love feels happiness, pain, turmoil, struggles. Love carries your emotions to us just as a vein would carry blood to your heart. Love flows all emotions through the veins of love back to our heart. I thought she'd like this, this view is for her especially, her nurse's mind. Tell her I'm smiling hugely thinking that was a good picture for her, I'm happy with this for her.

How interesting. This answer could have been written about anyone here. I have been amazed by how similar many parts of life in spirit are to our world. This answer made perfect sense to me because it's how I saw and accepted the range of variances between people and relationships here. Why should I be surprised by this answer?

November 10, 2011:

Five long, hard days later, I was still deep in a pit of despair. I could hear Carter's frustration in the day's writing. He wanted me to pay attention and pull myself together, and though I'd been trying, I hadn't succeeded. His message, though loving, was sent with strength as if delivered by a general rallying his troops for the courage to fight on for their purpose and to help their fellow soldiers.

C: Love you Mom.

Mom, use our strength, our love, let us help strengthen you through turmoil and low ebbs. We are here to help you first and foremost, our love reaches out, let it absorb into your being and enrich you. You fought to reach us, now let us fight to help you for the love we hold you within, and for the enrichment of your days and time there. Also without you, your commitment, strength, and determination, our hope to help is almost completely extinguished. We need you absolutely, as the component in form for us to reach out to others. You are an important, equal partner, as either of us here xxx

November 13, 2011:

I had been trying unsuccessfully for two weeks now to feel better. I couldn't seem to recover from the incredible sadness and vulnerability. During my morning meditation, I pictured myself carrying a bag of rocks then placing them onto the ground, hoping that I would be releasing my current struggles, but this hadn't helped either. After meditation, I connected and wrote with Carter.

C: Love you Mom.

You are not thinking positive and loving enough toward yourself. Step away from what frustrates and tires you. You need to do what will strengthen you, give you peace, move you forward each day clear and peaceful, and let your task be attended to. Be still but not in anxious frustration, but peaceful calmness. Even your body is tight and totally not at ease. Come on Mom, find a focus to move past these pointless frustrations and reach to us for help xxx.

As the day progressed, my anxiety continued to escalate. I went to a yoga class in an attempt to calm myself, but that also failed to help and by afternoon I was at the point of sheer desperation. I began to cry and felt very jittery; I knew that I really needed help because I couldn't seem to overcome the emotional after effects of the accident. I felt I was reaching a breaking point and I pleaded for Dad and Carter to help me. I meditated again, but this time I went back to what worked in the beginning and I did my original meditation. I brought the light around and through me then I "placed myself" at the start of the path, trying to bring as much detail as I could into this picture as I began to walk along the path. As I stopped by the stream to watch the water flow over the rocks, Dad and Carter "appeared" and from that point on they lead the meditation. I was no longer creating what I saw.

They asked me to lie down on the dirt path and then I watched as they reached under my outer clothing and began removing large rocks and stones. They didn't speak, but worked busily, removing rock after rock. Then they checked to make sure no more rocks remained under my clothing. During this process I was an onlooker, and I could see myself lying on the ground. I watched as both Dad and Carter stood up and looked down at me while dusting off their hands, seeming to be quite pleased with the job they had done.

Next Dad spoke to me, saying that I needed to go lie in the stream.

"The water is too cold, Dad, its November. I don't want to do this."

We argued back and forth, and he insisted. They both stepped into the stream when I did, then they helped me lie down in the icy water. They both stood beside me and watched the water turn brown as the remainder of the dirt and pebbles washed out from beneath my clothing.

When the water ran clear Dad said, "Okay that looks good, now let's get you up."

As they were helping me up the meditation ended. I was amazed as I opened my eyes, realizing that once I had placed myself in the woods, I had nothing to do but stand back and watch. Dad was definitely the one in charge, and to my amazement, I felt lighter. I instantly felt much better. I had sat in the chair to meditate, lost in desperation and pain, and rose when it finished feeling great. From that moment on, I was finished dealing with the stress of November's accident. I thanked them both in writing the next day.

November 14, 2011:

C: Love you Mom.

CH: Thank you so much for yesterday. I had been feeling worse every day. You and Dad coming to my aid yesterday in my original meditation was amazingly helpful, when it ended I was remarkably better!

C: That's okay, we're happy to help anytime. Of course, we have been trying but you were not trying hard enough, voiding your mind, clearing and opening for us, we can only do our best work for you then. In almost desperation yesterday afternoon you just totally opened and joined us. Earlier in the day you did try but you didn't see the help, but that did help also, it began to help guide you and yoga helped too. The less you do daily towards clearing your mind, letting go and the deeper you sink the harder it is to be helped. This is true for everyone. But isn't this a wonderful lesson to experience, to feel. You stood up from that meditation lighter, less burdened, able to function. Like a pill or a snap of the fingers [within the time span of the meditation] but it was like day and night, an immense and immediate difference in your emotional state.

CH: I had tried to visualize myself putting down a bag of rocks—my burdens, etc. Why didn't it work for me? Later during my afternoon meditation, when you and Dad removed the rocks from under my clothing then laid me down in the stream and let the water cleanse the remaining dirt away, it worked. Why did this work? I felt so much better, but my earlier efforts to do almost the same thing myself didn't work at all.

C: It was your call for us to help and truly be with us and allow us to help you. It was giving us this task and allowing it to be successful. You simply couldn't do it alone, your focus, effort, weren't complete enough or you should have been successful, why not! But you were so tired, weakened, the light helped heal you as did we. We simply removed the weight of burden from your emotional and spiritual elements. You're cleansed, refreshed, renewed and ready to rise and stride forward. It was an unpleasant time and of course, there will be more for you. You witnessed in body and spirit the physical and emotional change within you by your focus to get past it and your total connection to us. Though we are only in spirit you discovered the true help and relief we three achieved. You won't always be strong but remember we will always be there to help. Reach clearly and with trust and love, we will help.

The clouds of darkness had lifted from me just like that—amazing! Once again I realized that when I truly ask for help and was open to receive it, help comes to me. Two days later, Carter brought me this beautiful writing. After the tumultuous last few weeks, and my personal struggles, the lessons were uplifting, joyful, and true. I told myself to enjoy, learn and remember the message.

November 16, 2011:

C: Love you Mom.

Well done you have recovered, you're rejuvenated, see Mom. Believe in the power of spirit, yours and ours, you feel that almost immediate change of personal energy, peace of mind, depression eased. People need to see things to believe they happen, exist, are real and often won't even accept when things happen since they are unseen, unexplainable. The mind needs to open to the very real truth of reality beyond vision, beyond the physical presence and realm. That view can be stifling, limiting—so much is possible outside your vision, that doesn't mean it doesn't exist. The human reality, that life while there, is usually so narrow and bound by the human mind and reality of presence. Even scientists look to the heavens' boundless-ness and to the increasingly smaller units—cells, atoms, and wonder what in each direction bigger or smaller—what else is there just as yet unseen, undiscovered. Now take this educated view of the scientists and open to beyond their realm of thoughts to the existence of all within the "nothingness" of the space, the air, the universe, and beyond. The true form of our existence, beyond these brief interludes in form. Open to the wondrous possibility, to all that is possible and our probability of reaching and touching your human life.

November 22, 2011:

C: Love you Mom.

Happy Birthday Mom from both of us, BIG HUG, feel it now.

CH: I feel it. (A feeling of energy surrounding me begins at my waist and extends up to my chest. Next, within this area I feel the pressure increase, it's similar to the feeling of someone gently squeezing me and for a few seconds it became harder to breathe.)

C: This is great today Mom, finally a clear connection, of course we really want it to happen today—all three of us for your birthday, right Mom!

CH: Absolutely right.

C: OK really enjoy your day, the time throughout the day, knowing we're spending it with you. We will enjoy the family dinner gathering tonight too! So happy this year you're so much more comfortable with our assured presence. We love you so much Mom xxxx.

Carter gave great hugs, ask any of his friends, and he gave them often and freely. He would stand beside people and put his arm around them and they could feel his happiness and know he was thoroughly enjoying being with them. His natural ability to put others at ease and have fun with them now left a hole in every occasion, the space that he should fill.

He began my birthday with such perfection that all day each hug I received was strengthened in meaning. As the family each began their day with a hug for me, I felt their love envelop me with joy and I cherished each one. I wasn't longing for that missing hug because Carter had already given me his hug. I wanted each person to remember my hug from them as genuine, heartfelt, and enjoyed if I didn't get a chance to share another hug with them. Carter's hugs live on in everyone's memory, and they continue to matter. All day I thought of his words and his hug, and I was able to enjoy every moment with my family, trusting Carter and Dad were with me and being fully present, aware how special these moments were.

Hand in Hand

Love you Mom. Let us rise for purpose hand in hand. My presence felt in your hand, mes-
sages received within your hand and mind, this gift of knowledge, continuity, purpose,
love. Your hands receive and give back; both to me, for me and from me. A reaching out
from both of us till the reach was felt. An awareness of my presence with you, you felt me
arrive and leave. We, when in form grasp with our hands for love, comfort, support, guid-
ance (when a child especially). Now our roles have reversed, you lead and guided me as
your child, now I lead and guide you. The tables have turned, flipped, the bond though is
constant, just a shift of nurturer and student. The grasp of your hand holding me hasn't
been lost, only a reversal of role for this part of our lives. When you feel me take your hand
remember I am right with you, grasp onto my "hand" and smile, we walk into the future
together. Enjoyment felt in these moments spent together with the physical aspects of the
living touch giving comfort, sending and receiving love by holding your hand and you
holding me xxx. (Carter, writing received January 3rd, 2012.)

Christmas had come upon us once again, and though still difficult, we had regained
some of the joys of the season. As always, the family tried very hard for each other,
which was a blessing I found experiencing special occasions with my heart wide open,
though raw, allowed a deeper and richer connection of sharing with those I love.

The previous year, the girls managed to put up their Christmas ornaments and I
put up a few family ones, but my heart hadn't been in it. Since Carter's death, we had
not opened the boxes that held all the years of treasured ornaments that included his,
but unknown to any of us one of these boxes had been brought up from the basement
and sat open among the other boxes. One of my daughters unwrapped an ornament
and then stood motionless, staring at it. Without a word spoken the energy of the room
shifted and we all looked her way. Hesitantly she said, "this is Carter's ornament," and
we all stared at her in disbelief. I think we all felt the same rush of thoughts. First, what

do we do now? This shouldn't have happened when we were trying so hard to enjoy Christmas. Also, now that it was in her hand, we couldn't rewrap it and stick it back in the box like it hadn't happened; that would feel so disrespectful to Carter's life.

My challenge was to think quickly what would be best for everyone at that moment to prevent bringing Christmas to an emotional halt. Luckily I had already been talking to Carter in my mind, saying I know he was with us because he wouldn't miss this, and trusting he was in the room with us. I reached toward my daughter for the ornament and said I would put up Carter's ornament for him.

Hoping to relieve some of the tension I said out loud, "Come on and help me Carter. We will put up your ornament together." I pictured him right beside me, our arms reaching up in unison and placing it on the tree. I stood back and admired it. The family joined me, and I felt a sense of peace that it was the right thing to do.

I then astonished myself by saying, "I will hang Carter's ornaments this year for him. I know he's here, so let's make sure he's included. He won't want to be left out." I was happy to do this for him and hoped he saw how much growth I had accomplished with his help. I knew if we had discussed trying to hang Carter's ornaments, the answer would have been a resounding no. But the way it happened unexpectedly, having to react to the circumstances, pushed us to deal with it. The outcome made us face our fears and find a way through it while bringing Carter's presence back in the room with us as we acknowledged him; another mountain climbed.

The spirit of Christmas illuminated our house with love that evening and I basked in its warmth. When sadness came over me that holiday season, I thought of my special gifts. I had a lot to be thankful for this Christmas because of the power of love.

After Christmas, we all spent a few days at the cottage. The love and gratitude I experienced on Christmas remained with me and I believe strengthened my connection to spirit for these next two clear and meaningful writings. They completed my year wrapped in love from my son.

December 27, 2011:

C: Love you Mom.

Yes, love flows easily and constantly between us, you and I, it is an open channel linking us both. Love flows endlessly and has not ever ceased since my passing. I was pouring my love into you for strength, support, and to simply do all I could within my confines of existence now to help ease your pain and give you extra help as was Grandpa in a much more focused effort on his part. His love and guidance sent steadily and readjusting his effort constantly in the hopes some could begin to pierce the armour of grief that enclosed you. It's held you like a prisoner, trapped within its fortress, unable at first to see any exit route or even glimpse a gated window for even a glimpse toward the light. Little by little you glimpse a small window, high but out of reach, but you did begin to know it was there and with determination and sheer will the body inside (the spirit) began to expand, put pressure on the armour, enclosing you, trapping and suffocating you. Cracks began to form; small pieces began to fall away, the window with light lowered to within your reach. At first just your fingertips to touch it, now it's lowered so you view past the fortress of pain into the beauty and glory of the light, the sun, the night sky sparkling with golden orbs. You have found the escape route, love and effort by you, by me, by Grandpa, and many here and there who support you with love and kindness. A hope for freedom to be won with effort, valour and love. You are not to be held captive by grief, you are to be free and fight outside the bastion of grief for the freedom of others trapped within its walls but unable to find a way out, they need someone's help from outside to be freed.

This was a powerful message, and one that made their hopes clear for me; this would be hard for me to ignore. I was also aware that Carter gave this message just two days after Christmas when I was very conscious of how, with their help, my outlook and healing had progressed. Within the framework of a fairy-tale setting, he had told my story with detailed images and vibrant colours that flowed like a silent movie through my mind as his words took shape on the page. I stepped away from the writing, seeing yet again a bigger picture and purpose for myself, but not knowing how or what to do to accomplish this.

December 29, 2011:
I love this next writing. Carter used water as a way to explain life's shifts on many occasions, and for me it was this writing, combined with the view that deepened my belief and grasp of its meaning on a profound level. Several weeks earlier, I had received a wonderful writing where he used the river's journey with an elegance of thought that was very meaningful to me, and it was this writing that my thoughts went back to when I saw the mist this morning.

I had risen early and sat quietly looking out as the mist rose from the lake. I was enjoying the view when my mind was suddenly jolted into thought as it began to process what I was witnessing. I leapt from the couch to get my camera before the mist vanished. I was talking out loud excitedly as I took the photos: "I can see exactly what Carter was talking about; this is amazing to see this now and be able to have a completely new view of what I have seen so many times before." I am so glad I thought to take a photo. I feel I never convey Carter's messages as well as I received them, partly because the images I receive with the writing are locked away in my mind. This photo allows others to see beyond words to the truth in his message. I rushed into his cottage bedroom and I continued to see the mist rising through his window as I spoke to him.

CH: Carter, I'm watching the mist rise from the lake this morning. It is my visual truth to your words on December 20, 2011—water rising to another realm—it means so much more to see that today after your writing.

C: Love you Mom.

Yes, yes I see it too, wonderful Mom, for you to sit still with a mindset of peace and serenity and to see and truly witness this truth, the visual presence that you there hold so tightly to. Yes, the rivers have journeyed to the lake, that journey within the form of water has finished but not ended. That singular journey of water is complete. The physical presentation changes, it is no longer at this moment water, yet it visually has changed to today's vision of a seen vapour as it rises and disappears unseen. Once it has risen into the air and becomes unseen, does that mean it has ceased to exist? Absolutely not, its presence and existence is absolutely, though quite amazingly, still there. We can no longer see the water, it is "gone" to us in form, yet it exists within the true composure of its existence, constant and unending just like a chameleon changes, an invisible cloak, though still present. This is a great view of our journey from the physical life. We exist as water, we rise and within special conditions as today in the mist, some people can witness the shift, but we rise to become unseen for the most part, to most people. But we exist absolutely unchanged and unchangeable in our true essence, waiting for our time within the existence to alter once again as rain, snow, mist, cloud, and be seen once again. We only step in and out of visual presence; our true presence is all around you. Part of your daily lives, though mostly not acknowledged or accepted within the daily journeys. The visual today is great, we rise, we fall, it is not sad or burdensome if seen within the reality of what this is, a natural part of a recurring cycle but not an ending of life, a shifting of how a part of life is lived xxx.

I felt Carter becoming wiser and teaching to a higher level. His latest writings showed growth within enriched imagery and phrasing, his symbolism was getting much stronger and it helped enhance my understanding. His favourite element was always water to easily explain our journey in form, and the visuals he gave me were increasingly rich and powerful. One day Shannon made a statement that I cherish, and it's in line with these thoughts. She said that she could hear Carter maturing through his writings, and although she would always see him as nineteen, she had found it so sad to watch her sons, who were his friends, mature and grow and think Carter never had that chance. She now realized that he was still growing and maturing as he would have done here.

January 3, 2012:

My New Year's resolution had been to stay more focused and attentive on my work with Carter. Carter's message today was nudging me forward within loving and well-chosen thoughts. I have used the writing from this day at the beginning of this chapter.

Throughout 2012, Carter continued to amaze me with his writings. My meditations also seemed to be reaching a higher quality as I floated free from my thoughts and connected easily to this unseen realm of existence. I continued to be blessed with many unique experiences with spirit, but I have only included a few key writings because I hope by now, just like me, you don't need as much proof. Choosing events that move the story forward, I leap forward a few months.

March 6, 2012:

CH: Thank you both for speaking to Olivia on her birthday yesterday. Dad, it was a lovely surprise when you spoke.

DAD: Yes Charm, of course. I thought Olivia was ready and it wouldn't be startling or upsetting, but would make her happy. She's not so desperately searching for Carter now, but finds hoped-for joy in the connection. I wanted to speak to her for the love and joy I hold her with and reassure her I too am part of her life also, always with love, of course.

CH: It was a fun talk; did you see her face when I said you were coming in to speak to her?

DAD: Yes, but more than that I felt her heart. A love of peace, happiness, excitement, an instant reaching out from her of happiness within love sent toward me.

CH: I was startled at first when I was hearing two people speaking at the same time. You were saying how proud you were of her, and Carter started talking over top of your voice. I could hear you both, but the writing stopped. It was a new experience, but it felt like you were both here in the room; it had the natural feel of a conversation.

DAD: It is just you are not hearing it with your ears, but within your mind through spirit. Carter, of course, is excited to be able to speak to Olivia and on her birthday, so he is full of fun for both reasons. You know what he gets like. He actually can still liven up any conversation here too with his enthusiasm and thrill of the moment. Carter is uncontainable like a firefly, even when held within bodily form he is lighting up that jar. Set him free as he is now, release him from the container and his joy and happiness is heightened. He throws his light farther, zips here, there, and everywhere, throwing his light for others to witness. Follow the path of his light; it moves with joy and exuberance, it's just such a pleasure to witness and enjoy.

CH: I love this Dad, what a beautiful vision to give me of Carter. I will treasure it and hold it in my mind to help give me strength. I love you Dad xxx.

DAD: And I love you, Charm xxx.

May 30, 2012:

Victoria had been studying in England for a semester on a university exchange. At the end of her semester, I flew to England and John and Olivia joined us one week later. While the plane was still on the runway, I watched the TV screen as it showed a route map listing Toronto, Buffalo, and Chippawa. Chippawa! I only saw it briefly, because at that moment the screen changed. I questioned if I actually saw the word as I waited for that screen to return. Chippawa was a very small village where my father was born that had long been part of the city of Niagara Falls. It had been my parents' favourite place, where we had gone to swim and picnic every day in the summer. As I waited, I noticed all the other screens showed only big cities like London, Dublin, and Paris, and finally, the screen returned and it did say Chippawa; that's so weird! I believed Dad was telling me he was with me, and as soon as I had that thought the top of my head started tingling. As the plane lifted off I realized this trip was already a success. I knew Dad was with me.

I was so happy to arrive in England and be with Victoria again. After going to her favourite tea room, we returned to her residence where we were chatting with one of her roommates when the doorbell rang. We all went to answer the door, but no one was there. The girls were puzzled. Moments later, as we continued to look out through the glass panel, the doorbell rang again but this time it was one long ring. We could all see there was nobody there ringing the doorbell, which unsettled Victoria's roommate quite a bit. I smiled, but said nothing as I thought, *hello guys, thanks for letting me know you're here with us in England; this is perfect.*

Sadly, Mom broke her hip as I flew to England. I tried to book a flight home immediately, but Mom insisted that I stay as planned with Victoria. John and Olivia did everything they could while they were still at home, but she was firm that they not alter their plans either. Her positive messages and attitude helped us all have a great time with Victoria, but when we returned we saw how frail she had become, and I now devoted most of my time to her. I found it increasingly hard to keep up with my events journal, so I decided that I would only make special entries, but I want to acknowledge how important keeping these journals is to me. They have allowed me to see the frequency and consistency of the signs and events received from both Carter and Dad in spirit. They were a structural keystone as I tried to understand if any of this was real and helped me see Carter and Dad were absolutely still present with me.

After returning from England, I felt more confident and comfortable with my connection to Carter and Dad. I accepted that I had somehow become part of a wonderful connection to spirit and I needed to try my very best with this opportunity. I understood that there would always be people who would criticise or voice their disbelief, but I knew there would be many like me who I could help. This vacation had allowed me to come to terms with how important this part of my life had become for me and the profusion of wonderful experiences and writings continued to erode my human doubts and hesitation.

I resumed my daily writings with Carter and several weeks after returning from England. I thought I'd make an attempt to see my aura again, which led to this lovely writing. After the writing ended, I added a note for myself—this writing took thirty-five minutes! This is a wonderful example to show how within this short time frame an amazing writing was formed; there were no stops or pauses, I received the writing as one continuous thought.

July 21, 2012:

CH: Carter, as I was practicing to see my aura, the energy layer appeared and disappeared from my view. It was a bright light in a thin layer around my head, then it would move and shift, and a few times it lifted or spiked (with less intensity) higher above my head. It reminded me of northern lights, the Aurora Borealis.

C: Love you Mom.

Yes well done Mom, an understanding seen and witnessed by you with no help from us. It is the wonderful mindset you are walking toward. For it is being seen within the oneness and similarities we all live within, you and I, humans and planets, microbes and the heavens. All has been created from the spark of love, and certain constants and similarities embody all things, though not witnessed within that thought so much. I am proud of you Mom, you with this thought show a leap toward the reality that is. You are showing growth beyond normal concepts and learned truths to see truth with eyes wide open to the truth held within existence unseen, normally unwitnessed or realized. It is a moment of thought within vision, an awareness and then connection to all within existence. So let's explain this thought Mom.

Both exist within existence; both have been created for the task of a journey, a trip of love within a unity with love. All are created from energy and are part of the energy of all, a constant of all. We come from energy and are energy, therefore we give off energy and when substance fails or ends we return to energy. So these physical presentations we see, in this case, the earth and you are physical, we see them, they have substance of a finite nature. Both are part of the heavens, in both cases they emit an energy (usually unseen). Energy is stronger often from the top and bottom, head and feet, north and south poles, for they will reach for sustenance and connection. Energy is released continually but in special circumstances (the northern lights or you seeing your aura) they come within human view. They are a visual statement: I am more than I am seen to be. I am continually truly connected to the energy from where I was formed and never separate from. And from seeing both "auras" of human and planet, I can stand witness to the fact we are all living energies reaching from the substance of form to our natural state, our "parents," our home. All energy is eternal and eternally connected for its movement is constant and ever flowing. It does not disappear or end, but reaches beyond form. Whether a planet mighty and massive sailing through space laden with countless forms of existence, or the human body perfect but smaller, laden with the life force of countless cells, atoms, molecules (forms of existence). Both are different yet similar, they both are single units within space yet not single, because of the entirety of their composition. Single units yet units of uncountable substance, all exist for each life to move forward, each a single though compound unit and each unit part of the compound of existence. Existence itself is only another single unit made up of uncountable substance. Whether you see the human life—the body or the earth—the planet or the entirety of the universe and all that exists within it, seen and unseen. All is complete, yet one and truly there is only one, we all beat as one heartbeat, the life force of light, the pulsing rhythm of energy and light. There is only one living thing and we are inside of it, part of it, whether in form or spirit we are part of the life that pulses, is within us, exudes unseen from us as part of the universal body. Both earth and people are only part of this single life force and the light energy you realize coming off both shows you the truth. Both have the same forces emitting back from them, energy released from form reaching to connect to what they have come from until they are reabsorbed unseen into the completeness of the existence that is truth and endures eternally. Yours was an amazing realization to allow you this lesson today.

You witness again Mom how we are all together, never truly apart or separated, all just part of all that is.

My Mother's Love

Love you Mom. Grandma knows, she reaches deep into herself now for strength. It shows in her smile to those around her, to those helping her, marking their kindness, appreciating and accepting their help. She wants them to know it touches her soul and she reaches out to theirs. Love flows through her no matter how fragile and tired she is and she adores the time and effort you and her family support her with constantly now. She sees the effort, she feels the love. She pours love out of her as best she can to all of you. She knows the outcome nears, but remember Mom it is only her body that fades and fails. Grandma will step out of it whole, happily strengthened by all the love and her life effort—well done! (Carter, writing received September 16, 2012.)

On January 13, 2013, my mother died at ninety-three, after seven difficult months.

January 15, 2013:

C: Love you Mom.

Love to all of you from all of us here. Grandma is here. We reached for her, grasped her "hands" and lead her forth into the light of spiritual life. She did not "travel" it alone, but with us plus others. She was tired, weakened by her final phase of struggles, but a marvellous life effort on the whole. Trials, turmoil, tests, and troubles, but she shone through with effort, faith, persistence, kindness, and an outreach of love. Grandma's marathon was definitely run, a complete marathon—long, with moments of great happiness and parts of the race arduous and difficult. But she completed it and ran it well, skillfully, and now is happy the race is complete, for she needs time to rest, restore, recover, and enjoy the tumultuous applause expressed in the outpouring of love by so many here who have loved and supported her, and now hold her tight in the enthusiastic hugs at the "finish line." Don't worry Mom, she is tired but happy and glad to see so many she has missed but always loved through her life. Kisses and hugs to you all from all three of us.

I was once again in an emotional tailspin. To lose my mom from my life was devastating, and she was the first person in my family to die since my connection to Carter. I knew she was okay, and for the first time, this belief comforted me. Over the next few days Carter talked of her passing, and as he brought me her messages I heard her voice. The words written resonated so true that once again I questioned whether it was me writing what I wanted to hear. Even though I knew I hadn't written them, I couldn't shake those lingering doubts. I needed to hear her through someone besides me to once again reassure myself that it was her speaking to me. I scheduled an appointment for a reading with Sandy in May. For several weeks before my appointment, I repeatedly pleaded with Mom to bring messages at this reading to assure me that what I was hearing from her was real. I needed reassurance the writing hadn't been created by me to meet my needs. After all, I had been given I shouldn't have had doubts, but I did and though I felt bad for asking, I trusted she would do this for me.

Mom was amazing for me as she led a reading through Sandy that confirmed both events and statements within my writings since her passing; it was exactly what I needed. The next day Carter and Mom gave me a clear message to stop searching and reach out to others.

The Pearl Necklace

May 28, 2013:

CH: Carter, Grandma came through at the reading yesterday with such wonderful messages. You did also, but this time it was Grandma that I most needed to hear from.

C: Love you Mom.

That was therapeutic, helpful for both of you. Grandma knows you now know she is okay, happy, but she also knows that you needed it to come through Sandy, not just yourself. She feels that you closed that loop from physical to spiritual presence—on a pearl necklace Grandma is telling me to say to you.

CH: Of course, that is a perfect image from her, she loves pearls; thanks Mom.

C: It is not just a loop on the necklace, that meeting with Sandy is the clasp on the necklace. Your search first for me, then to hear from me, you to connect to me, our knowledge leading and guiding you toward your purpose within this belief and knowledge. Now you have heard from Grandma, perfect details and thoughts of love flowed outward from her and within these messages, the clasp closed around the hook—which is us leading you toward your hoped-for purpose. You now strongly believe; feel more comfort and ease, feel more thrust to help. The circle is complete, solid and eternal with the knowledge, kindness, love, and understanding seen visually amongst the loops of chain as iridescent, luminous pearls—nature's beauty as this is perfect when held in focused vision. Grandma is telling Victoria it is the pearl necklace Victoria made for her, also to hold as a good view—pearls and strength in lengths of chain and of course her beloved pearls given to my sisters. A loop of her love seen giving view to her eternal love wrapping them within.

I had been writing with Carter for three years now. Over and over he's had to prove to me it's him. Each time I struggled with doubt and weakened into my logical mind once again. Since the writing began, friends kept telling me that I needed to write a book, and during the spring and summer of 2013 I felt they were pushing me harder to do this. I could now see that a book could be helpful to others, and perhaps I should write one, but I had no idea how to do this. I always told friends to find me someone in publishing, then I would tell them my story.

September 13, 2013:
When I returned from a girls' weekend at our cottage, John told me there was a message on the phone for me from a publishing company. Immediately I got goosebumps. *Carter, what have you done now?* Instinctively I knew Carter had something to do with this, but I was tired, and after a nice weekend I didn't want to deal with this emotional stress. Three days later, when no one was home, I was finally ready to listen to the message and return their call.

The woman at the publishing company who left the message thanked me for calling and said, "I've been trying to reach you on your e-mail address but it kept saying that it didn't exist."

I didn't know what she was talking about, and I struggled to respond. "What was the e-mail address?"

When she said what it was, I could barely contain myself; of course it doesn't exist, it never existed, it's ridiculous. I was now surer than ever this was Carter's work. He would have loved creating that to get my attention.

"That is not my e-mail address, but you're telling me you were given that silly email with my real home phone number?" I wasn't sure what Carter had done, but I knew without a doubt that he had done this somehow. I explained to her that I had never contacted them, or any publisher, and asked how this would have been done. She was very matter-of-fact as she stated that I did it through their website and I must have filled out an application. No, I definitely had not, I said. To convince me, she read me my application. It stated that I would have a book ready to be published in five to six months and that it was a children's book. I stumbled for words, saying that I might have a future book, though it's not a children's book (but it was written by my child!). As she began giving me publishing details I stopped her.

"I can't talk to you now because I didn't apply, and I have to find out who did."

Several bereaved mothers I had helped through Patricia had wanted me to write a book because they felt I had helped them cope with their grief. I asked Patricia to see if any of them had done this; but they only knew my first name and not my family name or where I lived, so they couldn't possibly have done it even if they wanted to. Now that was a good answer! I know the obvious thing was to ask Carter, but I already believed it was him. I needed to find out if he guided someone to do this for him, three days later, without me asking the question, Carter began to speak about opening the pages.

September 28, 2013:

C: Love you Mom.

Let the witness begin. Open the pages so others can see and add to the library of books to guide, love, and support people's journey and time there in form. The book is like others. It is not totally unique or an origin of new truth. No, for truth is truth, and has been told and retold. All books are attending to different concerns, aspects, or thoughts of part of the total composition. But like any library, there are many books capable of teaching and will teach in often slightly or completely different styles. These books teach—would you not agree Mom?

CH: Yes, I have learned so much from you.

C: And others too who would choose these books would learn at different levels, but all can be guided to truth.

CH: Okay—so it sounds like you want me to try to publish these journals.

C: Yes.

CH: Should I try to begin to do this soon?

C: Yes Mom!

CH: Carter, did you arrange that call from the publishing company? I wasn't planning on asking you, but you've brought up the topic today. When I was told there was a message, then again a few days later when I listened to the message on the telephone, every fibre of my being knew that it was you, so I didn't feel I needed to ask. This is the first time we have talked since I called them back, and now you're talking about publishing!

C: Yes! I arranged the contact, the call.

CH: Is this the publisher I am to use?

C: No not necessarily—you find the path, the one you feel comfortable with. But the time has come to move forward on this, please Mom.

CH: I will begin to try; it is all new to me.

C: Yes but like our journey now, look what effort to find me has given to you. Your life and mine together still and once again. For love we work into our future. Love you.

With a sigh of exasperation, I put down the pen and thought, *this is just great Carter, another one of your big ideas for me, and just how am I supposed to do this?*

After several minutes I told him, "Well if you want me to try to do this I'm going to need lots of help."

"Yes Mom, yes of course, this is a combined effort by us three."

One month later, on October 28, Shannon called me, quite excited. She had met Martin, a man who had been in publishing for twenty-two years, and he was very interested to meet me. She wondered if was I was still interested in writing a book. Absolutely!

Into the Light

Love you Mom. You absolutely grow more comfortable within this acceptance and under-standing. Be peaceful within yourself, with your fought for and hard won knowledge and growth of understanding. Be happy in your easing within the endless toil of grief and be thankful in what we now approach together. We stand on the path that runs ahead of us into our future, us three. Do you see the vision Mom?

    CH: Yes, it is lovely Carter.

    C: We walk it together, we pause to watch the sunrise, it is a huge ball of golden and pinkish glow. It dominates the horizon that we three see, it is rising, its presence seen. We are mere shadow outlines if you were to see us from behind; we are silhouettes upon the rising sun. It is the sun that dominates the vista but we are imprinted upon it for we are part of it, and this view from behind us shows us as part of it, enlightened as we visu-ally submerge into it, we are not lost within it but stay imprinted upon it. We are visually still seen but are part of its greatness. (Carter, writing received October 7, 2012.)

I now live my life with the absolute conviction and ease that Carter is with me as our journey together continues to unfold. I strive to live in the present, knowing every moment of time is a gift and each will be eternally followed by another. I know I'm always connected to my son and all of existence. It's impossible for me to completely grasp this, but I'm able to see it through a smaller perspective. I know the trillions of cells in my body all work individually yet also together so they function as one body. I can expand this thought to view myself and the unseen countless other parts that together form existence, including Carter.

Carter continues to teach and guide me, and still surprises me and others with his gifts from spirit. Although I am past the point of needing them to be convinced he exists, I cherish every event as much as the first. I'm happy when others have their own experience with Carter, and as I hear them speak with wonder and enthusiasm I smile and say, "I know, isn't it incredible!" Every connection from him still makes my heart soar.

After I began writing this book, I started learning mediumship, although I had refused to even think about it, in fact I was quite upset when Carter originally suggested I do this. As in the rest of my journey, I had to find my own acceptance, and then it happened quite naturally. As I shared my story with other grieving parents, they always hoped I could connect to their children. I understood their pain. Although Carter had always made the connection to their children for me, I had no awareness of their loved ones, other than Carter's words. The more secure I became that Carter wouldn't leave me completely, the more I thought perhaps somehow I could learn to do this. Apprehensively, I stepped away from him to become more helpful to others in their grief. I shouldn't have been surprised when he merely stepped aside as he faithfully continues to be with me. Carters love of people and life was and still is his greatest asset

After the writing began I wondered how I ever managed to get to this point. The answer is with unstoppable determination and great love from family and friends in both realms as I struggled to find my way out of the darkness and into the light.

I know Carter has fought to help me through grief, but I'm certain now he was always working toward a bigger plan, the hope to help all of you. I realize most people won't experience the continuous series of events as I did, but don't be disheartened, I share my journey in the hope it can help you find your path into the light. I believe that learning to communicate with spirit is possible for anyone, I am no one special. I believe you can do it too if you set your mind to it.

Regardless of any personal conclusions, reflect on how you live within this world. Ask yourself what you can take away from this book to enrich your life. I've taken much more than learning of Carter's continued existence from my quest.

You can think of all your blessings and be grateful for what they add to your life. You can focus on positive thoughts, realizing negativity weighs you down. You can face life's challenges and see how you can grow as a person through them, don't be beaten down by life. You can live each day in the present, aware of the moment. You can continue living your life with family and friends no matter what you're facing, it is the quality of our life that we take from this earth. For those who don't believe in an afterlife, that's an equally good reason to focus on love. It brings value and joy to our life here and this brings us back full circle to living in the moment. For those who believe in an eternal life, relax and enjoy the moment. You have all the time in the world. For those that don't believe, enjoy the moment; it is your only guarantee.

And for those who put up barriers because you believe love brings pain, you are depriving yourself of life's greatest experience. I agree it was my love for Carter that brought me unfathomable pain, but it is only because of this love that I discovered the true value and joy of the greater love, all else pales in comparison.

These tidbits of good advice have been retold countless ways, but I hope it is within the uniqueness of how my story unfolds that these points are strengthened for you. This story is a testament to the love between parent and child and my role in it is as both parent and child. For it's my son and father in spirit whose love has nurtured me through grief. The love I felt for them during our time together has now expanded beyond knowing. I hope by sharing this amazing story of love that I can help ease others' journey through grief, and even if you find my story unbelievable it might light a spark of hope in your heart as you face life's struggles.

I will be forever thankful for the blessing of love and support that I have been given, and I hope I'm able to reach out with love through these pages to help others.

Epilogue

November 14, 2013

Love you Mom.

And ... and ... and ... do you see it Mom? The rhythms of life, joyously for both of us now, THIS, this writing, our connection, talking, this too is now in the rhythms of our lives. Isn't that FANTASTIC Mom!! Yes! It too, I think has become one of your natural rhythms, part of the endless, countless, innumerous natural rhythms of your universe. I am excited to think of it now, today, this way for our talk. Think of it Mom, you inhale and exhale, the heart pumps and relaxes, the sun rises and sets, the summer turns to winter, birth and death, eat and sleep, we connect to talk, we disconnect, we inhale we exhale. Beautiful, it is now part of your rhythms. Another naturally occurring, automatic progression through your days and time there now, natural, Mom. It is part of your existence and what your heart and soul need to move forward as you move through your time there. It is becoming like your body's need to breathe. You are doing it more often and without even conscious awareness always now. As you walk through your days you often connect and disconnect, just as you inhale you exhale. We are part of your life and we help give you life. Spirit and growth through love becoming more the air to sustain you and as you breathe, a natural and often effortless way to sustain you there. We love and support you Mom xxx. Let us help you breathe.

I could feel the excitement from Carter as I received this writing. The pen was pushing ahead very fast; it was hard to contain him. When Carter wrote and ... and ... and ... I understood it to refer to the daily routine or repetition of our writing together. Love you Mom ... again and again on a daily basis, and the rhythm of this writing now in our lives. Since meeting Martin, I kept getting visions of a journal being tossed into the air. I feel it is being set free as I watch pages drop loose and float toward the ground beneath a crystal clear blue sky.

Helpful Steps for Me

1. **Meditation:** It is a fundamental cornerstone to build on.
2. **Journal:** Write down events you question. Maybe you will see patterns forming as I did. When you think the timing is important or something happens and you think right away of your loved one, write it down. It was by writing down events that helped cement in my mind that there was definitely something unexplainable going on! I could also refer back to these notes when I frequently had doubts, which helped.
3. **Stillness:** Spend time within stillness separate from meditation. Stillness gave me an increasing ability to shut out the noisy clatter of the world and find more purposeful thought, though truly, in the beginning, I sat for hours at a time because I was unable to do anything else. Everything upset me, so I would have to stop even the simplest of tasks and just sit and look out the window, yet in hindsight, this was helping me.
4. **Mindfulness:** Focus your awareness in the present moment. Be conscious of the thoughts, feelings and emotions you experience without judgement towards yourself or others.
5. **Suspend your beliefs:** Don't be tied to what you believe is possible or impossible. Allow your mind to be open to new ways of thinking and accept that maybe you don't know what's possible. Don't say that can't happen, say *can* that happen? And think about the circumstances. When I thought *that can't be, it's impossible*, I would go over the events and time and time again I'd realize they did happen, though seemingly impossible to believe. The text messages, the dream after I felt the mattress move, the hummingbirds, etc. If I had shut my mind and said that's just a coincidence, then I would not be where I am today.

And for those people that will say to you it's not possible, well maybe they're wrong. Come to your own conclusions; you don't have to convince anybody else. People would often say to me, "that can't happen," and I'd reply, "I know it can't, but it did!"

6. **Examine events:** Put each event under a microscope and examine it with as much clarity and detail as you can. I would examine each event in detail, for example, if a car fan came on—where were my hands, did I touch anything. To believe something that wasn't what it seemed to be was only going to harm my goal to understand. How could I believe anything if I was fooling myself about even just one thing? It diminishes the possibility of all the other occurrences being from Carter. I was the only one who knew everything that I'd experienced as I explored new thoughts, and maybe this task was only for me to do, so I could convince myself with complete inner conviction for my journey ahead, which I hope includes helping others through grief.

7. **Spend time in nature:** Nature is like a symphony orchestrated with perfection. It produces a world so sublimely cohesive it creates a masterpiece that intertwines and flows seamlessly. You and I are made up of the same elements as the nature that surrounds you: carbon, hydrogen, oxygen, etc. Align your thoughts with the similarities between you and your environment, and be enriched by the perfection and magnitude of which you are a part.

8. **Patience:** Grief is an unbelievably hard journey. Don't put pressures on yourself or others; everyone deals with grief differently. Give yourself the gifts of time and kindness, allow yourself to experience your grief. It isn't easy but it won't go away either, blocking these feelings only pushes them away; they need to be felt and worked through.

9. **Death didn't beat us:** Death is part of the natural process of life. It does change your life forever, but see it as a fork in the road, not as an end of the road, because it isn't. Find a way that works for you to see past it whether it is simply living with more joy and humanity in the moment or letting your mind expand into the wonders of existence. You are living in this physical world now, find a path to live it with joy.

10. **Gratitude:** Find at least one thing every day to be thankful for and acknowledge your gratitude.

11. **The power of love:** Send your loved ones in spirit all the love you feel for them. Open your heart and ask to receive their love to help you heal through grief. Try

to believe and acknowledge that love is a force of existence that's here to help us all, and allow the power of love and the love from those you're grieving to help you as you struggle through this most difficult journey. My love for Carter has driven me to write my story, and this love has flowed through its creation, I hope it will help serve in your healing. I hope that you find a path to grace, peace, and happiness in your life.

Life is blessed with many gifts. It is an added blessing to have the eyes to see them xxxx.

Carter, October 20, 2011

Yes, I have had the help of many and hopefully this may help many. I was only part of this picture, of this singular improvement; I would not have reached this state without the progress of all that came before. Have the wisdom to see it is not your discovery to claim, as it is not a child's "discovery" to walk or talk. They and others are thrilled for them, but they have had help and support and it is the journey of that child's life, a natural progression. Be wise in seeing all is accomplished as a united growth and is to serve many. We are not accomplishing anything ever on our own, without all who are part of creation's journey, we would not accomplish anything. (Carter, writing received May 22, 2012.)

Acknowledgements

I wish to thank the many people who have helped and supported me on this journey through grief. I could not have created this book alone; you are all important to its creation.

I thank my family for blessing me with a life filled with love. My husband John and I were fortunate that I was able to be at home for many years to raise our children. Our family life was enriched by this. He also helped me to become a stronger person and see how important this search had become for me. I thank my daughters Victoria and Olivia. You were my reason to fight for each day when I couldn't do it for myself. You have filled my life with joy since the moment of your births, and I am honoured to be your mother. You have remained kind and considerate people who have grown through this tragedy to see the importance of life, friendship, and the value of love. I thank my parents for their infinite love and faith in me. They always lived with generosity and thoughtfulness to everyone and showed us how to weather life's storms and live by their example, always holding strong to their belief, "we are all people, we are here to help each other."

I wish to thank my friends Janice, Lyn, Maria, Nancy, Pam, and Shannon. You listened with compassion and caring, and encouraged me to explore my thoughts. I could say to you what I couldn't say to anyone else at the time. Thank you, Patricia, Sandy, Sharon, Lauren, and Heather, I believe you were brought into my life to help me move forward on my journey. To all the people who have touched my life, if you think I have in turn helped you, I am humbled. My life has also been enhanced by our time together in whatever circumstances. A special thank you from me to Carter's friends, they enriched his life here and he loves you all and you continue to be a blessing in our lives. Thank you to Martin, Kim, and Dee for believing in me, guiding me, and encouraging me to create this book.

Finally, I want to thank Carter for the boundless joy and enthusiasm he brought to my life. And for the endless love and compassion he has sent to me as I struggled to live life without him. He continues to be an inspiration to us all. I thank him for the constant love *and effort he and my father have nurtured me with since he left. Ultimately, I was able to grow into the person I am now, able to see life with an expanded view of its rich tapestry. This is a story of the power of love that is beyond my understanding, but I have learned enough to live my life knowing beyond any doubt in my mind that Carter has never left my side.*

To reach Charmaine you can find her at **loveyoumomblog.blogspot.ca** or you can email at: **loveyoumomblog@gmail.com.**

About The Author

Charmaine Roud lives with her husband and two daughters. Charmaine now spends most of her time at their cottage in Muskoka. She has filled eleven journals with her communications with Carter and continues to write.

CPSIA information can be obtained
at www.ICGtesting.com
Printed in the USA
LVHW051944051219
639468LV00002B/2/P